Rethinking Ethnicity

How are dominant ethnic groups, whether majority groups or dominant minorities, responding to the pressure of our global era? Are such groups in decline or are they successfully negotiating or resisting the challenge of new global values?

The winds of liberal globalisation and multiculturalism have compelled nations to transform their identities from an ethnic to a civic mode. This has led, in many cases, to dominant ethnic decline, but also to its peripheral revival in the form of Far Right politics. At the same time, the growth of mass democracy and the decline of post-colonial and Cold War state unity in the developing world have opened the floodgates to assertions of ethnic dominance. This volume investigates both tendencies and argues forcefully for the importance of dominant ethnicity in the contemporary world

Rethinking Ethnicity begins with four conceptual chapters, rich in examples from the past and present, which outline the theoretical foundations of dominant ethnicity. Two further sections present detailed case studies exploring dominant ethnicity in decline, transition and resurgence in North America, the Middle East, Europe and Asia. This book will appeal to everyone interested in ethnic conflict, citizenship and nationalism.

Eric P. Kaufmann is a Lecturer in Politics and Sociology at Birkbeck College, University of London. He is also the author of *The Rise and Fall of Anglo-America: The Decline of Dominant Ethnicity in the United States* (Harvard University Press, 2004).

Rethinking Ethnicity

Majority groups and
dominant minorities

**Edited by
Eric P. Kaufmann**

Routledge
Taylor & Francis Group

LONDON AND NEW YORK

First published 2004
by Routledge
11 New Fetter Lane, London EC4P 4EE

Simultaneously published in the USA and Canada
by Routledge
29 West 35th Street, New York, NY 10001

Routledge is an imprint of the Taylor & Francis Group

Typeset in Times by
Taylor & Francis Books Ltd
Printed and bound in Great Britain by
TJ International Ltd, Padstow, Cornwall

British Library Cataloguing in Publication Data
A catalogue record for this book is available from the British Library

Library of Congress Cataloging in Publication Data
Rethinking ethnicity : majority groups and dominant minorities /
[edited by] Eric P. Kaufmann.
        p. cm.
Includes bibliographical references and index.
 1. Pluralism (Social sciences). 2. Ethnicity. 3. Majorities.
4. Minorities. I. Kaufmann, Eric P.
  HM1271.R47 2004
  305.8–dc22
                                    2003027167
ISBN 0–415–31542–5 (hbk)
ISBN 0–415–31543–3 (pbk)

For Steven and Carmen Kaufmann

Contents

Illustrations

Figures

Tables

Contributors

Chetan Bhatt is a Reader in Sociology at Goldsmith's College, London. He is the author of *Liberation and Purity: Race, New Religious Movements and the Ethics of Postmodernity* (Taylor & Francis/UCL Press, 1997) and *Hindu Nationalism: Origins, Ideologies and Modern Myths* (Berg, 2001). He co-edited a special issue of *Ethnic and Racial Studies* with Parita Mukta entitled 'Hindutva Movements in the West: Resurgent Hinduism and the Politics of Diaspora' (vol. 23, no. 3, 2000), which focused on the relationship between 'homeland' and 'diaspora' nationalism. He has also written on various aspects of social theory, ethnicity and post-colonial nationalism.

Steve Bruce is Professor of Sociology and Head of the School of Social Science, University of Aberdeen, Scotland. From 1978 to 1991 he taught at The Queen's University of Belfast. He has also held visiting posts at the Universities of Virginia and Edinburgh. He is the author of sixteen books on the sociology of religion, religion and politics, and terrorism, including *God Save Ulster: The Religion and Politics of Paisleyism* (Oxford, 1986), *Conservative Protestant Politics* (Oxford, 1998) and *God is Dead: Secularization in the West* (Blackwell, 2002). His latest book is *Politics and Religion* (Polity, 2003).

As'ad Ghanem is a Senior Lecturer in the Department of Political Science, University of Haifa. His most recent books are *The Palestinian Regime* (Sussex University Press, 2001) and *The Palestinian Arab Minority in Israel* (SUNY Press, 2001). He is currently writing a comparative work on ethnic politics in Estonia, Canada and Israel.

Geoffrey Hosking, FBA, is Leverhulme Research Professor in Russian History, School of Slavonic and East European Studies, University College London. In 1988, he delivered the Reith lectures on the BBC. He is the author of numerous books on Russia and the USSR, including *A History of the Soviet Union* (Collins, 1985, 3rd edn 1992), *The Awakening of the Soviet Union* (Heinemann, 1990), *Russia: People and Empire, 1552–1917* (HarperCollins, 1997) and *Russia and the Russians* (Allen

Lane/Penguin Press, 2001). He has also edited or co-edited, among other books, *Church, Nation and State in Russia and Ukraine* (Macmillan, 1991) and *Russian Nationalism, Past and Present* (Macmillan, 1998).

Danielle Juteau is Professor of Sociology at the Université de Montréal, where she held a Chair in Ethnic Relations from 1991 to 2003. She received a Research Fellowship from the Pierre Elliott Trudeau Foundation (2003–6), and is working on the theorisation of ethnic relations in the world system. She has published on topics related to ethnic relations and ethnicity, pluralism, citizenship, and gender. Her recent publications include: *L'Ethnicité et ses Frontières* (Presses de l'Université de Montréal, 1999) and 'The citizen makes an *entrée*: redefining the national community in Quebec', *Citizenship Studies* (vol. 6, no. 4, 2002). She is on the editorial board of *Ethnic and Racial Studies* and is a member of the executive of the Research Committee on Ethnic Relations (RC05) for the International Sociological Association. During the academic year 2001–2, she held the Chair in Canadian Studies at La Sorbonne Nouvelle in Paris.

Eric P. Kaufmann is Lecturer in Politics and Sociology, Birkbeck College, University of London, and holds a PhD from the London School of Economics. He is the author of *The Rise and Fall of Anglo-America: The Decline of Dominant Ethnicity in the United States* (Harvard University Press, 2004). He has written nine journal articles on aspects of dominant ethnicity. Most recently, his work has appeared in *Ethnic and Racial Studies* (vol. 23, no. 6, 2001), *Historical Sociology* (vol. 14, no. 1, 2001), *Geopolitics* (vol. 7, no. 2, 2002) and *Global Society* (vol. 17, no. 4, 2003). He is an editor of the Blackwell journal *Nations and Nationalism*. He is presently working on an ESRC-funded study of the Orange Order in Northern Ireland, Canada and Scotland (http://www.kpdata.com/epk/index.html).

Ralph R. Premdas is Professor of Public Policy at the University of the West Indies, Trinidad and Tobago. He has previously taught at the University of California, Berkeley, the University of Papua New Guinea, the University of Ife, Nigeria, McGill University and Brown University. His work on comparative ethnic conflict has taken him to Fiji, Guyana, Trinidad, Papua New Guinea, the Solomon Islands, Belize, Northern Ireland, Quebec, Nigeria, South Africa and Sri Lanka and has involved an examination of various mechanisms of ethnic conflict management including decentralisation, secession, power sharing and affirmative action. He is the author of *Ethnic Conflict and Development: The Case of Fiji* (Avebury, 1995), *Comparative Secessionist Movements* (Pinter, 1990) and numerous articles on Fiji's politics and society. His most recent works include *Ethnic Conflict and Public Policy* (UNESCO, 1996), *Modes of Ethnic Conflict Regulation* (UNRISD, 2001), and *Identity, Ethnicity and Culture in the Caribbean* (2001).

Dominique Schnapper has been Professor at the École des Hautes Études en Sciences Sociales, Paris, since 1981. She was a member of the Nationality Commission, chaired by Marceau Long, vice-president of the French Council of State, in 1987, and other official commissions. She has also been president of the Société Française de Sociologie (1995–99). She has published over ten books, many in the field of ethnicity, citizenship and national identity, including *La Communauté des citoyens: Sur l'idée moderne de nation* (Gallimard, 1994), which was awarded the Prix de l'Assemblée nationale and was translated into English (Transaction, 1997). Her most recent work is *La démocratie providencielle* (Gallimard, 2000). She was awarded the Balzan Prize for sociology in 2002.

Anthony D. Smith is Professor of Ethnicity and Nationalism in the Department of Government, London School of Economics. A pioneer in the study of nationalism, his work, among other themes, highlights the connection between dominant ethnic groups and nations. In addition to numerous journal articles, he has published a considerable number of books on the subject of ethnicity and nationalism. These include (by no means a comprehensive list): *Theories of Nationalism* (1971), *The Ethnic Origins of Nations* (1986), *National Identity* (1991), *Nationalism and Modernism* (1998), *Myths and Memories of the Nation* (OUP, 1999), *The Nation in History* (Brandeis, 2000) and, most recently, *Nationalism: Theory, Ideology and History* (Polity, 2001).

Andreas Wimmer is Professor of Comparative and Historical Sociology at the University of California, Los Angeles. He was the founding director of the Swiss Forum for Migration Research at the University of Neuchâtel and later directed the Centre for Development Research of the University of Bonn, Germany, where he was Professor of Political and Cultural Change. His research interests include ethnicity and nationalism, migration, social change, history of thought, culture and globalisation. His most recent book is *Nationalist Exclusion and Ethnic Conflicts: Shadows of Modernity* (Cambridge University Press, 2002). He is currently working on a new book on globalisation and ethnicity, to be published by Polity Press.

Theodore P. Wright, Jr, is Professor Emeritus of Political Science at the State University of New York at Albany. He received his doctorate in International Relations from Yale University in 1957, and has been working on the politics of the Muslim minority in India and Muhajirs in Pakistan for forty years. He was a visiting fellow at the Institute of Commonwealth Studies of London University, then under the direction of the late Professor W.H. Morris-Jones, the UK's leading expert on post-independence Indian politics. Besides his published dissertation on 'American Support of Free Elections Abroad' (1964), he has published sixty-five articles and contributions to symposia in, among others, the *Journal of Asian Studies*, the *American Political Science Review* and *Comparative Politics*.

Keiko Yamanaka is a Lecturer in the Department of Comparative Ethnic Studies at the University of California, Berkeley, and is also a Research Associate at the Institute for the Study of Social Change. In 1993 she was awarded an Abe Fellowship from Japan's Center for Global Partnership to study issues of immigrant labour in Japan. She has published widely in both English and Japanese, in journals such as *Ethnic and Racial Studies* and *Diaspora*, and contributed to a number of successful edited volumes. In 2003 she co-edited (with N. Piper) 'Gender, migration and governance in Asia', in a special issue of *Asian and Pacific Migration Journal* (vol. 12, no. 1–2). In that volume, she authored an article on Brazilian immigrant women's community activism in Japan.

Oren Yiftachel is Professor of Geography at Ben-Gurion University of the Negev, Beer-Sheva, Israel. He teaches political geography, urban planning and public policy, and is a research fellow at the Negev Center for Regional Development. His main research areas explore the links between ethnonational politics and urban and regional development and conflict. He is the author of *Planning as Control: Policy and Resistance in a Divided Society* (Pergamon, 1995); *Ethnic Frontiers and Peripheries* (with A. Meir, eds, Westview, 1998), and *Ethnocracy: Territory, Politics, Identities in Israel/Palestine* (University of Pennsylvania, forthcoming). He is currently working on two main projects: studying the historical and political development of Israel's land system; and comparing and contrasting different ethnocratic regimes.

Acknowledgements

First, I would like to acknowledge the support of Steven and Carmen Kaufmann, without whom this project could never have been completed.

This project also owes a great deal to the support of the Economic and Social Research Council (ESRC), which furnished me with a generous two-year fellowship that allowed me, among other things, to complete this project. I would also like to acknowledge the support of the British Academy and the Association for the Study of Ethnicity and Nationalism (ASEN) in helping to sponsor a conference on 'Majority Groups and Dominant Minorities' at the London School of Economics in December 2002. Taking place at a time when many contributors had written first drafts, it gave both ourselves and our audience an opportunity to exchange ideas. More details and synopses from the conference can be found on the fellowship website at:

http://www.kpdata.com/epk/subtheme_C__Dominant_Ethnicity.html.

I am also grateful for the feedback I received from all contributors, notably my former doctoral supervisor Anthony Smith, whose retirement from the LSE in 2004 marks the end of an important era in nationalism studies. I have also gained from discussions with contributors and with my colleague Oliver Zimmer of the Department of History at the University of Durham.

Finally, I wish to thank Heidi Bagtazo and the editorial team at Routledge for their efficiency and support.

Introduction

Dominant ethnicity: from background to foreground

Eric P. Kaufmann

Today's nations are experiencing an unprecedented degree of pressure from the forces of globalisation. In particular, the spread of human and collective rights discourse since the 1960s has mounted an increasing challenge to the model of ethno-national congruence. Nations, nearly all of which were formed on the basis of a dominant, 'core' ethnic group, are thus facing pressure to shift their self-definitions from 'ethnic' to 'civic' criteria. They are encouraged to look to their future rather than their past, to treasure their cultural diversity (past and present) rather than their homogeneity, to recognise the autonomy claims of minorities and to be open to foreign trade, foreign immigration, and foreign ('multi') cultural influences. In short, global narratives of liberal multiculturalism, embedded in both global and national institutions, are driving an ever-greater wedge between modern nations and their dominant ethnic groups.

Meanwhile, the aftermath of the Cold War and the attendant loss of ideological discipline have led to a fracturing of many fragile ex-communist and post-colonial regimes along ethnic lines. The new wave of democratisation in the former communist bloc and many parts of Africa and Asia has given a boost to ethnic party systems, accentuating the trend. Iraq and Afghanistan are exhibiting similar tendencies post-9/11, suggesting yet a further dynamic of dominant ethnicisation. Never before have dominant ethnic constituencies been appealed to so narrowly and directly. Add the aforementioned globalising pressures that are denuding the national covering from dominant *ethnies*, and we uncover a picture in which dominant ethnicity appears more exposed than ever.

Much has been written about ethnic minorities and their relationship to state structures and abstract 'host societies'. There is also a voluminous literature on nations and nationalism. Burgeoning studies in the fields of citizenship and migration add to the debate.[1] Yet there has been virtually no consideration of the living, breathing ethnic communities which gave birth to, but are by no means coterminous with, the nation-state. These dominant ethnies – no less than their minority counterparts – are engaged in a process of reviving, constructing and adapting their identities and political strategies to the evolving context of late modernity. Due to their indigenous legitimacy and emotive power, such groups are arguably more central to explaining cultural and political developments than either subaltern minorities or professional state elites. We must therefore make every effort to improve our understanding of dominant ethnicity. How are ethnic majorities like the French of France, the Japanese of Japan, the Hindus of India and the Jews of Israel responding to the pressures of our global era? Are such groups in decline or are they successfully negotiating (or circumventing) the challenge of new global structures and values? These questions comprise one axis of our analysis.

The other concerns the place of politically dominant (or formerly dominant) *minorities*. As with ethnic majorities, evolving global norms pose a challenge to dominant minorities. In this instance, our post-colonial, post-communist era has generated renewed legitimacy for the idea of democratic self-determination. Notions of suzerainty and hegemonic control have been de-legitimated, and dominant minorities have been forced on the defensive. Rhodesians, Afrikaners, Baltic Russians and North Indian Muslims (see this volume) – all share a sense of loss, and face a crisis of ethnic legitimation. Even so, other dominant minorities, like the ethnic Fijians (see Chapter 12 by Premdas), Tutsis, Alawis or Gulf Arabs, appear as robust as ever. Once more, the focus of this work will be to probe the response of dominant ethnic communities to the new 'stimuli' in their environment, to examine whether such groups are in decline, or are successfully negotiating the latest wrinkle of global modernisation.

The development of the specialist literature in the field of ethnicity and nationalism studies has been astonishingly rapid in the past two decades. Indeed, many of the contributors to this volume are recognised as leading figures in this scholarly revolution. Since 1980, great strides have been made toward differentiating the concepts of state, nation, and ethnic group, and sketching the linkages between such phenomena.[2] *States* place the emphasis on the instruments of coercion, government and boundary demarcation within a territory. *Ethnic groups* refer to communities of (supposedly) shared ancestry, almost always accompanied by notions of an ancestral homeland and cultural boundary markers. *Nations* comprise an uneasy hybrid of elements from ethnies and the *modern* state: they are better integrated, more politically self-conscious and spatially demarcated than ethnies, but can employ a myth of political or ideological origins which is not specifically genealogical. In addition, nations do not always control their own political apparatus, nor must they maintain a monopoly of organised violence over their territory, hence the possibility of 'stateless nations'.

The connections between these entities are equally subtle, and are the subject of intense controversy between those of constructivist and historicist bent. Broadly speaking, this epistemic debate does not provide a central focus for this volume, though it enters into the discussion of several of our authors.[3] According to 'ethno-symbolist' theorists, some ethnies were transformed into nations in the modern era, while others, often due to their territorial dispersion, lack of political ambition or low level of self-consciousness (i.e. Balinese, Cajuns, Aragonese), did not emerge as nations.[4] Moreover, of those ethnies that successfully achieved nationhood, many (such as Scots, Tibetans) have failed to achieve modern statehood. Dominant ethnicity refers to the phenomenon whereby *a particular ethnic group exercises dominance within a nation and/or state*. Notice that the dominant ethnie need not dominate the state in which 'its' nation resides. This is the case, as Danielle Juteau points out in her chapter, with the *pures laines Québécois*, who dominate the nation of Quebec but not the Canadian state. In fact, it is possible for a culturally dominant nation to be politically subordinate (for instance, Euzkadi and Catalonia under Franco's Spain).

This of course flags up the variety of ways in which an ethnic group can be dominant: demographic, cultural, political, and economic. In pre-1960s Quebec, for instance, *pures laines Québécois* dominated culturally and politically but not economically. Today, many ethnic minorities (e.g. Chinese, Indians, Lebanese and Whites in developing countries) control the local economy but are politically weak, hence, argues Sino-Philippine Amy Chua, their vulnerability to genocide in a world of economic liberalisation and populist democratisation (Chua 2003). In many colonial settings, settler ethnies like the Rhodesians, Americo-Liberians and Afrikaners have enjoyed political, but not cultural dominance. In the medieval Baltic and Czech lands, German-speakers dominated the high culture, economy and polity, but the folk culture of the peasant masses remained as a springboard for the development of future Latvian, Czech and Estonian dominant ethnicity. Demography is also illusory since certain culturally dominant ethnies, like the pre-2003 Iraqi Sunnis (see Chapter 3 by Wimmer), Surinamese Creoles or Melanesian Fijians (see Chapter 12 by Premdas), do not even comprise a plurality of the population.

The two sides of dominant ethnicity: indigenousness and power

This brings us to the two key ingredients of ethnic dominance: indigenousness and power. Richard Schermerhorn's concept of an 'elite minority' (1970) and Anthony Smith's articulation of the term 'core ethnie' (1986) are cardinal points of departure for this investigation. The tradition that follows from Schermerhorn stresses the political side of the equation, concentrating on the raw political power of ethnic groups (minority or majority) and their ranking within ethnic power systems. Donald Horowitz's (1985) work is in this tradition, and Ashley Doane's important sociology of 'dominant-group ethnicity' (1993, 1997) maintains the focus on politico-economic hegemony as the metre of dominant ethnicity.

Yet what remained to be crafted in the 1980s was a conceptual framework for *cultural* dominance which related ethnie to nation. In fact, it was not until 1986 that the term 'core ethnie' was first used by Anthony Smith, who had refined the concept sufficiently to be able to provide a definition of 'dominant ethnie' within the pages of his *National Identity* (Smith 1986: 138; 1991). In this work, Smith emphasised that nations are built around 'ethnic cores' or 'dominant ethnies' which furnish the nation with its legitimating myths, symbols and conceptions of territory. 'Though most latter-day nations are, in fact, polyethnic,' notes Smith:

> many have been formed in the first place around a *dominant ethnie*, which attracted other ethnies or ethnic fragments into the state to which it gave a name and cultural charter ... since ethnies are by definition associated with a given territory ... the presumed boundaries of the nation are largely determined by the myths and memories of the *dominant ethnie*, which include the foundation charter, the myth of the golden age and the associated territorial claims, or ethnic title-deeds.
>
> (1991: 39, emphasis added)

Smith's argument would suggest that the critical element in dominant ethnicity is indigenousness, the idea that this is 'our' nation, and that 'we' deserve to be in control of its government and territory. In many ways, such an argument is especially potent in the modern, post-imperial age, when 'foreign' rule is deemed illegitimate. As Theodore Wright notes in Chapter 2, this is an owl of Minerva that has flown at dusk for numerous aristocratic ethnies (i.e. the Anglo-Irish, Zanzibari Arabs, Indian Mohajirs). Few nationalist conflicts are not in some way related to a struggle over whose territorial claim has priority, and the international legitimacy of self-determination claims is partly grounded in questions of indigenousness. Even where two groups can trace their history back for many centuries or even millennia (for instance, Tamils and Sinhalese, Jews and Palestinians, Serbs and Albanians), questions pertaining to indigenousness are central – and express themselves in archaeological, linguistic and historical controversies. Similarly, one of the engines behind anti-immigrant politics and attempts at cultural purification (especially *vis-à-vis* language) is a sense that foreign cultural borrowings are not really 'authentic' or indigenous, hence their illegitimacy in the eyes of Romantic ethno-nationalists in the Herderian mode.[5]

Given the increasing relevance of indigeneity-driven dominant ethnicity in the post-colonial and post-Berlin Wall epoch, it is surprising that little has been written on dominant ethnicity. Instead, the focus has been on the larger but fuzzier targets of nationalism and citizenship. Certainly no major conceptualisation of dominant ethnicity has taken place beyond an encyclopaedic definition and one journal article.[6] This book is therefore the first of its kind, and represents a new step in the maturation of ethnicity and nationalism studies, away from both the Anglo-centric equation of 'ethnic' with 'minority' and toward a more precise elucidation of the concept of dominant ethnicity within its conceptual atmosphere of ethnicity, nationalism and statehood.

Part I of the book, 'Conceptualising dominant ethnicity', makes this aim explicit. In Chapter 1 Anthony Smith expands upon his ground-breaking concept of the dominant ethnie and places it in historical, geographical and theoretical context. Theodore Wright examines the fate of formerly dominant ethnies in Chapter 2 and in Chapter 3 Andreas Wimmer places dominant ethnicity within his theory of ethnic closure – as an intrinsic component of the modernisation process. Though the first three chapters are explicitly conceptual, they are far from labouring alone in this task. All of our contributors engage with the concept of dominant ethnicity, and in many cases authors suggest new ways in which dominant ethnicity may be theorised. Here, for the first time, hermeneutic light is being directed towards dominant ethnic groups, which are interrogated not as abstract states, nations or host 'societies', but as ethnic communities like any other.

This volume is deliberately catholic in its geographic reach and disciplinary focus. Furthermore, our essayists disagree on many normative points, and most would certainly take issue with many observations made in this Introduction! Interdisciplinarity is especially evident: contributors span the humanities and social sciences. Consequently, we see discussion of dominant ethnicity as it relates to discourses in anthropology, sociology, politics, geography, international relations and history. We are thus interested in such cultural questions as the narration of dominant ethnic myths, symbols and histories, the operation of ethnic boundaries (i.e. endogamy, residential segregation, immigration restriction, assimilation), the interplay between traditional and modern concepts of identity and space, the intersections between dominant ethnicity and other identities like region or class, and the way in which dominant ethnicity is nested and mobilised in the private and public spheres.

Politically, our contributors are interested in the mechanisms by which dominant ethnies control their state or provincial governments. Is violence used, or is hegemony effected through majority ethnic party mobilisation and/or control of key posts in the legislature, executive and judiciary? Why have some dominant ethnies yielded power to subaltern groups while others appear to have strengthened their hand in recent decades? The precarious nature of dominant ethnic unity is also an important theme: Mancur Olson (1982), famously writing from a rational choice perspective, suggested that large groups tend to fragment and are less effective than smaller political actors. Yet certain dominant ethnies seem to be successful in their ecumenical strategy of mobilising their members across lines of region, class, and even language or religion.

There is also the international environment to consider: global or supra-national institutions can exert diplomatic and economic pressure (e.g. in Fiji or South Africa), while foreign governments can sustain short- or long-distance influence over the dynamics of dominance (e.g. the USA in Liberia, Syria in Lebanon). International norms, whether of self-determination, state sovereignty or individual rights, similarly intrude into our picture. The influence of norms of self-determination, for instance, helped to hasten the collapse of empire in the nineteenth and twentieth centuries, along with the European and Turkish ethnic elites who ran them. However, the application of international norms may be uneven; thus while European colonial elites are no longer in power in many developing countries, dominance by one ethnic group (or a coalition of groups, as in Jordan) appears to be a *de facto* norm that basks within the protective shell of state sovereignty.

Dominant ethnicity, ethno-nationalism and national identity

A number of themes run through this volume. The first involves the distinctiveness of dominant ethnicity as a concept. Dominant ethnicity is not ethno-nationalism, though there is overlap between these two concepts.[7] First of all, dominant ethnies pre-date our modern age of nations.[8] Second, many states are characterised by inter-ethnic conflict over power, wealth and symbolic recognition in which nationalism plays little part. Turning first to the former phenomenon, many empires were controlled, at least in part, by an aristocratic ethnie. Theodore Wright, in his fascinating chapter, mentions the role of the Mohajirs in the Mughal Empire, but we could devise an extensive list that includes such ethnies as the Austro-Germans and Magyars in the Habsburg Dual Monarchy and Anatolian Turks in the Ottoman Empire. In addition, tribal confederation or a position on a religious or imperial frontier often crystallised the ethnic identities of groups as diverse as the Armenians, Zulus, Swiss-Germans, Poles and Vietnamese – groups which occasionally held sway in their particular region (Armstrong 1982; Smith 1986).

Cycles of integration and disintegration characterise many empires and the occasional combination of ethnic unity and imperial disunity meant that many pre-modern ethnies enjoyed periods – however fleeting – of ethnic dominance within their homeland. It is therefore the case that many if not *most ethnies have been dominant somewhere at some time in their history*. Indeed, this near-universal experience typically becomes grist for the ethno-nationalist revival mill, a template for ethnic elites in search of a 'golden age' of unity and strength (Smith 1997). In the more recent epoch, dominance is sometimes achieved by minority groups as formerly centralised nation-states devolve power to regions or federal units. Danielle Juteau's discussion of *pures laines Québécois*' dominant ethnicity in the province of Quebec in Chapter 5 provides a case in point. The Welsh, Flemish, Catalans and others furnish similar examples, though dominance in these cases is rarely complete.

This brings us to a second important difference between dominant ethnicity and ethno-nationalism. Even if ethno-nationalism (i.e. separatism) is not evident, ethnic competitors usually jockey for the prize of dominance, both in their regional homeland and in a state's economic, political and symbolic arenas. This was especially pronounced in the run-up to decolonisation but is nearly everywhere a pervading theme. In Donald Horowitz's words: 'Evidence that control of the state is a central ethnic conflict objective is abundant.' In the immediate decolonisation period, for instance, Maronites demanded a Lebanese state with a Christian character and control over Lebanon Mountain, the Hausa-Fulani jealously guarded their claims over northern Nigeria, Sinhalese and Tamils struggled for dominance in Sri Lanka, and North African states like Chad, Mauritania and Sudan were riven by rivalries between Arab and African ethnies for control (Horowitz 1985: 187–9). In some cases, a dominant ethnie like the Kikuyu in Kenya or Tutsi in Rwanda emerged; in others, as Wright points out in this volume, formerly dominant ethnies lost power, while in still other cases, ethnic systems remained unranked and contested.

Horowitz's path-breaking work on ethnic dominance considered struggles over demographic increase (manifested in 'winning' the census and restricting migration into homeland regions), and also detailed the way in which groups clamour over economic resources, government posts and symbolic status. Struggles over symbolic status, though often concerned with official language or religion, also tend to involve conflicts over indigenousness. For instance, in highly multi-ethnic settings such as Trinidad, Mauritius, Suriname or Belize, the question of which group became 'dominant' was very much a matter of chance, since a diverse array of groups arrived within a relatively short space of time. However, the relative timing of migrations (which saw African slaves arrive first, followed by Asian indentured labourers), the tendency of colonial elites to favour Creoles in the colonial power structure as well as the stronger propensity for African descendants to adopt European culture have given African-Creole groups the edge. Neither the more 'indigenous' Amerindians, the more numerous Asian Indians nor the more politically and economically dominant Europeans possessed the requisite degree of indigenousness and power to prevail. As a result, creolised Dutch or English has emerged as an assimilative *lingua franca* and the national identity, shaped in the image of the Creole dominant ethnie, has achieved significant assimilative success among subaltern groups (Eriksen 1993; St. Hilaire 2001).

Other analysts have probed the twin-track strategies of dominant ethnic groups who simultaneously narrate both their own ethnicity and the broader national identity in fragmented societies. Such groups often take the lead in suppressing separatist claims in the name of 'national unity'. In Ghana, for example, David Brown remarks that the nation's leaders, who hail from the Akan dominant ethnie, tend to stress an ecumenical national unity. Yet the appeal to a sense of dominant Akan ethnicity has accompanied this quest. Whereas such an appeal first manifested itself in the demonisation of the Ewe minority, subsequent leaders like Jerry Rawlings managed to soften this rhetoric. Even so, frequent appearances in Akan costume helped to assuage the dominant ethnie (Brown 2000: 110–25). Likewise, in cases as diverse as Indonesia (presidents in Islamic dress), Singapore ('speak Mandarin' campaign), the USA (nearly all presidents have been WASP) and China, a recognition of 'diversity' does not preclude the leadership's overtures to the dominant ethnie.

Expansive and restrictive strategies

Just as dominant ethnicity may be expressed in either political or cultural terms, it can take on either expansive or restrictive form. *Expansive* dominant ethnic strategies seek to project dominance outward to new lands, and in so doing may be content to let dominant ethnic particularity lapse in favour of a broader national or imperial construct. *Restrictive* strategies focus on purifying the dominant ethnic core of external influences and often involve instruments like immigration restriction, deportation, endogamy and cultural refinement. Restrictive dominant ethnies will not, in contrast to their expansive cousins, trade their 'soul' for power, and are in principle prepared to accept the secession or federation of minority ethnies. Many situations involve both strategies: the winners of the First World War (i.e. those that chose the correct side, like Romania) were only too pleased to enlarge their territories and deal later with their new-found heterogeneity through the high-pressure assimilation tactics of the 'nationalising state'. In response, irridentist 'homeland nationalisms' among losing nations like inter-war Hungary or Germany attempted to enlarge the ethnic homeland by annexing adjacent territory inhabited by co-ethnics in other states (Brubaker 1996; Zimmer 2003: Chapter 4). Serbian ambitions to carve out a Greater Serbia through ethnic cleansing or Indonesia's policy of sending Javanese settlers to East Timor or West Irian suggest that other groups wish to have their cake and eat it too.

Usually, such strategies fail, thus the frequent decision to opt for power over culture in expansive fashion. If dominant ethnicity remains expansive, the preferred method for maintaining its boundaries is through assimilation rather than exclusion (Barth 1969). In such cases, dominant ethnicity remains 'hidden' and a broader nationalist or imperial appeal takes place, though this can ultimately lead to a decline of dominant ethnic consciousness or its disappearance altogether. The British, Ottoman, Habsburg and, as Geoffrey Hosking details in Chapter 8, Tsarist/Soviet empires often submerged the identity of the dominant ethnie in their quest for power and territory. Ethnic decline is especially likely in the case of empires which engaged in large-scale cultural borrowing or slave labour importation (i.e. the Assyrians, the Romans, the Normans) (Smith 1986). It is perhaps indicative that many of the cases which experienced a decline of dominant ethnicity (i.e. the USA, Canada and arguably Britain) were or are expansive in nature.

With the collapse of empire, rump states like Hungary, Britain or Turkey were faced with crises of identity. They could either return to imperial scale (a 'greater' strategy that involves more power/territory but less ethnic homogeneity) or turn inwards towards a 'little' nationalism that stresses the dominant ethnie's cultural particularity. Israel's choice between a more homogeneous pre-1967 state or an expanded occupied territory (see Chapter 10 by Yiftachel and Ghanem) presents one form of this dilemma. The renewed focus on 'little' Englandism in Britain in the wake of de-colonisation and devolution suggests that a different route is possible (Bryant 2003). The American and Anglo-Canadian examples (see Chapter 2 by Wright and my Chapter 4 on this), in which ethnic homogeneity was 'traded' for the increased politico-economic power which immigrants brought to the country, might be viewed as a 'third way' forward.

Dominant ethnicity: why now?

Numerous restrictive–expansive dilemmas are now being created for dominant ethnies by today's separatist movements and immigration inflows which open up space between ethnie and nation. Given the post-colonial, post-Berlin Wall collapse of empire, and the surge in international migration associated with globalising technologies, it is not surprising that so many dominant ethnies find themselves under pressure to choose between restrictive 'ethnic' and expansive 'national' strategies. We can add to this a dominant ethnic 'legitimation crisis' brought on by the new post-1960s' Western discourse of cultural liberalism and multiculturalism. This current of thinking, inflected by the New Left and carried by a post-industrial, post-materialist educated elite, has come to prominence in Western culture and its global institutions.[9] The result, as Dominique Schnapper notes, is an attack on *both* restrictive and expansive boundary-maintenance techniques, especially in the West. Such a stance splits ethnie from nation, precluding both an expansive recourse to republican nationalism (see Schnapper's Chapter 6) and a restrictive focus on protecting the dominant ethnic core.

Part II of this book, 'Dominant ethnicity in transition', considers these challenges as they pertain to cases where empires have collapsed (i.e. Britain, Russia/USSR) or immigration has surged (i.e. WASPs in Canada and the United States, the French in France and *pures laines Québécois* in Quebec). Such groups are unused to thinking of themselves in ethnic terms, having long since viewed 'their' nation as an extension of themselves (Resnick 2001). Dominique Schnapper suggests that the French nation tried to transcend its ethnic base to embrace a wider community of citizens, while Danielle Juteau avers that such a transformation is an illusion, and republican nationalism merely provides a foil for dominant ethnicity – a shift from restrictive to expansive boundary-maintenance. Hence the difficulty of *pures laines Québécois* in retreating from the national podium to ethnic 'lower ground'. Like Ted Wright, I point to the importance of liberal-egalitarianism in fomenting ethnic decline among WASPs in North America, while Steve Bruce in Chapter 7 suggests that similar tendencies, along with the fissiparous nature of the Protestant faith, were among the factors that led to a decline in the Protestant identity of the Scots, English and Welsh in Britain.

Part III, 'Dominant ethnicity resurgent', adjusts the focus to a new, and probably more widespread, set of cases. In Japan, as Keiko Yamanaka makes clear in Chapter 9, or in Israel (see Chapter 10, Yiftachel and Ghanem), the new norms of universal personhood have generally failed to unseat a well-entrenched 'ethnocracy'.[10] This does not mean there are no liberal constituencies: Yamanaka's focus on local progressive actors in Hamamatsu and the persistence of a robust 'post-Zionist' sector of opinion in Israel illustrate the tension between dominant ethnicity and the new multicultural liberalism[11] (Hazony 2000; Yadgar 2002). In Chapter 12 Ralph Premdas's fascinating work on Fiji highlights the important role played by liberal norms and their transmission through global/supranational institutions like the IMF and the British Commonwealth in checking some of the more flagrant Fijian ethnocratic tendencies.

Even so, only in the West can one truly describe dominant ethnicity as in retreat: it is both more visible (due to a questioning of the ethnie–nation link) and weaker (due to its legitimation crisis). On the other hand, the steady resurgence of the ethno-nationalist right in Western Europe, coupled with the wider anxieties over immigration which powered the Schengen agreement, suggest that the fault-line between dominant ethnicity and cosmopolitan liberalism runs through the Western world as well. Indeed, Andreas Wimmer, in considering the Swiss case, proffers that ethnic closure is a principle which, far from being opposed to modernisation, actually helps to constitute *modernity itself*.

A second major focus of attention in Part III rests on new trends that are largely to be found in the developing world. During the Cold War, many regimes in the developing and communist world were predicated on an ideological consensus which suppressed fissiparous ethnic tendencies. Nkrumah's Ghana, Congress India and Tito's Yugoslavia provide three examples. The post-Berlin Wall rise of separatist movements and the mobilisation of ethnic parties in the democratising regimes of Eastern Europe, Asia and Africa have exposed the dominant ethnic underpinnings of many Second and Third World states. Unlike the situation in the West, the 'outing' of the dominant ethnie has frequently strengthened it, and sharpened its focus on mobilisation, exclusion and hegemony. In Part I Wimmer draws our attention to the steady tightening of Sunni domination in pre-2003 Iraq and Mestizo hegemony in Mexico. In this Part, by contrast, Ralph Premdas suggests, in Chapter 12, that dominant ethnicity in Fiji has more path-dependent, colonial roots and thus transcends more recent developments. Chetan Bhatt's analysis of Hindu nationalism in India, Theodore Wright's focus on the deprivation of the once-dominant Indian Muslims (see Part I) and Oren Yiftachel and As'ad Ghanem's piece on Judaisation point to another source of dominant ethnicity: the Diaspora. Though long associated with minority nationalisms (i.e. Irish, Greek), diasporan ethnic minorities such as overseas Hindus and Jews (not to mention Serbs or Croats) can play a leading role in the resurgence of dominant ethnicity (dominant ethno-nationalism in the Serbo-Croat cases). Communications technology, therefore, provides another medium by which modernity can *enhance* dominant ethnicity.

Given the geographical limits inherent in any comparative work on ethnicity and nationalism, we are unable to treat a wider array of cases. It would have been useful to include cases from Sub-Saharan Africa (i.e. Kikuyu in Kenya, Tutsi in Rwanda, Baganda in Uganda) or to consider more Arab Middle Eastern examples such as the Saudis, Gulf Arabs, Transjordanians or Syrian Alawi. South America and much of Eastern Europe are barely touched upon. To some extent, a wide range of groups are treated in the first four theoretical chapters. However, there is little question that more research is needed in this area. If this book can help to generate new insights and stimulate further scholarship, it will have been worth the effort.

Coda: normative questions

Though the focus of this work falls squarely within the ambit of 'empirical' theory and investigation, there are many normative questions raised by our contributors. Is dominant ethnicity always malign, or are there forms that may be important for human well-being? On a practical level, Brendan O'Leary contends that dominant ethnies lend stability to power-sharing systems (O'Leary 2001). More poignantly, Yael Tamir (1993: 11) has written that:

> Liberals often align themselves with national demands raised by 'underdogs', be they indigenous peoples, discriminated minorities, or occupied nations, whose plight can easily evoke sympathy. But if national claims rest on theoretically sound and morally justified grounds, one cannot restrict their application: They apply equally to all nations, regardless of their power, their wealth, their history of suffering, or even the injustices they have inflicted on others in the past.

Putting to one side Tamir's use of the term 'nation', we might easily apply the argument to ethnic groups. However, as I have pointed out elsewhere, liberal culturalist political theorists like Will Kymlicka, Charles Taylor, David Miller and Joseph Raz tend to focus on the interplay between nation-states and minority ethnies while neatly sidestepping the difficult issue of dominant ethnicity (Kaufmann 2000a). After all, it is much easier to reconcile a 'thin' version of national identity with minority claims than to deal with competing 'thick' ones. Yet it is extremely difficult to see how the particularism and diversity associated with ethnic cultures can survive without some form of 'deep' cultural dominance over a particular territory.

On the other hand, it is by no means clear that ethnic groups need to control the levers of political and economic power. Here I agree with Danielle Juteau's conception, in which dominant ethnic groups recognise themselves as ethnic groups like any other and take their place alongside, rather than on top of, fellow ethnies in the state. Perhaps we might conceive of a new global configuration, in which 'national ethnic groups', shorn of their dominant politico-economic position, agree to participate in trans-ethnic networks of national and supranational governance.

Notes

1   The explosion of academic journals in this area is one indicator. *Nations and Nationalism, Nationalism and Ethnic Politics, National Identities, Citizenship Studies, Ethnic and Racial Studies, Journal of Ethnic and Migration Studies* and numerous others service this vital field of scholarly endeavour.
2   Leading works in this area include Smith (1971, 1986, 1991), Gellner (1983), Anderson (1983), Hobsbawm (1990) and Connor (1994).
3   See Chetan Bhatt's Chapter 11 in this volume for a constructivist challenge to the notion of dominant ethnicity.
4   The classic exposition of the 'ethnie-to-nation' argument appears in Smith, (1986). See also Hutchinson (1987). A critique of ethno-symbolism can be found in Ozkirimli (2003).
5   On the role of archaeology, see Díaz-Andreu (2001). Linguistic controversies currently plague the former Yugoslavia, where Croatian, Bosnian Muslim and Serbian scholars have recently marked out their own separate versions of Serbo-Croat (see Conversi 1997). In the nineteenth century, 'Anglo-Saxonist' philologists and literature scholars in England and the United States tried to emphasise Anglo-Saxon as opposed to Latin or French-origin words, a practice common in many countries in the Romantic period (Niles and Frantzen 1997). German Romantic scholar Johann Gottfried von Herder, though an advocate of anti-imperial, polycentric pluralism, stressed that territorial-linguistic integrity was critical, and that authenticity inhered in linguistic rather than political boundaries. A more general discussion on the role of archaeologists, philologists, linguists, historians and other antiquarian scholars in helping to revive, embellish or invent ethnicity and nations appears in Smith (1991).
6   See Kaufmann (2000a) for definition, Doane (1997) for article. A number of important area studies touch on the concept obliquely, as with Allworth (1980) (Russia) and a more recent edited volume on Asian majorities by Gladney (1998). Authors like Brendan O'Leary and George Schopflin have made use of the term 'Staatsvolk' in their writing, and Ernest Gellner staged a conference on formerly dominant ethnic minorities at the Central European University in Budapest in 1995 (O'Leary 2001).
7   Dominant ethnicity, when it uses the nation as its vehicle for political ambitions and employs nationalist rhetoric, approximates to the term 'dominant ethnic nationalism'. However, ethnic nationalism is usually used to characterise sepa-ratist movements like the Welsh or Flemish which are subordinate in political terms. All of which suggests that ethnic nationalism and dominant ethnicity are relatively distinct, and that it is a mistake to use the former term to describe the latter phenomenon.
8   If we accept the admittedly contentious view of mainstream (for instance, modernist and ethno-symbolist) nationalism scholars that nations are modern. This position is contested by many medievalist historians and some theorists like Adrian Hastings (Hastings 1997).

9 For more on post-materialist value change, see Inglehart (1990).
10 This term was first coined by Oren Yiftachel, and carries a similar meaning to dominant ethnicity.
11 Though liberalism and multiculturalism are frequently seen as opposing concepts by political theorists, they are united in their opposition to dominant ethnicity. Moreover, the more expansive concepts of liberal culturalism developed by Will Kymlicka dovetail nicely with a 'soft', cosmopolitan multiculturalism which eschews ethnic boundaries and celebrates hybridity and diversity (Kaufmann 2000b).

References

Allworth, E. (ed.) (1980) *Ethnic Russia in the USSR: The Dilemma of Dominance*, New York: Pergamon Press.

Anderson, B. (1983) *Imagined Communities: Reflections on the Origin and Spread of Nationalism*, London: Verso.

Armstrong, J. (1982) *Nations before Nationalism*, Chapel Hill, NC: University of North Carolina Press.

Barth, F. (ed.) (1969) *Ethnic Groups and Boundaries: The Social Organization of Culture Difference*, London: Allen and Unwin.

Brown, D. (2000) *Contemporary Nationalism: Civic, Ethnocultural and Multicultural Politics*, London: Routledge.

Brubaker, R. (1996) *Nationalism Reframed: Nationhood and the National Question in the New Europe*, Cambridge: Cambridge University Press.

Bryant, C.G.A. (2003) 'These Englands, or where does devolution leave the English?', *Nations and Nationalism*, 9(3): 393–412.

Chua, A. (2003) *World on Fire: How Exporting Free Market Democracy Breeds Ethnic Violence and Global Instability*, London: Heinemann.

Connor, W. (1994) *Ethnonationalism: The Quest for Understanding*, Princeton, NJ: Princeton University Press.

Conversi, D. (1997) *The Basques, Catalans and Spain: Alternative Routes to Nationalist Mobilisation*, London: Hurst.

Díaz-Andreu, M. (2001) 'Guest editor's introduction: nationalism and archaeology', *Nations and Nationalism*, 7(4): 429–40.

Doane, A.W., Jr. (1993) 'Bringing the majority back in: towards a sociology of dominant group ethnicity', paper presented at the annual meeting of the Society for the Study of Social Problems, Miami Beach, FL.

—— (1997) 'Dominant group ethnic identity in the United States: the role of "hidden" ethnicity in intergroup relations', *Sociological Quarterly*, 38(3): 375–97.

Eriksen, T.H. (1993) *Ethnicity and Nationalism: Anthropological Perspectives*, London: Pluto Press.

Gellner, E. (1983) *Nations and Nationalism*, Oxford: Blackwell.

Gladney, D. (ed.) (1998) *Making Majorities*, Stanford, CA: Stanford University Press.

Hastings, A. (1997) *The Construction of Nationhood: Ethnicity, Religion and Nationalism*, Cambridge: Cambridge University Press.

Hazony, Y. (2000) *The Jewish State*, New York: Basic Books.

Hobsbawm, E.J. (1990) *Nations and Nationalism since 1780: Programme, Myth, Reality*, Cambridge: Cambridge University Press.

Horowitz, D.L. (1985) *Ethnic Groups in Conflict*, Berkeley, CA: University of California Press.

Hutchinson, J. (1987) *The Dynamics of Cultural Nationalism: The Gaelic Revival and the Creation of the Irish Nation-State*, London: Allen & Unwin.

Inglehart, R. (1990) *Culture Shift in Advanced Industrial Society*, Princeton, NJ: Princeton University Press.

Kaufmann, E. (2000a) 'Dominant ethnie', in *The Companion Guide to Nationalism*, London: Transaction Publishers.

—— (2000b) 'Liberal ethnicity: beyond liberal nationalism and minority rights', *Ethnic and Racial Studies*, 23(6): 1086–119.

Niles, J.D. and Frantzen, A.J. (eds) (1997) *Anglo-Saxonism and the Construction of Social Identity*, Gainesville, FL: University Press of Florida.

O'Leary, B. (2001) 'An iron law of nationalism and federation? A (neo-Diceyian) theory of the necessity of a federal Staatsvolk, and of consociational rescue', *Nations and Nationalism*, 7(3): 273–96.

Olson, M. (1982) *The Rise and Decline of Nations: Economic Growth, Stagflation, and Social Rigidities*, New Haven, CT: Yale University Press.

Ozkirimli, U. (2003) 'The nation as an artichoke? A critique of ethnosymbolist interpretations of nationalism', *Nations and Nationalism*, 9(3): 339–56.

Resnick, P. (2001) 'Majority nationalities within multinational states: the challenge of identity', in F.C. González (ed.) *El espejo, el mosaico y el crisol: Modelos politicos para el multiculturalismo*, Barcelona: Anthropos-Universidad Autónoma Metropolitana.

St. Hilaire, A. (2001) 'Ethnicity, assimilation and nation in plural Suriname', *Ethnic and Racial Studies*, 24(6): 998–1019.

Schermerhorn, R.A. (1970) *Comparative Ethnic Relations: A Framework for Theory and Research*, New York: Random House.

Smith, A.D. (1971) *Theories of Nationalism*, London: Duckworth.

—— (1986) *The Ethnic Origins of Nations*, Oxford: Blackwell.

—— (1991) *National Identity*, London: Penguin.

—— (1997) 'The "Golden Age" and national renewal', in G. Hosking and G. Schopflin (eds) *Myths and Nationhood*, New York: Routledge.

Tamir, Y. (1993) *Liberal Nationalism*, Princeton, NJ: Princeton University Press.

Yadgar, Y. (2002) 'From the particularistic to the universalistic: national narratives in Israel's mainstream press, 1967–1997', *Nations and Nationalism*, 8(1): 55–72.

Zimmer, O. (2003) *Nationalism in Europe, 1890–1940*, London: Palgrave-Macmillan.

Part I

Conceptualising dominant ethnicity

1 Ethnic cores and dominant ethnies

Anthony D. Smith

In the burgeoning literature of the 1950s and 1960s on 'ethnicity', as it came to be called, one bedrock assumption was almost universally endorsed. Ethnicity adhered to numerical and sociological cultural minorities, never to numerical and sociological majorities in a given state. National states, it was conceded, were rarely monoethnic. The great majority consisted of a nation and one or more ethnic minorities. On the one hand, there was the historic 'nation', the most populous, the wealthiest and the politically dominant of the cultural groups in the state, even if it was not indigenous. On the other hand, there were the minority populations, immigrants of a different culture, if not religion, each of them less populous, poorer and without power, acculturating to the national Way of Life and in the throes of assimilation. These were 'the ethnics', in contrast to the 'nation', into which they were to be incorporated and integrated, if not melted down.

This was, broadly speaking, the image of the 'national state' held by American sociologists at the time, and it was clearly drawn from the peculiar experience of immigrant societies, notably the United States. We see it even in more sensitive treatments like those of Nathan Glazer and Daniel Moynihan. How far the image conformed to the reality is another matter; and in particular, I leave aside the rather different issues raised by the history and status of the Blacks in the United States, defined in terms of 'race', from which sociologists and politicians alike wished to differentiate other non-Black minorities, partly through the use of the term 'ethnicity'. Here I want to show how this specifically American image and usage of the term 'ethnicity' have distorted our overall understanding of the dynamics of ethnicity and nationhood, and how historians and social scientists have tried to produce a more valid and useful framework for the analysis of the interrelations of ethnicity and nationhood, as well as for our understanding of the origins and development of nations.[1]

A critique of 'minority ethnicity'

We might start with the term itself. Although as a noun the term 'ethnicity', signifying, like social class, either a sub-field of the study of stratification, or a type of status group, or both, seems to have originated after the Second World War, its roots in an adjectival concept referring to the origins and culture of a group are far older. They reach back to the first Greek usage, in Homer. Here, *ethnos* refers to a band or host or tribe – be it of friends or fighting men or a swarm of bees, or of named groups like *ethnos Lukiōn*, *ethnos Achaiōn*. In Pindar we read of the *ethnos* of men or women, in Herodotus of the *to Medikon ethnos*, and in Plato of the *ethnos* of heralds.[2]

What these usages appear to have in common is that the groups in question possess certain common cultural, and in some cases physical, attributes. The named groups also appear to have some territorial referent. Herodotus seems to have thought that the cognate concept of *genos* referred to a smaller kinship group, a sub-division of *ethnos*, but he sometimes uses *gens* interchangeably with *ethnos*, much as the Romans tended to use *genos* to refer to larger civilised peoples, other than themselves, the *populus Romanus*. For the Romans, the concept of *natio*, on the other hand, was reserved for distant, usually barbaric tribes, and only in the Middle Ages did it begin to acquire its modern usage, alongside the old Roman usage of *gens*. However, no such consistency informed the ancient Greek usage in respect of *ethnos*. Though, like the apparent Jewish opposition between the *'am Israel* and the *goyim*, the Greeks clearly distinguished *Ellenes* from *barbaroi*, their use of the term *ethnos* covered all 'peoples' who possessed common cultural traits.[3]

These ancient usages, untidy as they may appear, were nevertheless highly influential for the ways in which later epochs sought to describe relations between cultural and territorial groups. Thus, in the New Testament and Church Fathers, the *goyim*, or Gentiles, rendered by *ta ethnē* (which in turn were translated into the *nationes* of the Vulgate), referred to all peoples apart from the Jews and Christians. This suggests a considerable overlap, if not identity, between *ethnos* and *natio*, in contrast to the opposition between ethnic groups and nations, and ethnicity and nationhood, in modern Western, and specifically American, usage. Of course, terms frequently change their meaning. But here we have two diametrically opposed traditions, in one of which the terms 'ethnic' and 'national', and ethnic group and nation, overlap or are even synonyms, while in the other, they are radically different and opposed concepts.[4]

The argument from etymology brings us immediately to that from history. Here I think it useful to contrast two kinds of historical development, the one endogenous, the other exogenous, the one based on long resident communities, the other on recently arrived populations, the one claiming to be indigenous and autochthonous, the other immigrant and pioneering. I refer, of course, to the Middle Eastern and European societies, on the one hand, and, on the other hand, to the immigrant societies of North America, Australia and Argentina.

In the first of these, we are confronted by an evolution of long resident ethnic groups or, in the French term, *ethnies* in the formation of nations over *la longue durée*. The concept of *ethnie* refers to a named human population with a myth of common origins and ancestry, shared historical memories, one or more elements of common culture, and a measure of solidarity, at least among the elites. This slow development from *ethnie* to nation was often accompanied by the use of force on the part of the centralising state of a dominant *ethnie* who constituted the state's core against adjacent *ethnies* and its conquest of their territories, as occurred in England, France, Spain, Sweden and Russia. Throughout this long-drawn-out process, the leading personnel of the state were largely drawn from the members of its core *ethnie*, and, equally important, its social, religious, military and political institutions, as well as its customs and codes, were those of the dominant *ethnie*'s elites. To this, largely European, evolution I shall shortly return, for it has been pivotal to the formation of nations and national states.[5]

In the second kind of trajectory, one or more *ethnies* pioneered the development of a new territory and attracted immigrants from many other *ethnies*, who formed the nation through voluntary submission to common myths, symbols, norms and codes and with differing degrees of social mobility and intermarriage. Of course, we should be careful not to exaggerate the historical differences between the two models of nation-formation. Even in immigrant societies, there was a pioneering or leading *ethnie*, which soon assumed a position of dominance in the nineteenth-century state. But, apart from the much shorter time-span involved, there was no forcible incorporation of long resident *ethnies*, except for the indigenous peoples; while, on the other hand, there was a clear desire for integration into the state by successive waves of immigrants. As a result, it was much easier to oppose the concept of the territorial nation or national state to the ethnic groups formed by incoming migrants eager for rapid integration into the host culture.[6]

Here, the argument from history finds its complement in that from sociology. There is an important difference between *ethnies* whose attachments to particular territories, for example Euzkadi or Slovenia, appear to be 'immemorial', their origins being lost in a haze of legends, and the fairly recent and relatively well documented arrival of immigrant groups who have no particular attachments to this or that territory within the large host state and no wish to politicise their cultures and historical mythologies in opposition to the national state into which they seek rather to be integrated.

It is little wonder if, in the latter case, quite different terms are used to denote the immigrant communities, the ethnic groups, from the total community of the host state, or nation. The relations between ethnic groups and the nation differ greatly from those obtaining between a peripheral *ethnie* and the state in long-resident national states. In immigrant societies, the governing impulse, with a few exceptions among indigenous and Black peoples, has been to integrate, if not assimilate; and this has been more or less acceptable, the return to a 'symbolic ethnicity' notwithstanding. Whereas, in long-resident societies, no such mutual understanding has prevailed in the case of resident or 'homeland' *ethnies*. Even in the French case, where the republic has sought to homogenise its citizens, there has been considerable resistance by the resident *ethnies* – Bretons, Corsicans, Alsatians and the like. This has demonstrated the historic dominance of the French *ethnie* within the French national state, something that its members have taken for granted in equating France and the French national state with the French *ethnie*. And, from the standpoint of the Scots and Welsh, not to mention the Irish, the same might be said of the English, for whom Britain and Britishness was simply an extension of their own identity.[7]

Ethnic cores and nation-formation

Despite these historical and sociological contrasts, the consequences of these two trajectories for the creation of nations and for their internal relations may not, after all, be that different.

Let me start with nation-creation. It has often been argued that in Europe the state, together with nationalism, forged nations, not the other way round. This is, in general, the thesis of political modernists like John Breuilly, Charles Tilly, Michael Mann and Anthony Giddens. It is also, quite explicitly, the message of Eric Hobsbawm, and more subtly that of Ernest Gellner. In all their theories and approaches, the modern, centralised, professional state plays the central role in the drama of nation-creation. If, for Gellner, the state mediates modernisation, for the other theorists it provides the impetus and engine for modernisation and nation-creation, a process that becomes increasingly an intended outcome of mass mobilisation by elites.[8]

But this was clearly an over-simplification. For one thing, it overlooked the fact that the strong Western states, which provided the buttress and proof of the 'theory', were themselves founded on a degree of ethnic and cultural homogeneity at the centre during the period of their foundation and initial development. It was this relative ethnic homogeneity of the core that enabled the state to expand without internal ethnic fissure, such as we have witnessed in Sub-Saharan Africa. Religion provided a second unifying factor. We do not have to embrace Hastings' view that nations are a Christian product and phenomenon to see how a widely accepted biblical and providentialist reading of the role of dynastic kingdoms helped to buttress these Western medieval Christian states. The drive for religious, and cultural, homogenisation by absolutist states was predicated on a long history of divine chosenness of the ethnic core. Third, the growth of shared historical memories and an 'ethno-history' among the elites of dominant ethnic cores has helped to underpin and legitimise the dynastic state and its wars. It has also provided a repertoire of ethnic myths and symbols of heroes and saints, exploits, battles and sacrifices, on which later generations of the dominant *ethnie* have been able to draw when they and their state have been under threat.[9]

While many factors encouraged, and impeded, the growth of strong states, the combination of ethnic bonds, biblical religion and shared ethno-history, which so often produced a sense of ethnic election and mission, constituted a powerful support, indeed a necessary condition, for the states that would later help to forge nations. In other words, viewed diachronically, the state could be seen to play a mediating role between an initial ethnic core which it helped to consolidate and the subsequent formation of nations. For this reason, in some cases, France and England among them, it is no easy matter to discern the shift from ethnic core to nation. What is clear is that the strong aristocratic state built upon this ethnic core began to expand both through conquest of outlying areas and through *bureaucratic incorporation* of the middle (and much later the lower) classes of the state's population, imposing the language, culture and religion of the dominant *ethnie*, and drawing a large part of its administrative personnel from that same core *ethnie*. Such a complex process, involving the state, ethnic core, aristocracy and religion, represented the first, and perhaps the most influential, of the trajectories of nation-formation, and at its centre we can discern the pivotal role of an ethnic core.[10]

It might be thought that the second major trajectory of nation-formation, that of *vernacular mobilisation*, denoted not just a different, but a diametrically opposed, role for *ethnies*, one that is perhaps more akin to that of ethnic minorities in immigrant societies like the United States. After all, their sociological point of departure is quite different. Unlike the 'lateral', aristocratic *ethnies* whose members built up the strong states of western and northern Europe, much of eastern and south-east Europe, as well as parts of Asia, consisted of 'vertical' or demotic *ethnies*, which were generally smaller, more compact and more exclusive than their lateral counterparts. Some, it is true, like Bohemia, Bulgaria and Serbia, could point to a history of medieval statehood, or, like the Greeks, to a special role in a wider Orthodox empire. But most of them were subject *ethnies* of far-flung empires, often submerged and with only shadowily documented histories. In these cases, it was an enlightened intelligentsia which, touched by Romanticism and attracted to an historicist nationalism, sought to return to an ethnic past, and recover it for themselves and their 'people', along with a vernacular culture and language. But, as a consequence of their mobilising endeavours, a remarkable transformation occurred. Like the ugly duckling that became a swan, several of these neglected erstwhile minorities, once roused and politicised, became dominant *ethnies* in the new national states that were created by the Great Powers – in Hungary, Czechoslovakia, Yugoslavia, Bulgaria, Romania and Georgia. The point, of course, is that in Europe, and in parts of Asia, these long-resident 'peripheral' *ethnies*, on becoming masters in their own houses, transmuted into dominant *ethnies* in national states, or indeed into dominant nations – with or without small ethnic minorities and peripheral *ethnies* within their borders. So that, though their starting-point and trajectories were quite different, these demotic *ethnies* arrived at much the same dominant-*ethnie* national end-point as their Western European 'lateral' counterparts.[11]

Other kinds of polity later followed the Western bureaucratic route, often quite deliberately. In later Tsarist Russia and Meiji Japan, for example, the dominance of the ethnic core was clearly displayed in an admittedly multi-cultural setting, and in the late nineteenth and twentieth centuries policies of cultural homogenisation were increasingly enforced. The Young Turks, too, attempted a Turkification of the Ottoman empire, in line with an integral nationalism, with disastrous results, preparing a way for what would amount to a secession of the Turkish core from the Ottoman empire.[12]

This tendency for nation-formation to be closely bound up with the position and transformation of the role of the dominant *ethnie* might lead us to think that all nations are founded on strong core *ethnies* and their symbolisms and mythologies. That constitutes the strong claim of 'ethno-symbolism'; and one can certainly think of many cases that demonstrate such an intimate connection. I do not think the evidence allows us to go that far. On the one hand, there are cases like the Slovak where ethnicity was too weak, ethno-history too shadowy and ethnic symbolism too undifferentiated (from that of the Czechs and others) to allow us to posit any progression from *ethnie* to nation; the ethnic elements appear to have been forged in the crucible of the nation-creation process itself. On the other hand, there are cases like Eritrea, where a prior association and unity of the designated population were based on a history of political ties through, in this case, periods of Italian and then British colonisation – ties strong enough to differentiate the Eritrean populations from those of neighbouring Ethiopia. But it remains to be seen how far such state-based 'nations' will survive and flourish, in any more than a juridical sense.

As a result, we can only advance a weaker claim: to build, create or forge nations, it greatly helps the creators to be able to point to and make use of a relevant prior core *ethnie*, or at least strong ethnic networks; and that not to be able to do so greatly hinders the tasks and processes of nation-formation. The point at issue here is the well-known problem of popular 'resonance'. To mobilise people to make the necessary sacrifices for the nation-to-be, one needs ethnic ties – shared memories and common myths, symbols and codes, as well as some widely held values and traditions – which can underpin the new national 'construct' and show the members of the core *ethnie* that they are one historical people of common devotion, and preferably that they are ancestrally related, however fictively. And, even then, in highly polyethnic states, the chances of forging successfully integrated nations may be slender.[13]

Dominant *ethnies* versus peripheral *ethnies*

Let me turn to the politics of dominant *ethnie* nations, and more particularly in Africa and Asia. Here, these difficulties of resonance and mobilisation are all too apparent. Policies similar to those employed by Meiji Japan and Tsarist Russia have been attempted in some post-colonial states, for example in Burma, Kemalist Turkey, Zaire and, in respect of Africanisation, in Uganda and perhaps now in Zimbabwe. But, in these cases, the project of national unity around the culture of a core *ethnie* has met with only limited success. Instead, we find an uneasy, even conflictual, relationship between ethnic cores and peripheral *ethnies*, as in states like Malaysia, Indonesia and the Philippines, sometimes leading to open ethnic wars, as in Burma, Sudan and Zaire. Here, the dynamics of nation-formation have foundered on the inability of core *ethnies* to forge sufficiently strong states which can accommodate peripheral *ethnies*. To this, we must add the novel impact of nationalist ideology. The epoch of Western nation-formation predated the emergence of national*ism*, and hence the ideological blueprints which it subsequently afforded to *ethnies* that were dissatisfied with their lot. In today's world, the lure of potential nationhood has meant that, in addition to their economic and political weakness, post-colonial states based upon a core *ethnie* are faced with threats of secession, at least as a bargaining counter in the struggle for political offices and the redistribution of scarce resources. In consequence, core *ethnies* are often locked in a struggle to establish their dominance, in some cases by force, further weakening their chances of creating unified national states, let alone nations.[14]

A similar, if somewhat more muted and peaceable, tension can be found in the national states of Western Europe and Canada. Ethnicity, which for many had seemed to be obsolete in the aftermath of the War and its genocides, suddenly re-emerged as a political force in the 1960s and 1970s – to be followed by a second wave of more strident ethnic revival in Eastern Europe and the former Soviet Union after 1989. Suddenly, long established nations found that they were viewed from the periphery of 'their' states as dominant *ethnies*, and that the larger identity, which they had assumed to be merely an extension of their own national identity, was no longer an exclusive property, if indeed it ever had been. Thus, the English, so long accustomed to think of the British nation and British identity as an historic extension of their own national identity, found themselves swiftly disabused by Scots and Welsh of such proprietary notions; and much the same occurred in France, when Bretons and Alsatians, Provencals and Corsicans attacked the centralist Jacobin ideal of a unitary France dominated by Paris and the historic north-central French *ethnie*. Even in more federal states like Belgium and Spain, the old dominance of historically hegemonic *ethnies* was challenged by autonomist movements of peripheral but long resident or 'homeland' *ethnies*, sometimes violently. And, further east, in the former Yugoslavia, the project of Greater Serbia culminated in a series of horrifying wars and carnage, as Tito's federal state swiftly unravelled under the pressures of ethnic nationalism.[15]

One consequence of these movements has been to underline the mixed nature of conceptions of the Western nation and national identity. Non-immigrant Western states have increasingly thought of themselves and their nation as territorially based and civic in orientation, their nationalism firmly entrenched in a liberal conception of individual rights. But the 'ethnic revival' of the 1970s (if that is the right term) revealed the ethnic underpinnings of even the most liberal and civic states, if not in the eyes of the members of their dominant *ethnie*, then in those of its peripheral ethnic communities. The sense of alienation and exclusion felt by many members of peripheral *ethnies*, of a combination of bureaucratic interference and social and economic neglect, highlighted the ethnic divisions within the national state and the often unconscious bias on the part of central government towards the needs and interests of members of the dominant *ethnie*, who in virtue of their great numerical majority or political hegemony, or both, appeared to receive a disproportionately high share of jobs and resources. And, given the vital role of perception and sentiment in the sense and understanding of ethnicity, that appearance of bias and sense of alienation has defined the ethnic nature of Western states as much as, if not more than, any overt discrimination by the elites of the dominant *ethnie* against peripheral *ethnies*.[16]

A second consequence of the ethnic revivals in the West and the East has been to reinforce the ideological commitment to civic, and even multicultural, conceptions of national identity, at least on the part of elites. Given the desire of the majority of the members of peripheral *ethnies* to oppose the historic bias towards the dominant *ethnie*, but not to secede from the state in which they had been incorporated, state elites who are largely recruited from the dominant *ethnie* have found it politic, if not necessary, to accentuate the equality of all the members of the polyethnic state and even to recognise the separate rights and cultures of peripheral *ethnies*. This occurred most dramatically in France, where during the 1960s the western half of France, including Brittany, had been designated as 'parkland' by the Debré government, but which was subsequently accorded a more equal share of industrial development. Of course, this change in policy was hastened by the influx of immigrants of radically different culture from that of the majorities of most Western states, placing multiculturalism within an overall civic national identity on the agenda. But, once again, this has only served to highlight the ethnic nature of Western European national states, and the perceived ethnic basis of their national identities.[17]

Dominant ethnicity: erosion or revival?

How useful in today's world are concepts like 'ethnic core' and 'dominant ethnicity'? Has globalisation altered, once and for all, the nature of national states, as it has diluted their power and efficacy? In a post-modern epoch of mass migration and cultural assimilation, can ethnicity, dominant or otherwise, play any but the most folkloric role?

This is a huge subject, and only a few comments can be made here. Much of the discussion is centred on the West, meaning North America and West/Central Europe, which is then generalised globally. But even the most cursory global survey suggests that ethnicity and especially dominant *ethnies* remain a powerful force in most states outside the West. One might just as well posit the contrary claim: the conflict between dominant and peripheral *ethnies* is not only becoming fiercer and more entrenched, it is actually part and parcel of the cultural and political pluralism of the world order, as it has evolved since Westphalia and the French and American revolutions. Where states remain largely sovereign, at least in matters of society and culture, and where their scope and penetration are much greater than before, the likelihood of conflict between the ethnic powerholders at the centre and the parties of marginalised *ethnies* in the periphery is that much greater – and endemic. The ways in which colonial territorial lines were drawn, and the advantages accruing under colonialism to some *ethnies*, who tended to be the most central and hegemonic, if not the most populous ethnic groups, were reinforced by the norms of the inter-state order and the increasing power of the modern, centralised state, which controlled the sources of patronage and became a prize of bitter rivalry. The result of such high stakes has been the intensification of conflicts between dominant *ethnies* and peripheral ethnic minorities, on the one hand; and, on the other hand, a range of measures and attempted solutions for conflict management, including arbitration, minority rights, consociation, autonomy and even federalism.[18]

A second point concerns immigration, especially in the Western context. While there has been a continual ebb and flow of migrants throughout recorded history, the scale and cultural mixing of current migration flows are probably unprecedented. So at the very moment when some European states have shown themselves willing to surrender some of their sovereign powers and functions to a supranational authority, particularly in the economic sphere, there is a determined contrary trend to a stronger delineation of controls by these same national states over immigration and related areas, to avoid labour conflicts and cultural backlashes. Similarly, at the societal level, while we are witnessing an undoubted fraying and erosion of widely held traditions of national identity on the part of members of the dominant *ethnies*, we are also periodically reminded of the limits to such erosion, not only by violent displays of xenophobic resentment, but also by often passionate discussion and defence of a national identity based on the symbols, memories, values and myths of the dominant *ethnie*.

Much the same can be said about the cultural effects of a third factor, globalisation. The voluminous literature on this vast topic seems, on this point, to be at best inconclusive, insofar as, on the one hand, it documents the loss by the national state of many of its major economic functions and some of its political controls, while, on the other, it highlights the resilience of local ties and the revitalisation of ethnic bonds, aided by the uses of intermediate technology and urban and media networks. But this applies equally to dominant *ethnies*, insofar as through their control of major economic, media and political networks, they are able to increase their resources and power, and determine the agenda for regional and minority *ethnies*. Far from over-riding and dissolving ethnic differences, the evidence suggests that globalising trends, including mass migration, sharpen cleavages and inequalities, particularly where class and ethnicity are superimposed, and where nationalism is invoked as the ground and goal of revived ethnic aspirations.[19]

Undoubtedly the traditional sense of national identity is under siege today. So rapid has been the pace of cultural change since the War, that the foreignness of the past extends to the remoteness of the conceptions of national identity held by our grandparents, and even our parents. But there is really nothing new in this. There have always been rival ideologies of national identity and a succession of competing traditions of the sources and myths of the 'authentic' nation. This is a far cry from the claim that globalisation necessarily erodes all sense of national identity. If the idea of a monolithic national identity is a fiction, generated perhaps by a severe crisis of national existence such as the War, so is that of a general withering away of nations and national identities. What is perhaps new, at least for some Western states, is the degree and range of cultural recombinations to which a sense of national identity is now subject. This requires on the part of members of the dominant *ethnie* a much more radical rethinking of what they have taken for granted in respect of their national identity. In other words, from being implicit and tacit, the multiculturalism which is so much an expression of the diversity of ethno-cultural and religious groups within the contemporary national state has now been made explicit, and has become a matter of overt policy.

Conclusion

In conclusion, we should perhaps remind ourselves of the elusive yet durable nature of ethnic ties across the centuries. While particular ethnic categories, associations and communities have emerged, flourished and declined, with only a few surviving in some form the many vicissitudes of social, economic and political change, ethnicity and ethnic ties as such have been a recurrent feature of human history since records commenced in the third millennium BC. These ties take many forms. For the most part, they are fluid and mutable, embodied in oral cultures and 'tribal' networks. Often, they become visible simply as cultural and linguistic categories, noted by travellers and ethnographers, but without much in the way of shared memories or myths of common ancestry or solidarity. At other times, they coalesce into definite networks of association and symbolism; and in some of these cases, they become well-documented named communities with a distinctive culture and network of institutions.[20]

With the introduction of powerful state structures, first under agrarian empires and then in modern states, ethnicity became institutionalised, and even frozen into an 'ethnic mosaic'. That is to say, some ethnic communities found stable niches in the economic and political structures of empires, like the *millets* of the Ottoman empire, which helped, at least partially, to congeal them by assigning them a specific function in society. In the modern period, centralised, bureaucratic states, along with nationalist ideologies, tend to reinforce the role of ethnicity. But they also transform it. While they undermine the status of some *ethnies* and augment that of others, their overall thrust is to politicise ethnicity and create an interplay between dominant and peripheral *ethnies* competing for resources through the institutions of powerful, centralising states. Despite the present trend in some areas to greater unions of states, the cultural and political pluralism that underpins the inter-state order remains intact; and as long as it does so, the tensions between dominant *ethnies* and peripheral ones will continue, and will find expression in the ideals of the self-determination of peoples which nationalism has unleashed.

Notes

1   See Glazer and Moynihan (1964), Introduction; and Glazer and Moynihan (1975), Introduction. For the debate about the post-war resurgence of white ethnic minorities, see Greeley (1974); and for the issue of 'symbolic ethnicity' among third generation immigrants to the United States in the 1970s, see Gans (1979).
2   For these usages, see Liddell and Scott (1869), under *ethnos*, citing *inter alia* Homer: *The Iliad* 13, 354 and Plato: *The Republic* 290C.
3   Liddell and Scott (1869), under *ethnos*, citing Herodotus' *The Histories* I, 101, 125; and Lewis and Short ([1879] 1955), under *natio*. See also Geary (2002), Chapter 2, who argues that ancient historians after Herodotus failed to observe his methodology and value neutrality, and chose to objectify and rank ethnic groups outside the Roman *populus*, rather than capture the fluidity of ethnic experience.
4   For changes in the concept of *natio*, see Hertz (1944) and Zernatto (1944); also Greenfeld (1992), Introduction. Christian usages sharpened the contrast between '*am Israel* and *goy* (a term also used sometimes of Israel) in the Hebrew Bible.
5   For the concept of *ethnie*, see A.D. Smith (1986), Chapter 2. See also the comprehensive analysis in Horowitz (1985), Chapter 2. For this process of 'bureaucratic incorporation', notably in the West, see A.D. Smith (1989).
6   On such an immigrant 'plural' route, see A.D. Smith (1995), Chapter 4. For an illuminating recent analysis of national formation and ethnic reformation in the case of the United States, which emphasises the colonists' cultural homogeneity, see Kaufmann (2002).
7   For homeland communities, see Walker Connor (1994); and *idem* (1986), 'The impact of homelands upon diasporas', in Sheffer (1986). On the French case, see Suzanne Berger (1977), 'Bretons and Jacobins: reflections on French regional ethnicity', in Esman (1977), and Brubaker (1992), especially Chapter 7. On British and English nationalism, see Colley (1992) and Clark (2000).
8   See Tilly (1975), Introduction; Gellner (1983); Giddens (1985); Hobsbawm (1990); Breuilly (1993); and Mann (1995). For a critique of such 'modernist' approaches, see A.D. Smith (1998).
9   See Hastings (1997, 1999). On ethnic underpinnings of modern nations, see Hutchinson (2000). On war and ethnicity, see A.D. Smith (1981b).

10 On these different kinds of *ethnie*, and the routes of nation-formation, see A.D. Smith (1986: Chapter 4; 1989). For a processual analysis of nation-formation, see Uzelac (2002).

11 Eastern European nation-formation is discussed in Sugar and Lederer (1969), and Sugar (1980). For the route of vernacular mobilisation, see A.D. Smith (1989).

12 On Tsarist Russia and its minorities, see Kappeler (2001). On ideas of Japanese ethnic homogeneity in the Meiji and later periods, see Oguma (2002). For the Young Turk ideology, see Berkes (1964) Chapters 11–14 and Poulton (1997) Chapter 3.

13 For ideas of ancestral relatedness, see Connor (1994), especially Chapter 8. For the importance of myths, symbols and codes, see Armstrong (1982), and for a brief outline of an 'ethno-symbolic' approach, see A.D. Smith (1999), Introduction.

14 This process has been fully analysed by Horowitz (1985); see also the essays in Brass (1985).

15 There is a large literature on Western 'autonomist' movements; see especially Esman (1977), A.D. Smith (1981a), and Orridge (1982). For the Yugoslav débacle, see Ramet (1996).

16 The academic version of the grievances of peripheral *ethnies*, the 'internal colonialism' model of Hechter and others, derived via the *dependistas* from the case of Black exclusion in the United States, is presented in the essays in Stone (1979).

17 On centralism and ethnicity in France, see Coulon (1978) and Brubaker (1992). For 'civic' nationalism, see especially Breton (1988) and Miller (1995); for a critique, see Yack (1999).

18 On these conflicts, see Horowitz (1985). For the range of attempted solutions, see McGarry and O'Leary (1993).

19 On this literature, see M. Guibernau: 'Globalisation and the nation-state', in Guibernau and Hutchinson (2001). See also the essays in Featherstone (1990), and A.D. Smith (1995), Chapter 1.

20 On both the polyethnicity of empires rooted in labour needs, and the failed nationalist attempt to homogenise populations, see McNeill (1986).

References

Armstrong, J. (1982) *Nations before Nationalism*, Chapel Hill, NC: University of North Carolina Press.

Berger, S. (1977) 'Bretons and Jacobins: reflections on French regional ethnicity', in M. Esman (ed.) *Ethnic Conflict in the Western World*, Ithaca, NY: Cornell University Press.

Berkes, N. (1964) *The Development of Secularism in Turkey*, Montreal: McGill University Press.

Brass, P. (ed.) (1985) *Ethnic Groups and the State*, London: Croom Helm.

Breton, R. (1988) 'From ethnic to civic nationalism: English Canada and Quebec', *Ethnic and Racial Studies*, 11(1): 85–102.

Breuilly, J. (1993) *Nationalism and the State*, 2nd edn, Manchester: Manchester University Press.

Brubaker, R. (1992) *Citizenship and Nationhood in France and Germany*, Cambridge, MA: Harvard University Press.

Clark, J.C.D. (2000) 'Protestantism, nationalism and national identity, 1660–1832', *Historical Journal*, 43(1): 249–76.

Colley, L. (1992) *Britons: Forging the Nation, 1707–1837*, New Haven, CT: Yale University Press.

Connor, W. (1994) *Ethno-Nationalism: The Quest for Understanding*, Princeton, NJ: Princeton University Press.

Coulon, C. (1978) 'French political science and regional diversity: a strategy of silence', *Ethnic and Racial Studies*, 1(1): 80–99.

Esman, M. (ed.) (1977) *Ethnic Conflict in the Western World*, Ithaca, NY: Cornell University Press.

Featherstone, M. (ed.) (1990) *Global Culture: Nationalism, Globalisation and Modernity*, London: Sage.

Gans, H. (1979) 'Symbolic ethnicity', *Ethnic and Racial Studies*, 2(1): 1–20.

Geary, P. (2002) *The Myth of Nations: The Medieval Origins of Europe*, Princeton, NJ: Princeton University Press.

Gellner, E. (1983) *Nations and Nationalism*, Oxford: Blackwell.

Giddens, A. (1985) *The Nation-State and Violence*, Cambridge: Polity Press.

Glazer, N. and Moynihan, D. (eds) (1964) *Beyond the Melting Pot*, Cambridge, MA: MIT Press.

—— (eds) (1975) *Ethnicity: Theory and Experience*, Cambridge, MA: Harvard University Press.

Greeley, A. (1974) *Ethnicity in the United States*, New York: John Wiley.

Greenfeld, L. (1992) *Nationalism: Five Roads to Modernity*, Cambridge, MA: Harvard University Press.

Guibernau, M. and Hutchinson, J. (eds) (2001) *Understanding Nationalism*, Cambridge: Polity Press.

Hastings, A. (1997) *The Construction of Nationhood: Ethnicity, Religion and Nationhood*, Cambridge: Cambridge University Press.

—— (1999) 'Special peoples', *Nations and Nationalism*, 5(3): 381–96.

Hertz, F. (1944) *Nationality in History and Politics*, London: Routledge and Kegan Paul.

Hobsbawm, E. (1990) *Nations and Nationalism since 1780*, Cambridge: Cambridge University Press.

Horowitz, D. (1985) *Ethnic Groups in Conflict*, Berkeley, CA: University of California Press.

Hutchinson, J. (2000) 'Ethnicity and modern nations', *Ethnic and Racial Studies*, 23(4): 651–69.

Kappeler, A. (2001) *The Russian Empire: A Multiethnic History*, Harlow: Pearson Educational Publishers.

Kaufmann, E. (2002) 'Modern formation, ethnic reformation: the social sources of the American nation', *Geopolitics*, 7(2): 99–120.

Lewis, C.T. and Short, C. (eds) ([1879] 1955) *A Latin Dictionary*, Oxford: Clarendon Press.

Liddell, H.G. and Scott, R. (eds) (1869) *A Greek–English Lexicon*, 6th edn, Oxford: Clarendon Press.

McGarry, J. and O'Leary, B. (eds) (1993) *The Politics of Ethnic Conflict Regulation: Case Studies of Protracted Ethnic Conflicts*, London: Routledge.

McNeill, W. (1986) *Polyethnicity and National Unity in World History*, Toronto: Toronto University Press.

Mann, M. (1995) 'A political theory of nationalism and its excesses', in S. Periwal (ed.) *Notions of Nationalism*, Budapest: Central European University Press, pp. 44–64.

Miller, D. (1995) *On Nationality*, Oxford: Oxford University Press.

Oguma, E. (2002) *A Genealogy of 'Japanese' Self-Images*, trans. D. Askew, Melbourne: Trans Pacific Press.

Orridge, A. (1982) 'Separatist and autonomist nationalisms: the structure of regional loyalties in the modern state', in C. Williams (ed.) *National Separatism*, Cardiff: University of Wales Press.

Poulton, H. (1997) *Top Hat, Grey Wolf and Crescent: Turkish Nationalism and the Turkish Republic*, London: Hurst.

Ramet, S. (1996) *Balkan Babel: The Disintegration of Yugoslavia from the Death of Tito to Ethnic War*, Boulder, CO: Westview Press.

Sheffer, G. (ed.) (1986) *Modern Diasporas and International Politics*, London: Croom Helm.

Smith, A.D. (1981a) *The Ethnic Revival in the Modern World*, Cambridge: Cambridge University Press.

—— (1981b) 'War and ethnicity: the role of warfare in the formation, self-images and cohesion of ethnic communities', *Ethnic and Racial Studies*, 4(4): 375–97.

—— (1986) *The Ethnic Origins of Nations*, Oxford: Blackwell.

—— (1989) 'The origins of nations', *Ethnic and Racial Studies*, 12(3): 340–67.

—— (1995) *Nations and Nationalism in a Global Era*, Cambridge: Polity Press.

—— (1998) *Nationalism and Modernism: A Critical Survey of Recent Theories of Nations and Nationalism*, London: Routledge.

—— (1999) *Myths and Memories of the Nation*, Oxford: Oxford University Press.

Stone, J. (ed.) (1979) 'Internal Colonialism', *Ethnic and Racial Studies*, 2(3) (special issue).

Sugar, P. (ed.) (1980) *Ethnic Diversity and Conflict in Eastern Europe*, Santa Barbara, CA: ABC-Clio.

Sugar, P. and Lederer, I. (eds) (1969) *Nationalism in Eastern Europe*, Seattle: University of Washington Press.

Tilly, C. (ed.) (1975) *The Formation of National States in Western Europe*, Princeton, NJ: Princeton University Press.

Uzelac, G. (2002) 'When is the nation: constituent elements and processes', *Geopolitics*, 7(2): 33–52.

Yack, B. (1999) 'The myth of the civic nation', in R. Beiner (ed.) *Theorizing Nationalism*, Albany, NY: State University of New York Press.

Zernatto, G. (1944) 'Nation: the history of a word', *Review of Politics*, 6: 351–66.

2 The identity and changing status of former elite minorities

The contrasting cases of North Indian Muslims and American WASPs

Theodore P. Wright, Jr

The aim of this chapter is to explain the different outcomes, one violent and the other peaceful, in two cases in which dominant ethnies, one (North Indian Muslims) a minority of the population and the other (North American WASPs) originally a majority, lost their hegemony. The study of minority groups has been practically monopolized in the United States by academics who themselves come from subordinate but upwardly mobile elements of the population. They have quite naturally concentrated their sympathetic attention on subordinates in the narrow sense: those groups which lack both numbers and power in the United States, or which, like the Bantu of South Africa before 1994, had been reduced to subjection by outside colonizers (Wright 1972).

Thus, these theorists have produced what R.A. Schermerhorn, a pioneer of ethnic studies, called a sentimental 'victimology' (Schermerhorn 1970). He distinguished instead four types of minorities in a matrix of power and numbers: dominant majorities, dominant elites, subordinate mass subjects, and subordinate minorities. Our focus in this volume is on the first two, which have seldom been studied as ethnies because they are assumed, not least by themselves, to constitute 'the nation' or the 'natural rulers' respectively. The loss of political dominance in the Indian case has depressed the group into Schermerhorn's fourth category, a subordinate minority, while the Partition of British India in 1947 elevated it again to a dominant ethnie in Pakistan, where Muslims are an overwhelming majority of the population.

Within those categories of dominance, what I wish to draw attention to are cases of loss of dominance, amounting to 'group status reversal' and thus to the potentialities for cyclical change in the position and numbers of ethnies over time (Wright 1980). In this process of downward mobility, I can claim the empathy of the insider because in recent decades my own community in America, who have been somewhat pejoratively dubbed 'WASPs' (White Anglo-Saxon Protestants), have been rather condescendingly attacked in books like *The Decline of the Wasp* by Peter Schrag (1971) and *The Rise of the Unmeltable Ethnics* by Michael Novak (1972) or defended as in *The Dispossessed Majority* by Wilmot Robertson (1972). In my own discipline, Political Science, for instance, I calculated that the percentage of WASPs in the most prestigious university departments has dropped by 50 per cent in the past generation.

What other, analogous cases of group status reversal can be found for purposes of comparison? There are a few in Asia: the Manchus in China and the Tatars in Russia; in Africa pockets of former European colonists left in Kenya, the Maghreb and pre-eminently, since 1994, the Afrikaners of South Africa; the Watutsi of Rwanda and the Arabs of Zanzibar; in Oceania the Hawaiians, Fijians and Maoris; in Latin America possibly one could count the Spanish-descended Creoles after the Mestizos or mixed bloods seized power from them; in North America the French-Canadian Québécois; and in Europe the Anglo-Irish and the various German, Hungarian and Turkish communities which were left outside of their former homelands by defeat and boundary changes after the two world wars, most notoriously including the Sudeten Germans until their expulsion from Czechoslovakia in 1945. It is not a very sympathy-evoking lot for the typical American liberal academic to study.

Among these, North Indian Muslims, or more accurately their elites, the subject of my academic research for the past forty years, conquered and ruled most of their region, the subcontinent of India, as a dynastic state or states for six centuries (1191–1757) as a pre-modern dominant elite, then lost control to the British East India Company during just one hundred years (1757–1857). This ethnie is defined by its religion whereas WASPs, if taken literally, are bounded additionally by colour and place of origin. Within the Muslim community, however, a sharp social distinction has historically been drawn (for instance for purposes of marriage) between the Ashraf (noble), those of foreign Arabic, Persian, Afghan or Mongol origin, and the Ajlaf (dirty), those descended from indigenous Hindu converts, generally of low caste (Ansari 1960). The Hindu and Muslim upper classes had more in common with each other than with their lower class co-religionists. Only with the introduction of the modern democratic franchise, reserved seats and separate electorates by the British, which made total numbers of the community significant, did the elite Muslim politicians discover the low status majority of fellow Muslims and assert the existence of a Muslim nation transcending class and caste in South Asia (Hardy 1972). By 1947 they were a quarter of the population of British India.

Politically, the geographical core of this erstwhile dominant ethnie was not in the Muslim majority areas of what are now Pakistan and Bangladesh, but between those regions in the Jumna–Ganges *doab* (basin) called Aryavarta, then Hindustan, where a majority of the Muslim rulers' mass subjects had been unconverted Hindus. This happened also to be the core area of pre-Muslim Hindu empires. Thus it is an almost unique case of a national core shared by two national ethnies. (Israel/Palestine may qualify as another, although Palestine was never the centre of a Muslim state.) Since in departing South Asia in 1947 the British partitioned their empire according to modern criteria of majority 'national self-determination' and rule (except in Kashmir), North Indian Muslims were evenly split between our two principal categories: they became a dominant majority again in Pakistan, but a true minority (in both numbers and power), an irredenta, in the Indian Republic within a newly constructed and civically defined Indian nation. It must be added that the Bengali Muslims of East Pakistan claimed that they were treated as subjects by West Pakistanis and eventually in 1971 revolted and became the dominant ethnie of Bangladesh. The theretofore dominant Urdu-speaking 'Biharis' suffered another status reversal and became a dispossessed minority.

In the United States, if not in Canada (because of French-speaking, Catholic Quebec), WASPs, broadly construed to include Scots, Welsh and Scots-Irish Protestants, are estimated to have comprised about 90 per cent of the White population of the new republic at the time of the first census in 1790, 60 per cent of them from England alone (Anderson 1970). The rest were Dutch in New York and New Jersey and Germans primarily in Pennsylvania. The Native American peoples were decimated by European diseases and warfare. Black African slaves were totally subordinated. Hispanics were minuscule until the acquisitions of Florida (1819), Texas (1845) and California (1848). WASP dominance was expressed most clearly in Anglo-conformity, especially in the official use of English and the requirement of its knowledge to obtain citizenship. But you might be surprised to learn that knowledge of the Dutch language persisted in some families of Albany, New York, until the 1880s and of German (so-called 'Pennsylvania Dutch') until the Second World War.

Was there a geographical core area of WASPdom? As in the geographically divided Pakistan of 1947–71, one can say loosely that New England and the tidewater South were overwhelmingly English in origin until the Irish Catholic influx of the 1840s into the former; the Middle States (New York, New Jersey, Pennsylvania, Maryland) were much more ethnically and religiously mixed and a portent of the future pluralism of America. But the major regional enmity, unlike India vs. Pakistan, was between the two WASP sections, North and South, over slavery and the economy. Importation of Black slaves from Africa declined after the international prohibition of the slave trade in 1808. With the rapidly expanding frontier to the West, immigration from Europe was encouraged until after the First World War and the restrictive immigration Act of 1924. The decimation of WASP youth in the Civil War (1860–65) created a great need for immigrants to work in industry as well as agriculture, so waves of Irish, Germans, Scandinavians, Italians, Slavs and Jews further diminished the WASP share of the population in terms of both religion and language. By 1970 White Protestants comprised a bare majority (55 per cent) and in 1980 only 20 per cent in the census identified themselves as of English descent (Brookhiser 1991: 21). Nevertheless, policies of separation of church and state, democratic franchise, free public education, cheap land and assimilation (Gordon 1964) began quickly to create a new American nation. A melting pot, both cultural and genetic, flourished on the frontier and in the growing cities. I cannot stress enough the importance of the genetic melting pot because its very existence was denied by the neo-ethnicity movement of the 1970s (Glazer and Moynihan 1970). I have purposely in my autobiographical sketch noted that my ancestry is only 'about half English, the other half being Irish, Scots, Welsh, Dutch, French, German, Norwegian and Native American'. This is fairly typical of 'old migration' Americans. Fifty per cent of American Jews now marry outside of their group. The wedding announcement page of the Sunday *New York Times* illustrates how the post-1965 Asian immigration is also joining the melting pot at a high economic level. As I asked in a paper in Mumbai in 1995, 'How long can ethnicity survive exogamy?' (Wright 1995). On the other hand, with parentally arranged marriages among both Hindus and Muslims in India and Pakistan, outmarriage is very rare so the 'cross-pressures' created by exogamy are absent in South Asia. Hence the frequency and violence of the so-called 'communal' riots (Varshney 2002).

Thus one must ask: have the WASPs really lost their ethnic dominance in the United States? A recent study of 'Persistence and change in the Protestant establishment, 1930–1992' (Davidson *et al.* 1995), by measuring elite membership in several high status churches (Episcopal, Presbyterian, Quaker and Unitarian), concludes that WASP dominance has not declined much, although he admits that Jews have risen to a disproportionate role in both politics and culture and Catholics have largely overcome their previous disadvantage. This process has been facilitated by the dramatic expansion of the economy of the United States since 1945, so it has not been a 'zero-sum-game' in which your gain is my loss. The total number of WASP political scientists, in the study cited above, remained stable in 1948–68 because departments quadrupled in size. One has only to recall the names of the Presidents since I wrote my initial analysis in 1972 (Nixon, Ford, Carter, Reagan, Bush, Clinton and Bush) for evidence that the projected group status reversal of WASPs at the top is an illusion. What Davidson fails to take into account, besides the melting pot behind many of these surnames, are the well-known phenomena of change of religious affiliation accompanying social mobility, name changing especially among Jews (Maas 1956) and the lack of indicators for ethnicity-of-origin in the term WASP, which is both religious and ethnic. Sectarian affiliation is taken as a surrogate for ethnicity. What strikes me as more accurate is to posit the approaching assimilation, both culturally and linguistically, of all European-origin ethnies plus some Asian into an amorphous amalgam of Euro-Americans (Alba 1990), distinct from a huge underclass of African-Americans, Native Americans and the darker of Hispanics. So the dominant WASP ethnie has survived, if at all, by so weakening its boundaries in the past two generations and incorporating other groups that it is no longer the same group which was first named by Lawrence Fuchs in 1952. Only the English language has persisted as a defining characteristic, despite official attempts to institute bilingualism. Before that, most WASPs thought of themselves as the nation, as 'just plain Americans', not as just another ethnicity.

Another factor cross-cutting all religion and ethnicity in the post-modern United States is the gender revolution of the 1970s. The rise of WASP and other women to positions of political and economic prominence has, to some extent, been at the expense of WASP men. But affirmative action has tended to favour ethnic groups which support women's education and that has meant WASPs, Jews and Chinese, but not Hispanics.

By contrast, the Indian Muslims, Pakistanis and Bangladeshis (except for some in Kerala, e.g. Koya and Mumbai -walla suffixes) are readily distinguishable, by both friend and foe, by their Arabic names from their Hindu/Sikh/Jain neighbours. Indeed, some surname changing and 'Ashrafization' in the direction of the Arabic by Muslim quasi-caste 'O.B.C.s' (other backward castes; for instance, Julahas become Momin Ansaris) serve to further consolidate the Muslim community, and by the same token further differentiate it from the Hindu majority.

In recent decades the Hindutva ideology and movement, championed by the now ruling Bhartiya Janata Party, has sought to redefine Indian nationality in terms of religion, replacing the civic definition given it by Nehru and the Congress Party, thus excluding the Muslim and Christian minorities (Ghosh 1999).

Paradoxically, the survival of ethnic group dominance may be dependent, as in the WASP case in America, on failure of 'boundary maintenance', which eventually undermines or completely redefines group identity which is no longer from ancestral origins. Perhaps, since 'Hindus' in the broadest sense after 1947 constituted a four-fifths majority of the population of India, they do not need to assimilate or even integrate the minorities in order to remain dominant.

What then are some common characteristics of the formerly dominant elite ethnic mentality which may affect its political and social behaviour? The first thing that needs to be said is that the different circumstances, rapidity and stages for the group status reversal will affect the group's awareness of and reaction to its new condition. Most of the historic displacements came about through violence, either international or domestic. Presumably a sudden, traumatic descent from power would leave the group irreconcilable and eager for revenge and restitution by whatever means. Defeat in the First World War led to the break-up of a multinational empire like the Habsburg or Ottoman, leaving a segment of their dominant groups, German, Magyar or Turkish, as a discontented and suspect minority on the other side of new frontiers. Or an always numerically small ethnic elite is displaced by revolution from within (Manchus, Creoles, Watutsi, Zanzibar Arabs), tempting them to ally with any adjacent state which like peoples still control. Indian Muslims are often accused of disloyalty or treason to Pakistan by Hindu nationalists in India (Imtiaz Ahmad 1975).

However, it is possible for this 'ethnic succession' in power to take place more gradually and peaceably with a minimum of violence as the final confirmation of a long trend such as differential migration or birth rates as in the United States. Time may allow for enough assimilation and co-optation that there would be little 'identity crisis' in either the displaced group or individuals. At what point in history, for instance, does one say that the conquered English of 1066 displaced the French-speaking Normans in England? Chaucer (1350)? Henry V unable to court Catherine of France in French (1415)?

Recognition of decline may come at different stages: Shah Waliullah in Delhi saw what was happening in North India as early as the mid-eighteenth century and invited Ahmad Shah Durrani, the Afghan, to rescue the Muslims from the Hindu Mahrattas. The Muslim nobility of Oudh did not see what was happening until the British deposed the Nawab-Wazir and annexed the state in 1856. The reality of defeat did not come to Hyderabad until the Indian 'police action' in 1948 deposed the Nizam (Smith 1952).

Segments of the WASP dominant ethnie periodically have resisted mass immigration, which threatened to dilute their numbers and control. One thinks of the nativist 'Know-Nothing' movements of the 1830s and 1840s, the KKK in the South in the 1870s, the Red Scare after World War I, which produced the restriction of immigration from 1924 to 1965, and now the F.A.I.R. organization opposed to illegal immigration and the post '9/11' deportation of Muslims. But by and large the need for settlers in the West and for cheap labour have won out, although now 'outsourcing' of jobs abroad, such as to Bangalore, India, may become a substitute for immigration.

Second, the term elite in 'formerly dominant elite ethnicity' may in any objective sense be a misnomer. Manifestly the bulk of the members of the groups in question were not actually part of the ruling class, even though subjectively they regarded themselves as superior to subordinate Hindus. The ordinary Indian Muslim who was exempt from the jizya tax under the Mughal Aurangzeb, and the Manchu who was not required to wear a hair queue, were privileged more symbolically than materially compared to the Hindu and Chinese subjects of the respective emperors. Failure to compre-hend this psychological need of the downwardly mobile has confounded much Marxist analysis of Muslim communalism in India. They inveigh against the lower class Muslim for blindness to his 'real' economic interests. It is apt to be the poor or lower middle-class WASP or North Indian Muslim who actually earns vital 'psychic income' from identification with a decadent or modernising upper class with whom he shares some external characteristics and who were once the real elite. This point has been made by Gunnar Myrdal (1944) about the poor white 'rednecks' of the Southern United States as well as by others regarding the lower middle-class German supporters of Hitler in Nazi Germany.

Third, a formerly dominant ethnie may regard itself as especially fit to rule even if a loss of nerve or feuds among its leaders or foreign invasion had precipitated its downfall. As the late Professor Rashiduddin Khan, MP, from Hyderabad wrote in an unusually perceptive paper on 'the self-view of minorities: the Muslims in India':

> The Muslims in the sub-continent have never been a dormant or incon-spicuous minority, but on the contrary, had almost continuously been an active and for centuries also a leading segment of India's cultural and political life ... Muslim mass-psychology (however irrational and factu-ally untenable) ... reveals a subjective awareness of their collective superiority ... born out of the indelible memory of seven hundred years of Muslim hegemony in the Indo-Gangetic plain and in the Deccan.
>
> (Khan 1970)

In my own and Jonah Blank's studies of the Daudi Bohra community of Bombay, an Ismaili Muslim trading community, who, far from ruling Hindus, have been persecuted themselves by Sunni Muslim rulers, I found a striking contrast in attitudes and demands. Almost none of the usual stri-dent and disproportionate North Indian Muslim grievances are displayed; instead one finds the typical middleman minority inconspicuousness and desire to be left alone (Wright 1975; Blank 2001).

Fourth, a former dominant ethnie in the early stages of its decline exhibits a tendency to think of itself and its interests as identical with those of the whole country. It is unable to recognize itself as a minority and protect its interests as such. Peter Schrag (1971) observes of my group in *The Decline of the Wasp*:

> The Wasps never thought of themselves as anything but Americans, nor did it occur to others to label them as anything special until, about twenty-five years ago, their influence began to decline and they started to lose their cultural initiative and preeminence ... It is not that Wasps lack power and representation or numbers but that the once unques-tioned assumptions on which that power was based have begun to lose their hold ... The foundation of Wasp dominance in national politics and culture rested on the supposition that waspdom was the true America – no subculture or special group.

Fifth, the self-image of dominance and superiority, even after erstwhile subordinates have ceased to believe it, renders the declining former elite peculiarly lacking in adaptability, that characteristic *par excellence* of the middleman minority (Zenner 1991). The British and North American WASP is notoriously incapable of learning foreign languages and compla-cent about his own culture. I suspect that this is the real reason why Indian Muslims lagged behind Hindus in learning English instead of Persian in the nineteenth century rather than any religious fears or inhibitions about apos-tasy. After all, Arab traders have learned other languages when they needed them. This is still reflected in the hopeless struggle to preserve Urdu alongside Hindi with official patronage in North India (Wright 2002).

A sixth characteristic which I perceive in the North Indian Muslim, absent in the WASPs either because they are in different stages of decline or because of different original bases of power is the insistence on public office, overt channels of political expression and 'looking to government' for redress of grievances, a lack of self-reliance (Wright 1998). My Yankee ancestors surrendered Boston politically to the Irish long ago and retreated to business, banking and law from which they could exert indirect influence. This shrewd strategy allowed them to co-opt the Kennedys when that clan reached the top of Samuel Lubell's 'ethnic ladder' of offices (Lubell 1956). The North Indian Muslim has not had this option because even in his heyday the Hindu banias monopolized business. The difference reflects the fact that the New England WASPs stemmed from the Calvinist middleman minority in England and retained some of those skills. The more apt analogy for the North Indian Muslims is with the WASP elite of the American South, which also had a feudal self-image: only land, army and church were considered appropriate careers for the elite scions.

In conclusion, declining dominant majority groups like the North American WASPs may preserve some of their status by extending their boundaries to include kindred populations, but thereby jeopardize the survival of their distinctive identity. Formerly dominant ethnies like North Indian Muslims face a bleak future because of the thirst for revenge by their erstwhile subordinates and doubts about their loyalty, especially if there is a hostile neighbouring country in which that ethnie is still dominant.

References

Ahmad, I. (1975) 'Pakistan and the Indian Muslims', *Quest*, 93 (January–February): 39–47.

Alba, R. (1990) *Ethnic Identity*, New Haven, CT: Yale University Press.

Anderson, C.H. (1970) *White Protestant Americans: From National Origins to Religious Group*, Englewood Cliffs, NJ: Prentice Hall.

Ansari, G. (1960) *Muslim Caste in Uttar Pradesh*, Lucknow: Ethnographic and Folk Culture Society of Uttar Pradesh.

Blank, J. (2001) *Mullahs on the Mainframe: Islam and Modernity among the Daudi Bohras*, Chicago: University of Chicago Press.

Brookhiser, R. (1991) *The Way of the WASP*, New York: Free Press.

Davidson, J.D., Pyle, R.E. and Reyes, D.R. (1995) 'Persistence and change in the Protestant establishment, 1930–1992', *Social Forces*, 74(1): 157–75.

Ghosh, P.S. (1999) *The BJP and the Evolution of Hindu Nationalism: From Periphery to Centre*, New Delhi: Manohar.

Glazer, N. and Moynihan, D.P. (1970) *Beyond the Melting Pot*, 2nd edn, Cambridge, MA: MIT Press.

Gordon, M. (1964) *Assimilation in American Life*, New York: Oxford University Press.

Hardy, P. (1972) *The Muslims of British India*, Cambridge: Cambridge University Press.

Khan, R. (1970) 'The making of the Muslim mind', *Illustrated Weekly of India*, 91 (August 16).

Lubell, S. (1956) *The Future of American Politics*, New York: Doubleday.

Maas, E. (1956) 'Integration and name changing among Jewish refugees from Central Europe to the United States', *Names*, 6 (September): 129–71.

Myrdal, G. (1944) *The American Dilemma*, New York: Harper.

Novak, M. (1972) *The Rise of the Unmeltable Ethnics*, New York: Macmillan.

Robertson, W. (1972) *The Dispossessed Majority*, Cape Canaveral, FL: Howard Allen.

Schermerhorn, R.A. (1970) *Comparative Ethnic Relations: A Framework for Theory and Research*, New York: Random House.

Schrag, P. (1971) *The Decline of the Wasp*, New York: Simon & Schuster.

Smith, W.C. (1952) 'Hyderabad: Muslim tragedy', *Middle East Journal*, 4(1): 27–51.

Varshney, A. (2002) *Ethnic Conflict and Civic Life: Hindus and Muslims in India*, New Haven, CT: Yale University Press.

Wright, T.P., Jr (1972) *Identity Problems of Declining Former Elite Minorities: South Asian Muslims and North American 'Wasps'* (Muslim Studies Sub-Committee, Committee on Southern Asian Studies Occasional Paper Series), Chicago: University of Chicago.

—— (1975) 'Competitive modernization within the Daudi Bohra sect of Muslims and its significance for Indian political development', in H. Ullrich (ed.) *Competition and Modernization in South Asia*, Delhi: Abhinav Publications.

—— (1980) 'North Indian Muslims: the mobilization and demobilization of a former elite', in J.A. Ross and A. Baker Cottrell (eds) *The Mobilization of Collective Identity: Comparative Perspectives*, Lanham, MD: University Press of America, pp. 279–96.

—— (1995) 'How long can ethnic identity survive exogamy?', paper delivered at Bombay University, 28 December.

—— (1998) 'The Indian state and its Muslim minority; from dependence to self-reliance?', in Y. Malik and A. Kapur (eds) *India: Fifty Years of Democracy and Development*, New Delhi: APH Publications, pp. 313–39.

—— (2002) 'Strategies for the survival of formerly dominant languages', *Economic and Political Weekly of India*, 12 January: 107–14.

Zenner, W. (1991) *Minorities in the Middle: A Cross-Cultural Analysis*, Albany, NY: State University of New York Press.

3 Dominant ethnicity and dominant nationhood

Andreas Wimmer

Introduction

The editor of this volume merits our gratitude for having directed our attention towards an issue that remained absent, for a conspicuously long time, from the menu of the otherwise omnivorous social sciences. The reasons for this unusual restraint seem to be systematically tied to the subject matter itself: As long as the modern nation-state was the uncontested form of political organisation, the characteristic capture of this state by a particular ethno-national group – WASPs, Germans, Sunni Arabs, *mestizos* – did not appear as such, but as a perfectly legitimate form of representing 'the people' by its elite. 'Dominance' was a term reserved for the scandalous situations where one's own group was subject to the rule of ethnic others, either in the historical past before the nation shook off the yoke of 'foreign domination', or in neighbouring states where one's co-ethnics were not recognised as the *Staatsvolk*, but consituted an oppressed ethnic minority. Conformingly, the term 'ethnic' was reserved, in common parlance as much as in the social sciences, for those that were *not* seen as the legitimate owners of a national state but as political, if not demographic, minorities (Williams 1989).

'Dominant ethnicity' therefore represents, in the eyes of the established orthodoxy, an oxymoron – which should make it all the more powerful as an analytical tool, precisely because it may allow us to take off some of the blinders of what Nina Glick-Schiller and I have called, using a term coined by Herminio Martins, 'methodological nationalism' (Wimmer and Schiller 2002) – the naturalisation of the nation-state form and its ethnic power balance by the social sciences.

In order to reap the full analytical potential of a 'dominant ethnicity' perspective, we are well advised to avoid some of the pitfalls characteristic of the ethnicity and nationalism field in general. First, we should resist the temptation of conceiving ethnicity as a given basis for group formation and instead treat it as one among many other possible lines along which social closure may proceed. WASPs, to cite an example, may exist as a category of identification and few people so categorised hesitate to make a cross in the corresponding box when they sit in front of the census sheet – which does not make them a group in the sociological sense of the term. It may therefore be misleading to conceive of dominant ethnicity as a relationship between given groups, as many authors do, including the most outspoken critics of the ethnic power balance of liberal nation-states (Young 1990). In other words, we should beware of 'groupist thinking' (Brubaker, in press) when approaching the question of dominant ethnicity. We can avoid this pitfall by looking at mechanisms of boundary making and social closure instead of 'group relations'.

This also bears upon the notion of dominance that we may want to apply. The degree of domination varies not only with the absolute power differentials 'between groups', but also with the relative permeability of boundaries, as Theodore Wright makes clear in Chapter 2. When everybody is allowed to join a dominant group, such as an open assimilationism *à la française ou mexicaine*, we certainly have less domination than when the boundaries are defined in racial terms, such as the 'one drop of blood rule' prominent in the history of American race relations. Again, rather than looking at relations between groups, we should direct our attention to the historical process of opening and closing boundaries – to echo the classic formula coined by Fredrik Barth (1969).

A final point relates to the question of how dominant ethnicity relates to dominant nationhood. Most nations have ethnic origins and ethnic cores and thus rather approach Meinecke's ideal type of a *Kulturnation* – a point that Anthony Smith has made repeatedly and with great force and clarity, again in Chapter 1. In addition, even nations that approach the ideal type of a *Staatsnation* may not exclusively rely on civic bonds as criteria of membership, but colour this notion with an ethno-cultural semantic (Brubaker 1999) – such as the French nation which is supposed to be held together by an 'everyday plebiscite of its people', as long as this plebiscite is held, *hélas*, in French. Other civic nations refer to a plurality of *ethnic* origins, without melting them into a single national stream of history and identity. The Swiss are a case in point for this apparent paradox of a *Staatsnation* based on several *Kulturvölker* (Centlivres and Schnapper 1991). The nation is defined as being pluralistic, embracing French, German, Italian, and Romance speakers as well as Catholics and Protestants into what is officially termed 'a nation by will' held together, *faute de mieux*, by direct democracy, multiculturalism, federalism and the Alps. Foreigners, even those speaking German, French, or Italian, however, are excluded from this nation by will on the basis of laws tying citizenship to national origin and descendance.

If most nations are defined in ethnic terms and if even the most civic nations are 'coloured' by ethnic references, we may be well advised not to treat dominance by an ethnic group as something analytically completely distinct from dominance by a nation. Perhaps ethno-national dominance is a term which usefully can embrace both: dominant ethnicity and dominant nationhood. This is, to be clear, not a matter of mere terminology but, as

with most definitional problems, one of underlying theoretical and normative assumptions. By including dominance by a nation over non-national
others, we further reduce the space for naturalising ethno-national hierarchies. In this way, even the perfectly legal and internationally sanctioned
form of exclusion on the basis of national citizenship laws is moved onto
our analytical screen as a phenomenon as much in need of explanation –
albeit not of moral justification – as the obviously illegitimate domination of
a black majority by white South Africans during apartheid.

In this chapter, I should like to elaborate on this point by showing that,
independently of the formula that defines the ethno-national core – ethnic
blend as with *mestizo* or melting pot ideologies, ethnic pluralism as in the
case of Switzerland – the modern nation-state includes as one of its essential
characteristics an element of ethno-national dominance. In the following
section, I will offer some reasons for this universality of ethno-national
dominance in the modern world. The third section discusses three variants:
dominant ethnic minority, dominant ethnic majority and dominant nationhood. In the fourth section, each variant is exemplified with a case: Iraq,
Mexico, and Switzerland. Finally, I should like to address one of the guiding
questions of this volume in a more straightforward way: does the rise of
global standards for minority rights and the general drift towards more
pluralistic definitions of nationhood lead to a decline of dominant ethnicity
and nationhood?

The rise of the modern nation-state

How can we account for the prevalence and universality of ethno-national
forms of domination in the modern world? The following summarizes a
macro-historical framework of explanation that I have presented in more
detail elsewhere (Wimmer 2002). It radicalises what Anthony Smith (Smith
1998) and others have termed the modernist position in the field of ethnicity
and nationalism studies, by showing that nationalist and ethnic politics are
not just a by-product of modern state formation or of industrialisation.
Rather, modernity *itself* rests on a fundament of ethnic and nationalist principles. Modern societies unfolded within the confines of the nation-state and
strengthened them with every step of development. On the one hand, the
modern principles of democracy, citizenship, and popular sovereignty
allowed for the inclusion of large sections of the population previously
confined to the status of subjects and subordinates. On the other, shadowy
side, however, new forms of domination based on ethnic or national criteria
developed, largely unacknowledged by the grand theories of modernity as a
universalistic and egalitarian model of society. Belonging to a specific
national or ethnic group determines access to the rights and services the
modern state is supposed to guarantee. The main promises of modernity –
political participation, equal treatment before the law and protection from
the arbitrariness of state power, dignity for the weak and poor, and social

justice and security – were fully realised only for those who came to be regarded as true members of the nation.

By contrast, pre-modern empires integrated ethnic differences under the umbrella of a hierarchical, yet universalistic and genuinely non-ethnic political order, in which every group should have its properly defined place (cf. McNeill 1986; Grillo 1998). This pyramidal mosaic was broken up when societies underwent nationalisation and ethnic membership became a question of central importance in determining political loyalty and disloyalty towards the state.

This politicisation of ethnicity is the result of the overlapping and fusion of three notions of peoplehood, on which the project of political modernity is based: (1) the people as a sovereign entity, which exercises power by means of some sort of democratic procedure; (2) the people as citizens of a state holding equal rights before the law; and (3) the people as an ethnic community undifferentiated by distinctions of honour and prestige, but held together by common political destiny and shared cultural features; these three notions of peoplehood were fused into one single people writ large – replacing the Grace of God as the nadir around which political discourse draws its circles. Democracy, citizenship and national self-determination became the indivisible trinity of the world order of nation-states.

The exact relation between the three principles evidently varied according to historical circumstances and the nature of the political process. The French and the Swiss states emphasise democracy, deducing nationhood and citizenship from it. Germany, Greece, and Israel stress the principle of nationality, from which common citizenship and democratic inclusion flow. The order of the nation-state thus has its own doctrine of trinity, with innumerable variations and much sectarian fighting – nourished, as was the case with theological disputes, by vested political interests. Variation also characterises developments in the newly founded nation-states after decolonisation or after the dissolution of the communist bloc. Differential emphases on citizenship, democracy or ethnos/nation as defining elements of the state's people can be discovered, different time scales, different international environments, and domestic political dynamics.

However, a unifying motive can be discerned in the multicoloured fabrics of history and context. The fragmentation of modern society into its many national segments, held together by statehood, democracy, nationality, and citizenship, had everywhere a profound effect on the political role played by ethnicity. Since being a part of the sovereign body and a citizen became synonymous with belonging to a particular ethnic community turned into a nation, the definition of this community and its boundaries became of primary political importance. Who belongs to the people that enjoy equal rights before the law and in whose name should the state be ruled, now that kings and caliphs have to be replaced by a government 'representing' the nation?

The answer was easier to find where absolutist states preceded national ones and created large spheres of cultural, religious, and ethnic homogeneity.

Where the ethnic landscape has been more complex – usually the heritage of empires based on some sort of indirect rule and communal self-government – the politicisation of ethnicity resulted in a series of nationalist wars aiming at a realisation of the ideal nation-state where sovereignty, citizenry, and nation coincide.

Forced assimilation or the physical expulsion of those who have now become 'ethnic minorities' and are thus perceived as politically unreliable; the conquest of territories inhabited by 'one's own people'; encouraging the return migration of dispersed co-nationals living outside the national home – these are some of the techniques employed in all the waves of nation-state formation that the modern world has seen so far. What we nowadays call ethnic cleansing or ethnocide, and observe with disgust in the ever 'troublesome Balkans' or in 'tribalistic Africa', have in fact been constants of the European history of nation-building and state formation, from the expulsion of the Gypsies under Henry VIII or of Muslims and Jews under Fernando and Isabella to Ptolemy's night in France or the 'people's exchange', as it was called euphemistically, after the treaty of Lausanne between Turkey and Greece. Many of these histories have disappeared from popular consciousness – and maybe have to be forgotten, if nation-building is to be successful, as Ernest Renan (1947) suggested some hundred years ago.

Dominant ethnic majority, dominant minority, dominant nationhood

Eventually, this conflict-ridden, warlike process leads to the fully developed nation-state, as we know it from Western societies after the Second World War. It is, indeed, a more inclusive, more accountable, more equitable, and universalistic form of politics than humanity has known before – except for those who remain outside the doors of the newly constructed national home and for those who are not recognised as its legitimate owners despite occupying one of its rooms. Political modernity – democracy, constitutionalism, and citizenship – had its price, as has every form of social organisation based on strong membership rights. Inclusion into the national community of solidarity, justice, and democracy went along with exclusion and domination of those not considered to be true members of the sovereignty/citizenry/nation: those that became classified as foreigners, as guest-workers or stateless persons. Adjusting our terminology to this book's major preoccupations, we may call the constellation of power in fully nationalised modern states one of 'dominant nationhood'.

This process of nationalising the principles of social inclusion and exclusion is not self-generating or consequential to the introduction of modern forms of statehood or, as with functionalist theories (Gellner 1983), a by-product of the rise of the industrial mode of production. It depends on a successful compromise between the new state elites and the various component parts of society: an exchange of political loyalty for political participation, equal treatment before the law, and the symbolic capital associated with the rise from *plebs* to nation. If the state's elites are unable to provide these collective goods to the whole population of the national state, we expect similar processes of social closure to develop on a sub-national, ethnic basis. The polity will then be compartmentalised and fragmented into ethnic groups perceiving themselves as communities of shared destiny and political solidarity. Politicised ethnic groups and nations are thus both children of modernisation. They owe their contemporary appearance and political salience to the hegemony of the nation-state as the sole model of political organisation.

Perhaps I should outline the mechanisms of politicising ethnic differences in more detail here, since it most directly relates to the topic of this book. In weak states lacking the resources for a non-discriminatory treatment of their citizens and lacking an established network of civil society, ethnic ties become the channels through which the new elites distribute the collective goods of the modern state in order to legitimise their rule, now that the state should be responsive to the needs of 'the people'. In this way, the diffusion and rooting of a national identity are undermined, and ethnic groups are transformed into communities of shared political interest.

Two variants of this process of political closure along ethnic lines may be distinguished: dominant majority and dominant minority. In the first case, the elite of the most powerful ethnic group takes over the new state apparatus after the end of empire, while the subordinated groups continue to remain on the margin of political life and public culture. As part of the nation-building project, the state aims at assimilating these 'minorities' through education and language training and thus realising the vision of a unified citizenry, nation and sovereignty. Resulting from these endeavours, an educational elite of previously marginalised groups may emerge. It enters into direct competition with the established bureaucrats, who close ranks, particularly during hard times (Smith 1979), and make 'passing' into the dominant group through cultural assimilation difficult (Rothschild 1981: Chapter 5). The minority elite then begins to protest against discrimination and to question the ethno-national basis of the nation-state or demand one of its own. The Indian movements in Latin America, the ethno-nationalist awakenings of the Oromo in Ethiopia, minorities in the Soviet Republics, and Christian minority groups in southern Sudan are good examples of this process.

In the second variant, relations of power and demography are less clear. The new state apparatus becomes quickly compartmentalised on ethnic grounds and a fight erupts over which group will dominate the political centre. Depending on the previous position of the different ethnic elites in the colonial edifice and depending on shifting power balances and institutional arrangements, the outcome of this fight may be different, with varying degrees of inequality and domination between ethnic groups.

Perhaps the least dominant are so-called consociational democracies (Lijphart 1977), where a grand coalition of elites of differing ethnic origins negotiates a stable institutional compromise. Thanks to ethnic quotas in government and bureaucracy, reciprocal veto rights and regional autonomy, the power distribution may be balanced enough to classify this as a case of non-dominance, which may imply low intensity of conflicts and allow for mass political participation through elections without the destabilising effects that democracy often has in ethnicised polities. However, in resource-poor states with a weak tradition of civil society politics, these regimes proved to be rather unstable. If the power balance between ethnic elites changes, the capacity to renegotiate power sharing formulas is lacking (van den Berghe 1991: 191ff.). Unfortunately, as Simpson has remarked, 'the list of cases where consociational arrangements applied reads like an obituary page' (1994: 468).

In the dominant minority variant, representatives of different ethnic clienteles negotiate the price for political support behind the scenes, in the lap of a monopoly party or a bureaucracy where representatives of one region (such as 'those from the North') or ethnic category control key ministries and positions. Here, the ethnic clientelism does not manifest itself in public politics and the dominance of the state apparatus by persons sharing the same ethnic-regional background is not a matter of public contest. Donald Rothchild described this type of political system as the 'hegemonial exchange model' (1986). The one-party systems in Kenya under Kenyatta, the Ivory Coast under Houphouët-Boigny (Rothchild 1986) or Indonesia under Suharto (Brown 1994) are examples.

While such arrangements may prove to be stable and durable, they may break apart when the resources to satisfy the various ethnic clienteles run dry or when the political system is forced to 'democratise' and the emerging party system organises along ethnic lines. Politics then often centres on the question of which ethnic party – or coalition of parties – gains control and thus may exclude all others from the spoils of state power.

Finally, we find the most extreme case of dominance in authoritarian regimes where the elite is recruited from one single ethnic group, or most often even from one of its subgroups. Given the obvious break with the modern ideal of 'representing the nation', the ruler can only rely upon a narrow circle of relatives or ethnic acquaintances, which even further reduces his legitimacy and enhances the need for relying on 'his own' people. And so, often in a round dance of coups and palace revolts, ever smaller and more closely knit groups assert themselves (see Horowitz 1985: 486–501). Syria can serve as an example of this type of political regime. Its state apparatus is dominated by the Numailatiyya clan of the Matawira tribe, a small subgroup of Alawites (Batatu 1981). Until the American intervention of 2003, similar conditions prevailed in neigh-bouring Iraq, where the al-Begat section of the Al-bu Nasir tribe of the Sunni town of Takrit held all the threads of power in its hands (Batatu

1978: 1088ff.). And finally in Burundi, the Hima, a Tutsi subgroup, gained power following a number of coups and purges. The example of Burundi shows that minority regimes are often only able to hold on to power thanks to ruthless deployment of military and police forces. Yet repression increases the very tensions which it is intended to suppress (Kuper 1977).

The three major variants of ethno-national dominance certainly differ with regard to the constellations of conflict they entail and therefore also with regard to political stability. Dominant nationhood represents the most legitimate mode since here citizenry, nation, and sovereignty fully coincide and thus correspond to the modern ideals of statehood. Excluding non-national citizens on the basis of legal discrimination is perfectly sanctioned by international and constitutional law and wholly naturalised in the eyes of the world's population. Given this legal and moral legitimacy, dominant nationhood represents perhaps the politically most stable form of ethno-national dominance. Conflicts are expected to arise from major challenges to dominant nationhood. An enlargement of the circles of citizenship to include persons perceived as non-national others may be answered, by those most dependent on a privileged relationship to the state, by xenophobic or racist movements (Wimmer 2002: chapter 7). The modern anti-Semitic movement answering the 'emancipation' of Jews or the rise of scientific racism after the abolition of slavery are the most prominent examples. Xenophobia targeting refugees (in Europe) or illegal immigrants (in the USA) represents more recent attempts at reinforcing or re-establishing a hierarchical, dominant relationship between nationals and others.

In countries with a dominant ethnic majority, sovereignty and citizenry are not fully congruent with the nation, since the nation comprises a majority thought of as the true *Staatsvolk* and the ethnic minorities who contributed less to the heroic history of national liberation. Sometimes, as in the more exclusivist variants of dominant majoritarianism, they are barely tolerated and openly treated as guests rather than full residents of the national home. Sometimes, as with contemporary multiculturalist states, they are welcomed as permanent members of a colourful family. The distinction between more inclusivist and more exclusivist variants of dominant ethnicity already delineates a field of political tension, where the nature of the ethnic power balance is at stake. It is therefore a more contested, conflictive mode of ethno-national dominance than that previously discussed.

This is even more the case in dominant ethnic minority situations where the state apparatus is controlled by a group that is obviously not representative of the majority of the national population such that one of the fundamental principles of modern nation-states is violated: that of the ethnic-national representativity of government stipulating that 'likes' should rule over 'likes'. This lack of legitimacy produces a constant pressure on the

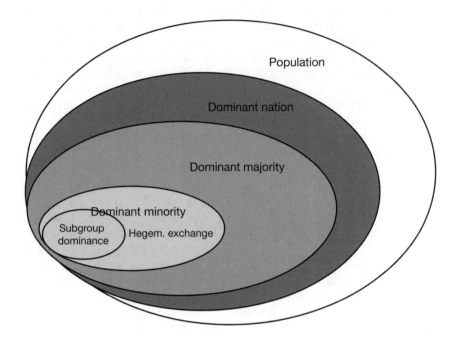

Figure 3.1 Three types of ethno-national dominance

ethnocratic regime and makes democracy a very risky and unlikely institutional companion to minority dominance.

In summary, we can grade the three types according to the degree of exclusiveness and to the degree of conflictivity and instability that they entail. Figure 3.1 illustrates this in a perhaps overly simple and straightforward way. The usual caveat of typologies applies: individual countries do not fit nicely into the three circles. A specific case may show traces characteristic of different types: a dominant minority, say South Africa's whites during apartheid, may be exclusivist towards non-national aliens as much as towards its own black majority. A sub-group (and hence: minority) of an ethnic majority may dominate the state apparatus while citizenship and immigration laws exclude large sections of the resident population. In the following section, I should like to save the reader from these complexities and present three rather more unequivocal examples.

Three examples

Mexico may serve as an example of a state with a politically dominant ethnic group transformed into a nation. Shiite Arabs and Sunni Kurds long contested the hegemony of Sunni Arabs in Iraq in vain – an example of a dominant ethnic minority. Switzerland illustrates dominant nationhood especially well, because here national closure entailed the integration of various ethnic constituencies without establishing a relationship of dominance between them.

Colonial Mexico was governed by other principles than those of the modern nation-state and ethnic distinctions conformingly played a different role from the one they played after the country became independent. They did not provide the main principles for defining membership in legal, political, and cultural terms, which were, instead, couched in the universalist language of religion that legitimised imperial rule – the integration of the Americas into the Christian (that is: Catholic) world and the eradicating of native customs contradicting 'natural law'. Universalist inclusion was combined with a hierarchical distinction between different status groups according to their 'purity of blood'. This so-called caste system differentiated the rights and obligations of the subjects towards crown and church. It implied unequal rights, indirect rule, legal segregation and paternalist protection with regard to these different status groups, including the Indian population.

The leaders of the Mexican independence movement destroyed the transnational structures of Catholic Church and Spanish empire, and abolished, in the name of the equality of citizens, the system of indirect rule and all the legal provisions that had kept the different groups apart. As a consequence, those groups that remained outside the newly defined nation of Creoles and (socially) white *mestizos* who enjoyed a privileged access to state power were rapidly subordinated, marginalised, and impoverished – they were now seen as remnants of another 'people', inferior in civilisational, and later also racial, terms compared to the newly born nation of Mexicans.

The politics of land reform and clientelist integration of post-revolutionary Mexico laid the basis for a more inclusive concept of nationhood encompassing the majority of the population. *Criollo* elitism was replaced with *mestizo* populism as the cornerstone of state ideology. However, the Indian population again remained excluded from this enlarged realm of the nation. They now became regarded as an 'ethnic minority' left over by the history of nation-building. They were to be absorbed into the melting pot of the *mestizo* nation by a benevolent politics of assimilation.

This classificatory divide between national majority and ethnic minority has become more and more politicised since it has been taken up by social movements led by a newly formed Indian intelligentsia. Its members started to challenge the dominant order according to which the Mexican state, its citizenry and the *mestizo* nation are seen as congruent, and to counter it with their vision of a multinational, pluricultural Mexico. The nationalism and social closure of the majority were finally contested and at the same time mirrored by the mini-nationalism of the excluded.

Iraq under the Ottomans shows certain structural similarities to premodern Mexico under the Bourbons. Under Ottoman rule, the universalistic, explicitly non-ethnic doctrine of religious integration into the *umma* was combined with a hierarchical system of ranks defining the rights, privileges and duties of the subjects, the amounts of taxes to be paid or to be received, the degree of political influence they would have, and the economic activities open to them. But contrary to the Spanish imperial model, these estates were not framed in racial, but religious and military, terms. The administration governed its domains through indirect rule, dealing with the notables of the various religious groups, at the end of Ottoman rule the well-known *millets*, but also of guilds, villages, and tribes or tribal confederations.

The introduction of nation-states, as was the case with Mexico, led to the politicisation of the dividing lines that had separated the mosaic pieces of imperial society, because the new national elites had to choose one of them as being the 'people' in whose name they would now rule. *Millets* were turned into ethno-national groups (Maronites, Shiites, Sunnis, Druze, Armenian orthodox, Greek orthodox, and so on), and the leaders of semi-independent tribal confederacies or emirates tried to forge nations out of their former subjects and allies.

In post-independence Iraq, the new elites narrowed their concept of the nation to those sharing their own background, i.e. to the Sunni Arab population. Accordingly, political closure quickly proceeded along ethno-religious lines. Exclusion from access to the increasingly Arabised state gave rise to a strong and militant Kurdish nationalist movement, which at various points in post-war history was able to secure control over large parts of the Northern territories. The Iraqi state was neither willing nor able to respond to the rise of Kurdish nationalism. A politics of accommodation and consociational power sharing, redefining the national character of the state by including the Kurdish as one of the state-embodying groups or integration through equal rights and political inclusion, might eventually have made the nationalist outlook attractive enough in order to motivate Kurdish speakers to join the Arab nation in greater numbers than they had over the previous decades – as with other processes of nation-building through ethnic amalgamation. Instead, the nationalist movement was received as a dangerous enemy of ethnic others residing within the newly constructed national home. The polity was more and more divided along ethnic lines, the ruling regime ever more exclusive with regard to its social bases of recruitment, and 'minorities' more and more estranged from the regime. At the end of this process stands a systematic attack on the Kurdish population by the Iraqi army (during the so-called *Anfal* operation of 1988). The Kurdish population was no longer considered part of the citizenry of the state, but an enemy population to be held in check by means of terror and force.

The modern logic of ethno-national dominance proceeds along a different and certainly much less exclusionist path in fully nationalised states, where a strong civil society had already been established and rights of participation and protection were accessible to all citizens independent of their ethno-national background.[1] Switzerland is our example here. I have shown elsewhere in greater detail that multi-ethnic, inclusive nation-building was made possible because early bourgeois patriotic associations, such as the Helvetic Society, the *Gemeinnützige Gesellschaft*, or the thousands of riflemen associations, had already spread across the entire territory and were firmly rooted even among the non-elite population *before* modern state-building had started. These provided the channels for political mobilisation for the new state elites, which therefore saw no reasons for appealing to *ethnic* solidarity in winning a following and legitimising their rule. The new state was also strong enough, in political and administrative terms, to guarantee equality before the law, political participation, protection from arbitrary violence, and later welfare benefits to all citizens irrespective of their ethnic background. In this way, a strong patriotic sentiment, later transformed into the civic nationalism of being a 'nation by will', could develop and overarch, if not entirely replace, older forms of political loyalty centred on the province and the commune.

However, this process of inclusion along national lines again had a shadow side. It excluded those who were not considered to be members of the multi-ethnic nation: travelling people and Jews until the 1870s and, up to the present day, immigrant workers and their families. The main mechanism that interlocks inclusion within and exclusion against the outside is, somewhat surprisingly, the establishment of the welfare state: the integration of the working classes into the national political framework, achieved through welfare state incorporation and power sharing, was paralleled by the deterioration of the status of immigrants and foreigners.

For the first sixty years after the foundation of the modern Swiss state in 1848, immigrants enjoyed almost the same rights and privileges – except voting rights – as citizens, and naturalisation was seen as a device fostering cultural and linguistic assimilation. With every step of the integration of the labour classes into the nationalist compromise, the distinction between foreigners and nationals became more and more important. The rights to sojourn and settlement, to free choice of profession and place of residence, to a family life, and to free speech were gradually taken away from foreigners and reserved for full citizens. Tellingly enough, access to citizenship was now made dependent on *previous* linguistic and cultural assimilation and usually not granted before at least a decade of permanent residence in the country.

The history of Switzerland shows that political modernisation may lead to ethno-national dominance even when the nation is conceived in almost purely political, plural, and multi-ethnic terms. One of the most republican, least ethnic, most democratic, least authoritarian state-building experiences of the Western world has given rise to a distinctively hierarchical and segregated relationship between different parts of the country's population, between nationals and foreigners.

Beyond ethno-national dominance? A few caveats

How deeply rooted is the relation between the modern nation-state and ethno-national dominance in the three forms that I have described above? And in which direction is it currently evolving, given actual trends of globalisation that put, in the eyes of most observers, a question mark against national sovereignty? A look at the historical origin of this relationship may help to determine its future. As Michael Mann has shown (1993: Chapter 4), the link between democracy and citizenship, on the one hand, and national self-determination, on the other, was greatly reinforced in the course of the Napoleonic wars. The allies of the cause of freedom had turned out to be oppressive conquerors. In much of central Europe and beyond, this constellation produced an enduring marriage between nationalist and democratic principles.

This marriage was also concluded, one could add, where Napoleon has never appeared, from South America at the beginning of the nineteenth century to India over a century later to Lithuania and Uzbekistan after the fall of the Berlin Wall. In all these different instances, national movements and eventually nation-states grew on imperial soil. The egalitarianism of nationalist thought, replacing earlier hierarchical conceptions of society, bears a family resemblance with democratic ideals of equal participation in politics. Political practice and discourse therefore mingled, claiming freedom from 'foreign' dominance with fighting for popular sovereignty, because both were opposed to the principles of imperial rule. Overthrowing kings and lords (or Napoleons, British colonialists or communist cadres) more often than not meant opposing peoples with other ethnic backgrounds, speaking other languages, 'belonging' to other nations. Thanks to this parallel logic of opposition, democracy and nationalism became the twin principles of modern nation-states. It is safe to assume that the world would look different today if the first modern states had emerged from within a framework of tribal politics or of city-states, where such a double logic would hardly have made any sense (Wimmer 2002: Chapter 3). The link between citizenship *cum* democracy and nationhood is therefore not a historical accident – contingent upon the birth of Napoleon – but part of the structural conditions of their emergence in all the successive waves of nation-state formation that have been set in motion by the collapse of great empires.

But how thoroughgoing is this relationship, if we look beyond the historical conditions of its emergence and focus instead upon its further trajectory? Once we break away from a view that takes the national state as the naturally given entity of modern politics and thus naturalises its particularities, we see that this relationship has affected far more realms of social life and plays a much more central role than it does in the standard accounts of the social sciences. Ethno-national criteria define the boundaries of inclusion and exclusion of most major subsystems in functionally differentiated modern societies. I will briefly relate to the legal, the political, the military and the territorial systems and take the dominant nationhood type as an illustration.

From the middle of the nineteenth century onwards, citizenship rights turned away from the medieval principle of *quidquid est in territorio est de territorio* and were more and more restricted to persons sharing a specific national background – whether defined in cultural or in civic terms (see Withol de Wenden 1992, for France; Franz 1992, for Prussia). Moreover, citizenship became a lifelong, inheritable status difficult to change, as France, Germany, Britain and the USA gradually included – albeit to varying degrees – elements of *jus sanguinis* in their legal definitions of citizenship (Bös 1997: 139–57), whereas, before, citizenship rights extinguished with permanent emigration.

Voting rights are in most countries restricted to national citizens and being elected to the highest government posts is usually reserved for persons *born* national citizens – a striking contrast to the transnational ruling elites of empires. Military service and duties are meant for national citizens only, since the *peuple en armes*, mobilised through general conscription, replaced the mercenary armies of diverse ethnic, religious, and national background. Full participation in the emerging welfare state was in most countries limited to legally employed persons, not to citizens. However, permanent, lifelong dependence on welfare is a privilege largely reserved for national citizens. Finally, the rules defining who is allowed to enter and settle on the state's territory were nationalised as well. On the one hand, citizens and non-citizens with appropriate national background were given the right to choose their domicile wherever it was on the entire national territory. And they obtained the right to leave the country and return there at any time without risking the loss of their civil rights. On the other hand, aliens were gradually deprived of the free choice of residence within a country and of the right of free entry and exit.

Nationalist principles thus deeply penetrated modern societies by granting most rights to members of the nation only and by excluding ethnic others. The marriage between ethno-national dominance and citizenship *cum* democracy may therefore be less arbitrary than most would have it. However, there are in principle no reasons why they could not divorce, institutional inertia and path dependency notwithstanding. And, indeed, there are actual signs of a decoupling. For citizens of Europe, equality before the law no longer depends on *national* citizenship. On the global level, we have witnessed the rise of a deterritorialised, transnational regime of citizenship rights (Soysal 1994; Kleger 1997). Supra-national institutions such as the UN, the Council of Europe or the OSCE have greatly contributed to the spread and enforcement of a pluralistic model of society as universally desirable, including ethnic and religious difference as a major dimension of diversity.

Multiculturalism is an important element of this vision of a post-hegemonic, tolerant liberal state stripped of its ethnocratic and nationalist characteristics. The principles of multiculturalism appear in the UN conventions against discrimination, in the UN debates on the development of a convention for indigenous populations, in ILO convention 107, in the Council of Europe convention regarding minority rights as well as in the recommendations of the OSCE. Development cooperation also increasingly ties aid to observance of 'liberal' guidelines with regard to minority issues. And this global system of both hard and soft law as well as various political pressures show their effects on all three forms of ethno-national dominance. It has become almost impossible to legitimate an apartheid-type regime based on extreme forms of minority dominance. Although many regimes of this type still exist around the world, they do so in the shadow of media and politics. Dominant majorities also face increasing challenges and have to treat minorities according to the new rules, granting parliamentary seats for the underrepresented, accepting minority languages as official idioms, allowing schools to educate children according to minority cultural traditions. The development of 'advanced' legal instruments of minority protection in the new member states of the European Union and the remaining candidate states in Eastern Europe testifies to the power of the 'liberal' international regime (see for Romania, Ram 2000). In fully nationalised states, too, the trend goes towards easier access to citizenship at least for second generation immigrants, with Germany's spectacular swing towards a *jus solis* regime representing the most visible of these developments. In addition, the legal discrimination between aliens and nationals has been greatly reduced in most Western countries (Mahnig and Wimmer 2000).

Thus, the supranational regime of minority rights and multiculturalism seems to compel nation-states to rethink the link between state and nationhood, forcing dominant ethnic groups either to loosen their grip on the state, open their ranks to members of other groups or de-ethnicise the state altogether (Joppke 2001). I wonder, however, if these changes indeed represent an epochal trend that eventually will take us to another type of society – or rather a momentum in the swing of a pendulum that may go back in the other direction as well. I thus would like to offer my company to Anthony Smith, who stands heroically alone facing a group of augurs that predict the arrival of the post-national age. Smith argues that there will be no alternative way of providing the sense of dignity and security that nations and nation-states have so far given to ordinary peoples (Smith 1995).

My scepticism is nourished from different sources, however. A second look at the modern history of nation-state formation reveals that post-war societies, with their characteristic exclusion of immigrants and a hegemonic stance towards ethnic minorities, do not represent the appropriate starting point from which we would then observe, as, for example, Hollifield (1992) does, how the liberal logic of inclusion unfolds its dynamics and finally also embraces immigrants and ethnic minorities. Largely forgotten in our mind is the much more tolerant, integrative, yet hierarchically structured stance that multicultural empires had towards minorities – as long as they accepted the superiority of the ruling elite and the legitimacy of their claim to power. Starting from such a basis of hegemonic tolerance, the exclusion of non-national others was, in most cases of nation-state formation, a gradual process. In addition, open borders for immigrants characterised most European and Latin American nation-states before the First World War. Immigrants enjoyed the same rights – except in the realms of politics and the military – as citizens. Open borders and equal treatment of minorities and immigrants came to an end when, from the 1870s onwards, the process of nationalising state and society gathered momentum. Rather than a linear trend, we thus have a curvilinear pattern starting from inclusive, relatively non-dominant modes of relating ethnicity and statehood, leading to a phase of closure along ethnic and national lines, accompanied by the three different forms of dominance discussed above, and finally the current phase of reopening.

Conforming to this movement of closure and reopening, the definition of peoplehood varied over time, being more 'civic', according to standard classifications, in times of opening, and more 'ethnic' in times of closing. In much of Western Europe the first half of the nineteenth century was characterised by an emphasis on the principles of citizenship. After the gradual extension of voting rights throughout the second half of the century, democracy became the most important defining criterion. The turn of the century, and even more so the outbreak of the First World War, saw the rapid nationalisation and ethnicisation of the notion of peoplehood, a process to be gradually reversed from the 1970s onwards. By the end of the millennium, most Western societies had apparently returned to older, de-ethnicised forms of defining those who belong to its people and those who don't (Joppke 2001), giving rise to the ideal of the post-hegemonic national state that was then projected to the global level by Western-dominated international institutions.

Much of the non-Western world, however, does not seem to be synchronised with this pattern, notwithstanding international pressures and post-national global discourse. The demise of the communist empires of Eastern Europe gave birth to a series of rapidly nationalising states that resembled early twentieth-century developments much more than the post-nationalist identity struggles of contemporary Western Europe. The global hegemony of the ideal of the civic, liberal state certainly tamed these developments and may be credited for having prevented a spiral of escalation into nationalist war and ethnic cleansing (van der Stoel, in press). But this has certainly not been enough to substantially modify the logic of nationalising states and ethnicising politics that dominated the course of history in Eastern Europe, the Caucasus, and much of Central Asia. A parallel reading of the chapters by Chetan Bhatt and by Theodore Wright (in this volume) offers a rich illustration of this 'simultaneity of the unsimultaneous' by juxtaposing the gradual de-ethnicisation of the US elite with the renationalisation of politics in India.

If we could observe processes of national closure and reopening from a global perspective, a very complex pattern would emerge. We would not only have to take into account the interrelations between various, desynchronised developments, but also allow for feedback mechanisms between closure and development which may well be of a non-linear type. More globalisation may sometimes leads to more closure, not less, while more closure may lead to more globalisation (Wimmer 2001). Despite these complexities, the basic tension between globalisation, especially of economic relationships, and national closure would perhaps still be visible as a guiding structural principle.

It may be a fruitful, while certainly not novel, hypothesis to see this tension as characteristic of the world system from the early nineteenth century onwards, i.e. since the parallel rise of capitalism and the nation-state. The balance between these forces depends on the factors alluded to in the preceding paragraph: on the interrelation of desynchronised developments in different world regions, on causal feedbacks, etc. We do not know what temporal pattern will emerge from this formula (and, unfortunately, we have only one unit of observation). It may be an oscillation between more globally integrated and less nationally closed societies, on the one hand, and less interconnected societies closed along national lines, on the other; it may be a pattern of bifurcation where several stable equilibria are possible at the same time; or perhaps a cyclical movement at the beginning that later breaks out into a linear trend; or we may enter into a chaotic pattern as soon as we achieve a certain degree of globalisation.

Leaving the technocratic language of non-linear systems theory aside, some of the main questions we may want to ask ourselves read as follows: are current trends of denationalisation and de-ethnicisation strong enough to break out of the back and forth movement between closure and openness that we can observe over the past 150 years? Should this be the case, which political and legal institutions will replace the nation-state if we tame our ethnocentric instincts and regard the European Union as an exotic exception not suited for export to the rest of the world? And if the trend is not strong enough to produce a new, post-national political regime, will we soon approach another peak in a cyclical development that will then tip over and produce a collapse of global interconnections, perhaps parallel to a demise of US hegemony, and a leap in national closure, similar to the period after the First World War? For the time being, the social sciences seem to lack the analytical precision and the empirical sophistication necessary to read the weather from the colours of today's sunset.

Note

1   Albeit not, for the first decades, for women and persons without property.

References

Barth, F. (1969) 'Introduction', in F. Barth (ed.) *Ethnic Groups and Boundaries: The Social Organisation of Culture Difference*, London: Allen & Unwin.

Batatu, H. (1978) *The Old Social Classes and Revolutionary Movements of Iraq: A Study of Iraq's Old Landed and Commercial Classes, and of its Communists, Ba'athists and Free Officers*, Princeton, NJ: Princeton University Press.

—— (1981) 'Some observations on the social roots of Syria's ruling, military group and the causes of its dominance', *Middle East Journal*, 35(3): 331–2.

Bös, M. (1997) *Migration als Problem offener Gesellschaften: Globalisierung und sozialer Wandel in Westeuropa und Nordamerika*, Opladen: Leske & Budrich.

Brown, D. (1994) *The State and Ethnic Politics in Southeast Asia*, London: Routledge.

Brubaker, R. (1999) 'The manichean myth: rethinking the distinction between "civic" and "ethnic" nationalism', in H. Kriesi, K. Armingeon, H. Siegrist and A. Wimmer (eds) *Nation and National Identity: Collective Identities and National Consciousness at the End of the 20th Century*, Chur: Rüegger.

—— (in print) 'Ethnicity without groups', in A. Wimmer *et al.* (eds) *Facing Ethnic Conflicts: Towards a New Realism,* Boulder: Rowman & Littlefield.

Centlivres, P. and Schnapper, D. (1991) 'Nation et droit de la nationalité suisse', *Pouvoirs*, 56: 149–61.

Franz, F. (1992) 'Das Prinzip der Abstammung im deutschen Staatsangehörigkeitsrecht', in Institut für Migrations- und Rassismusforschung *Rassismus und Migration in Europa*, Hamburg: Argument Verlag.

Gellner, E. (1983) *Nations and Nationalism*, Ithaca, NY: Cornell University Press.

Grillo, R. (1998) *Pluralism and the Politics of Difference: State, Culture, and Ethnicity in Comparative Perspective*, Oxford: Oxford University Press.

Hollifield, J.F. (1992) *Immigrants, Markets and States*, Cambridge, MA: Harvard University Press.

Horowitz, D. (1985) *Ethnic Groups in Conflict*, Berkeley, CA: University of California Press.

Joppke, C. (2001) 'Multicultural citizenship: a critique', *Archives Européennes de Sociologie*, 62(2): 431–47.

Kleger, H. (1997) *Transnationale Staatsbürgerschaft*, Frankfurt: Campus.

Kuper, L. (1977) *The Pity of It All: Polarization of Racial and Ethnic Relations*, Minneapolis: University of Minnesota Press.

Lijphart, A. (1977) *Democracy in Plural Societies: A Comparative Exploration*, New Haven, CT: Yale University Press.

McNeill, W. (1986) *Polyethnicity and National Unity in World History*, Toronto: University of Toronto Press.

Mahnig, H. and Wimmer, A. (2000) 'Country specific or convergent? A typology of immigrant policies in Western Europe', *Journal of International Immigration and Integration*, 1(2): 177–204.

Mann, M. (1993) *The Sources of Social Power*, vol. 1: *A History of Power from the Beginning to AD 1760*, Cambridge: Cambridge University Press.

Ram, M. (2000) 'Transformation through European integration: the domestic effects of European Union law in Romania', in J.S. Micgiel (ed.) *The Transformations of 1989–1999: Triumph or Tragedy?*, New York: East Central European Center.

Renan, E. ([1882] 1947) 'Que'est-ce qu'une nation?', *Œuvres complètes*, Paris: Calmann-Lévy.

Rothchild, D. (1986) 'Hegemonial exchange: an alternative model for managing conflict in Middle Africa', in D. Thompson and D. Ronen (eds) *Ethnicity, Politics, and Development*, Boulder, CO: Lynne Rienner.

Rothschild, J. (1981) *Ethnopolitics: A Conceptual Framework*, New York: Columbia University Press.

Simpson, M. (1994) 'The experience of nation-building: some lessons for South Africa', *Journal of Southern African Studies*, 20(3): 463–74.

Smith, A.D. (1979) 'Towards a theory of ethnic separatism', *Ethnic and Racial Studies*, 2(1): 21–37.

—— (1995) *Nations and Nationalism in a Global Era*, Cambridge: Polity Press.

—— (1998) *Nationalism and Modernism: A Critical Survey of Recent Theories of Nations and Nationalism*, London: Routledge and Kegan Paul.

Smith, M.G. (1969) 'Institutional and political conditions of pluralism', in L. Smith and M.G. Smith, *Pluralism in Africa*, Berkeley, CA: University of California Press.

Soysal, Y.N. (1994) *Limits of Citizenship: Migrants and Postnational Membership in Europe*, Chicago: University of Chicago Press.

van den Berghe, P.L. (1991) *The Ethnic Phenomenon*, New York: Elsevier.

van der Stoel, M. (in press) 'Looking back, looking forward: reflection on preventing inter-ethnic conflict', in A. Wimmer *et al.* (eds) *Facing Ethnic Conflicts: Towards a New Realism,* Boulder: Rowman & Littlefield.

Williams, B.F. (1989) 'A class act: anthropology and the race to nation across ethnic terrain', *Annual Review of Anthropology*, 18: 401–44.

Wimmer, A. (2001) 'Globalizations avant la lettre: isomorphization and heteromorphization in an interconnecting world', *Comparative Studies in Society and History*, 43(3): 435–66.

—— (2002) *Nationalist Exclusion and Ethnic Conflict: Shadows of Modernity*, Cambridge: Cambridge University Press.

Wimmer, A. and Schiller, N.G. (2002) 'Methodological nationalism and the study of migration', *Archives Européennes de Sociologie*, 53(2): 217–40.

Withol de Wenden, C. (1992) 'Fragen der citoyenneté', in Institut für Migrations- und Rassismusforschung *Rassismus und Migration in Europa*, Hamburg: Argument-Verlag.

Young, I.M. (1990) *Justice and the Politics of Difference*, Princeton, NJ: Princeton University Press.

Part II
Dominant ethnicity in transition

4 The decline of the WASP in the United States and Canada

Eric P. Kaufmann

Dominant ethnic groups may be resurgent, stable or in decline. Theodore Wright (1980) has drawn our attention to a number of formerly dominant groups – including White Anglo-Saxon Protestant (WASP) Americans and Indian Mohajirs. Most lost power due to military defeat. In other cases, dominant ethnic decline can be traced to demographic change and/or cultural assimilation (A.D. Smith 1986). In this context, the 'Decline of the WASP', to borrow the title phrase of Peter Schrag's book (1973), represents one of the most unusual reverses of ethnic fortune in history. Demographic change plays an important role in the story we are about to tell, but not in the usual way. For example, the demographic change that brought Chinese into Malaysia, Russians into the Baltic, Englishmen into Wales and Cornwall or European settlers to the New World occurred under the aegis of a colonising power. Yet the decision to alter the ethnic composition of the United States and Canada was taken, and is being taken, by the dominant ethnie itself – a deliberate policy within an environment of democratic deliberation and liberal self-consciousness.

To be sure, ethnies are not unitary actors. Elites tend to welcome immigrants and foreign culture to a far greater extent than the mass of the population. Whether they be Malaysian princes striking deals with the British as Chinese settle inland, Palestinian-Arab landlords selling land to Jewish settlers, Welsh and Cornish gentry adopting the English language or English kings importing Flemish craftsmen, ethnic 'treason' is most often committed by dominant group elites. While the United States and English-Canadian cases conform broadly to this pattern, a number of interesting differences remain. First of all, as democracies, ethnic minorities were able to have influence over the course of events, though less than many believe. Second, ethnic decline occurred as part of a deliberate ideological turn rather than for more mercenary reasons such as economic gain or political power. Indeed, ethnic decline is strongly linked to the rise of post-industrial (or 'post-materialist') liberalism after 1960.

The WASP case is becoming the paradigm rather than the outlier as globalisation and cultural liberalism bring migration to Europe on a scale unseen since the ancient waves of Celtic and Germanic colonists swept out from Central Asia. This latest North–South migratory trend is occurring during a period in which liberal-egalitarian thought is at its historic apogee. Together, these factors are driving a wedge between dominant European ethnies and the nations which, as Anthony Smith (1986, 1991) has written, 'they' spawned. In this sense, what is occurring on Europe's North American settlement periphery is coming home to roost. Just as developments in California serve as a beacon to the United States, the fate of the WASP in North America seems a harbinger of developments to come in Europe itself.

Defining WASPdom

The categorisation of White Anglo-Saxon Protestants (WASPs) as a dominant minority in Canada and the United States would strike readers at the beginning of the twentieth century as odd, for both groups still comprised a demographic majority of 'their' respective nation's population in 1900. In the United States, the amalgam of English, Scottish, Irish and Dutch Protestants that assumed the label 'old American' formed no less than 55 per cent of the population (Kaufmann forthcoming 2004b). In Canada, those of British and Irish background made up 60 per cent of the total, with British Protestants a majority in the English-speaking part of the country. The vast influx of non-British Europeans to North America in the twentieth century changed this demographic equation. Nevertheless, demographic decline might have been overcome through successful ethnic assimilation, as happened in Hungary after 1778 and in a vast array of other nation-building societies from Mexico and France to Turkey, where the dominant ethnie moved from a minority to a majority position. Why this did not take place in North America is of vital importance to any general theory of dominant ethnicity.

The rise and fall of American dominant ethnicity

Dominant ethnicity in the United States had its early foundation with the influx of thousands of Puritan Englishmen from East Anglia from the 1620s. Throughout the seventeenth century, settlers from England migrated to the English (later British) North American colonies. In the seventeenth century, this wave was joined by a slightly more diverse flow from Protestant Ireland, Scotland and north-western Europe. By the time of independence in 1776, 80 per cent of the free population was of British descent and 98 per cent were Protestant. This was hardly the global nation conjured up by foreign idealists like Crèvecoeur, Paine or Tocqueville. Nonetheless, the population was diverse in both regional and sectarian terms. David Hackett Fischer (1989) writes that the United States began as a collection of cultural regions based around core English settler ethnies. In New England the Puritans were dominant, Quakers influenced the Middle Atlantic States, in the Coastal South, Southern English Cavaliers held sway and in the Appalachian hinterland, Anglo-Scottish Presbyterians predominated.

Inter-colonial migration, trade and political links helped to integrate these regions during the mid-eighteenth century. Of greater significance, however, were cultural developments. The First Great Awakening, a New England-inspired Protestant revival movement that swept through the colonies during 1725–50, was an important mechanism here. In addition, as in Mexico, there was a growing inter-colonial sense of *Criollo* difference from 'Old Country' British officials and military officers – expressed through the increasing use of the term 'American' after 1740 (Kaufmann 2002). American independence in 1776 represented a step change in American identity and gave birth to the American nation-state.

Many contend that the United States was an 'exceptional' nation born in liberty, with a diverse culture and no founding ethnie (Zelinsky 1988; Greenfeld 1992; Lipset 1996). More recently, this sanguine Whig view has been challenged (Lind 1995; R. Smith 1997; King 2000). Low-church Protestantism and romantic Anglo-Saxonism were especially important revolutionary chords. Alexander Hamilton probably reflected the sentiments of many when he excoriated the Quebec Act of 1774, which, like the Proclamation Acts a decade earlier, protected the French Catholic population of the trans-Allegheny West from encroachments by Anglo-Protestant settlers. Hamilton went on to speak of the 'corruption of the British Parliament', and its implication in abetting the spread of 'popery' in the colonies (Hamilton [1768–78] 1961). The importance of Protestant religious identity at this stage derives from both the general currency of anti-Catholic ideas in the British population at large, and the Calvinistic American proclivity for viewing themselves as chosen servants of God. The latter, as much as anything, helps to explain the mass response to the call of revolution – especially among the Calvinist New Englanders and Scotch-Irish Presbyterians of the Backcountry settlements (Colley 1992; R. Smith 1995).

Romantic Anglo-Saxonism was more important for sections of the Whig elite in their attempt to narrate the break with British identity. Edmund Burke, John Wilkes and other English Whigs, many of whom supported the American revolutionaries, already tried to differentiate their 'Anglo-Saxon' inheritance from the supposed 'Norman' hierarchy imposed by Tories on their true liberal selves (Haseler 1996: 34). American Whigs took this reasoning a step further. By their account, the English of the Old Country represented a tired, hierarchical Norman influence, whereas the true Anglo-Saxon spirit migrated to the New World where it achieved its full flower. In Reginald Horsman's words:

> The various ingredients in the myth of Anglo-Saxon England, clearly delineated in a host of seventeenth and eighteenth-century works, now appear again in American protests: Josiah Quincy Jr. wrote of the

popular nature of the Anglo-Saxon militia; Sam Adams stressed the old English freedoms defended in the Magna Carta; Benjamin Franklin stressed the freedom that the Anglo-Saxons enjoyed in emigrating to England; Charles Carroll depicted Saxon liberties torn away by William the Conqueror; Richard Bland argued that the English Constitution and Parliament stemmed from the Anglo-Saxon period ... George Washington admired the pro-Saxon history of Catherine Macaulay and she visited him at Mount Vernon after the Revolution.

(1981: 12)

Thomas Jefferson was perhaps the greatest proponent of this creed, claiming that Americans were descended from the Anglo-Saxon chiefs Hengist and Horsa, and based his agrarian philosophy on the ideal of the yeoman farmer of King Alfred's period. Throughout the nineteenth century, particularly after 1840 as Romanticism deepened its influence, the Anglo-Saxon myth continued to gain currency among American intellectuals – a development that was only opposed in the antebellum Southern states[1] (Gossett 1963: 201–3; Ross 1984: 917; Frantzen and Niles 1997). Even twentieth-century presidents like Theodore Roosevelt and Woodrow Wilson were influenced by Anglo-Saxonist theories (Roosevelt 1889: 26).

While the lineaments of American 'WASP' ethnicity were evident at this point, it should be stressed that the absence of a significant non-British, non-Protestant threat retarded its development. This changed swiftly after 1815, when immigration resumed on a large scale. The attractiveness of the United States to non-British, non-Protestant immigrants after 1815 was to lead to profound changes in the nature of American dominant ethnicity. Previous immigrants were Protestant and mostly British, while those from Northern Europe – especially the Dutch and Huguenots – were readily assimilated. After 1830 this changed: most immigrants were Irish and German, and many were Catholic.

The Irish Catholics tended to settle in the growing cities of the northeast, where they quickly became demographically powerful. For instance, by 1853 Boston was 40 per cent Irish and over 50 per cent foreign white (Burkey 1978: 244). All this in the city that housed the Puritan elite that saw America in its own image. Since the American Constitution granted the franchise to all free whites, this ethnic bloc soon became a political force as well. This was symbolised by the rise of the Democratic political machine at Tammany Hall in New York. More to the point, the pro-Slavery Democrats helped forge links between the Southern plantocracy and northern immigrants, enraging northern WASP free soilers.

The result was the emergence of the Native American, or 'Know Nothing', Party, so called because of their secretive ways. 'The result was phenomenal', writes Ray Billington of the 1854 spring elections. 'Whole tickets not even on the ballots were carried into office. Men who were unopposed for election and who had been conceded victory found themselves defeated by some unknown Know-Nothing' (Billington 1938: 387). This third party movement won a quarter of the national vote in 1856, swept the Massachusetts and Delaware state legislatures and polled well in a number of other northern states. Even Catholic papers acknowledged the inevitability of a Know-Nothing president. Only the slavery issue and Civil War helped to avert a more complete affirmation of American ethno-nationalism.

As the nineteenth century progressed, immigrants began to arrive from a wider array of sources in Eastern and Southern Europe, eventually forming a majority of the flow (Easterlin 1982). New England WASP writers of the mid-nineteenth century like Ralph Waldo Emerson, though decrying the rise of the Irish presence, at least contented themselves with the knowledge that they had been spared the 'Black eyes and black drop ... the "Europe of Europe"' (Higham [1955] 1986: 65). Likewise, a new generation of writers in the late nineteenth century, like Theodore Roosevelt or Francis Parkman, subscribed to the idea that the Irish and Germans could combine with the English to re-form a new Anglo-Saxon compound akin to the English blend of Saxon and Celt. This would allow the WASP dominant ethnie to restore its congruence with the nation. Assimilation to Protestantism and the English language could thereby lead to a retention of the ethnic boundary in the face of massive migratory transgression. The shift in source countries from the north and west to the south and east of Europe threatened to upset this national vision, as did the potential of large-scale Chinese immigration post-1864.

It is vital, however, to focus upon the divisions that were emerging *within* the WASP or 'Native American' dominant ethnie by 1900. To begin with, the elite were more strongly pro-immigrant than the rural majority or urban working class. Abraham Lincoln had first given the nod to the importation of Chinese contract labour in 1864, and the Burlingame Treaty of 1868 placed Chinese immigration on a firmer footing. After the Civil War, Southern plantation owners, notably Ku Klux Klan founder Nathan Bedford Forrest, eagerly supported immigration, hoping to increase wage pressure on the indigenous black workforce (Gyory 1998: 33). 'All I want in my business is muscle', declared a large employer of labour in California in the 1870s. 'I don't care whether it be obtained from a Chinaman or a white man – from a mule or a horse!' (Gossett 1963: 294). The WASP cultural elite, both secular and religious, backed political and economic elites in their support for free Chinese immigration – a stance which crossed party lines. Meanwhile, business interests representing railroad and steamship companies as well as manufacturers pressed successive administrations to maintain the free flow of immigrant labour between 1890 and the mid-1920s.

Protestant workers and mechanics in the 1840s, 1850s and 1860s spearheaded the Know-Nothing movement in northern cities and towns (Foner 1970: 107; Silbey 1985: 149). Likewise, their descendants forged the Workingmen's Party, a Californian movement that brought Catholic and

Protestant white labourers together in a successful crusade to bar Chinese immigration in 1882. In subsequent decades, the American Federation of Labour provided the muscle behind the drive to limit immigration from southern and eastern Europe (Leinenweber 1984). The AFL's stance was reinforced by support from patriotic societies like the American Legion and WASP hereditary groups like the Sons and Daughters of the American Revolution (SAR and DAR). The rise of the agrarian, temperance-based, Populist and Progressive reform movements in the 1890–1920 period won many former *laissez-faire* elites to the cause of restriction.

This ultimately succeeded with the enactment of the Johnson–Reed Act (1924) which allocated a quota to each nation based on their proportion of the American population. In this way, the WASP dominant ethnie – through its 50 per cent British quota – hoped to maintain its ethnic position within the American nation, slowly strengthening it through 'Americanisation'. WASP ethnic activity in the 1920s was reflected in many ways. The Volstead Act (1920) introduced the prohibition of alcohol, a longstanding Protestant crusade. The Ku Klux Klan emerged as a mostly northern anti-Catholic (rather than southern anti-black) association with millions of members, some rural but most part of the urban WASP working class who felt threatened by Catholic immigration and secularism. There were Klan mayors and even one Klan president (Jackson 1967). WASP dominance, it seemed, had been consolidated.

The decline of the WASP in America

On the other side of the ledger, the 1920s marked the high tide of WASP control. Naturally, legislative success did result in a degree of institutionalised dominance along the lines suggested by Andreas Wimmer in Chapter 3 in this volume (Wimmer 2002). Immigration no longer posed such a serious threat to WASP control and Americanisation rested on a surer government footing. The history texts in the nation's schools, along with its popular magazines and films, reinforced the message that the true American type was Anglo-Protestant – a descendant of revolutionaries and westward-moving frontiersmen like Daniel Boone (H.N. Smith 1950). Finally, the political system allowed for the malapportionment of seats between rural and urban districts, ensuring the domination of rural America, where some three-quarters of the WASP population resided[2] (Erikson 1972; Schwab 1988).

Underneath this apparent self-confidence, though, new liberal-cosmopolitan currents of thought were emerging. Whereas cosmopolitanism in the nineteenth century tended to be the by-product of *laissez-faire* empire building and business interests, a new confluence of reformist and liberal WASP thought developed in Chicago and New York in the 1900s. This so-called Liberal-Progressive movement departed from the organic ethno-communitarianism of the Progressive movement. It advocated social reform, but felt non-WASP immigrants to be a source of richness rather than social ills. Rooted in rising non-denominational universities like the University of Chicago, Liberal Progressivism also expressed itself in educational outreach missions known as 'Settlements', which sprung up in deprived inner-city districts. John Dewey and Jane Addams were among the most important figures in this movement, which was the first to unite left-wing and liberal-cosmopolitan activists.

This ideological wind quickly gained political teeth as part of a caucus within, paradoxically, the federal government-sponsored Americanisation movement. Liberal Progressives founded The Immigrant Protective Association (1908), National Association for the Advancement of Colored People (1909) and joined business interests in the fight against immigration restriction legislation in 1912, 1917, 1921 and 1924. Liberal Progressives urged immigrants to treasure their ethnic heritage as a 'gift' to the nation and subscribed to Israel Zangwill's new vision (1909) of two-way assimilation in which both native and immigrant gave and received to forge a new cosmopolitan 'Melting Pot' (Lissak 1989). Meanwhile, a new generation of young Americans turned their back on westward settlement and celebrated the decadence of urban life. Beginning in 1912, New York's Greenwich Village served to incubate a modernist, Bohemian counter-culture which challenged the strictures of Protestant America. Ethnic cultures were lauded as liberating, and Anglo-Protestant mores lampooned (Abrahams 1986).

Though the 1920s saw many WASP legislative successes, the growth of left-liberal thought was exponential. In that decade, modern architecture, illegal drinking establishments and fashion innovations like the 'flapper' signified that many elite WASPs were flouting the moral code of small-town America. The popularity of anti-provincial, Protestant-bashing writers like Sinclair Lewis and H.L. Mencken heralded a new era. Along with drinking, bohemian innovations like watching black jazz in Harlem became increasingly popular middle-class pursuits. While many young, middle-class urban WASPs were drawn to Europe as part of the 'Lost Generation', their parents successfully launched a campaign against Prohibition which resulted in its repeal in 1933.

Arguably more important for the demise of WASP America was the stance of organised Protestantism in the form of the Federal Council of Churches (FCC). The churches embraced the ideas of the Liberal Progressives and were in the van of the ecumenical and interfaith movements. Rejecting the Protestant crusade as early as 1910, the mainline Protestant elite led the fight against Klan influence and immigration restriction. This increasingly critical posture led to a rejection of the entire missionary effort as imperialistic – a startling about-turn for the once hegemonic Protestant crusade (Cavert 1968).

The 1930s witnessed a continued division between the WASP elite – both secular and religious – and the mass of the Anglo-Protestant population. However, the high degree of cultural capital possessed by cosmopolitan

WASPs fed into the political system. Though unable to challenge the Anglo-Protestant hammerlock over the malapportioned legislature, liberal forces lapped at FDR's New Deal administration. The war effort, for instance, though it excluded black Americans, embraced Catholics and Jews as never before.

This was reinforced in a torrent of government-sponsored pamphlet literature and radio broadcasts which stressed the theme of 'Americans all' by the late 1930s (Savage 1999). The battle for the nation's soul was also fought over the contentious terrain of historiography. Accounts which preserved an Anglo-paternalist vision of the nation gave way either to critical or liberal-consensus historiography. The latter emphasised political unity and American exceptionalism and downplayed ethno-cultural pedigrees. The school system proved a harder row to hoe, but even here the newly powerful National Education Association (NEA), influenced by Liberal Progressivism, managed to face down patriotic societies like the DAR over textbook selection. Once central school texts like Muzzey's Anglo-Saxonist *American History* gave way, in the 1940s and 1950s, to books which applauded white ethnic contributions and reinterpreted the Statue of Liberty as a beacon to prospective immigrants (Strayer 1958: 69–71; FitzGerald 1979: 79–82, 175).

The aforementioned cultural revolution was followed by wartime films which, though privileging the WASP in lead roles, nevertheless suggested that others were also 'One Hundred Per Cent' Americans.[3] Meanwhile, the ecumenical interfaith movement was so successful that the Jewish-American writer Will Herberg could assert that though the American ideal remained the WASP type, a non-denominational religiosity embracing Protestants, Catholics and Jews defined the new Americanism (Herberg 1955). Dwight Eisenhower's election as the first German-origin president in 1953 and John F. Kennedy's 1960 triumph as the first Catholic to occupy the Oval Office demonstrate how much things had changed since 1928, when Al Smith's bid to become the first Catholic president foundered on the rocks of WASP dominance.

The last redoubt of WASPdom now lay in the political arena. Much work remained, for the McCarran–Walter Act of 1952 reaffirmed the ethnic exclusivity of the 1924 immigration act and malapportionment continued unabated. In their quest, WASP liberals were aided by a more self-confident Catholic and Jewish population in the northeastern cities. The Americanised, Irish-led Catholic Church and the multi-ethnic AFL–CIO labour movement helped to fuel the success of the Democratic Party, which held the lion's share of power during 1932–68.

Yet the ethnic lobby could never have achieved its goals without Anglo-Protestant stewardship. Moreover, Democrats relied on rural Southern Protestant 'Dixiecrats', who often voted with conservative Republicans to block changes to the ethnic and racial status quo. Only the intervention of the Supreme Court in the landmark Baker v. Carr (1962) case unlocked the potential for unseating the WASP 'ethnocracy', to use Yiftachel and Ghanem's phrase (see Chapter 10). A number of other decisions in 1964 established that nothing less than complete redistricting would be tolerated. Quite clearly, minority agitation, which is a feature of many societies, is an insufficient explanation of WASP decline.

Reapportionment enabled a restructuring of power in Congress as committee and sub-committee chairs passed out of the hands of conservative Protestants. Metropolitan Congressmen now controlled the fate of House legislation (Schwab 1988: 143–6). For instance, the chairman of the House Judiciary Subcommittee on Immigration until 1963 was Francis Walter (R-Penn.), a defender of the National Origins scheme and co-sponsor of the restrictive McCarran–Walter Act of 1952. His replacement in 1964 by the reformist Michael Feighan (D-Ohio) smoothed the way for the passage of the 'colour-blind' Hart–Celler immigration bill. Whereas President Truman railed unsuccessfully against the quota act in 1953, the Johnson administration was able to triumph with the enactment of the Hart–Celler Act of 1965 (Fitzgerald 1987).

The changed political terms of reference affected social relations as well. The rapid expansion of the university system in the 1950s, 1960s and 1970s and the rise of centralised mass television media helped to produce important liberalising attitude changes on questions of race, ethnicity and religion which have been charted in major surveys (McClosky and Zaller 1984; Mayer 1992). Protestant fraternal associations like the Freemasons faced membership losses while mainline Protestant churches haemorrhaged members (Anderson 1970; Roof and McKinney 1987; Putnam 2000) Catholic ethnic groups like the Italians, Poles and Irish achieved economic and educational parity with WASPs by 1980 (Alba 1990). The ranks of the elite were among the last to open up, but by the late 1980s Jews – just 2–3 per cent of the population – outnumbered WASPs among the ranks of the media elite, while Jewish, Italian and Greek millionaires (representing no more than 10 per cent of the population) outnumbered their WASP counterparts. Added to this, the proportion of WASPs in positions of corporate leadership and in academia was cut in half in a generation (Wright 1980; Christopher 1989).

A partial consequence of the above was a jump in inter-religious marriage: 91 per cent of Protestants married those of their own faith in 1957, but this changed greatly from the 1960s onward. Only a minority of European-origin Americans can claim single ancestry today. This is especially pronounced among youth – who frequently embody a mix of ancestries and ethnic identities. Theodore Wright and Richard Alba suggest that the new trend portends the emergence of a new 'white' or Euro-American ethnie. The decline in the non-Hispanic white proportion of the American population from 90 per cent in 1960 to 70 per cent today is seen as a stimulus to white dominant ethnic identification. The racialised politics of multiculturalism are touted as yet another spur to action (Lind 1995;

Gallagher 1997). Some view white nationalist far right movements (which include Catholic whites) as the edge of a rising wedge of dominant-group ethnic nationalism (Swain 2002).

Evidence for a rise in white nationalist activity is, however, scant (Kaufmann forthcoming 2004a). Instead, the main expression of this sentiment has been the 'white flight' of the native-born working class away from high-immigration metropolitan areas (Frey 1996). Certainly the level of white nationalist agitation, expressed through the Immigration Reform and Official English movements, pales in comparison with the stridency and success of 1920s' Anglo-Protestant nationalism. Is Wright correct in treating the decline of the WASP as a successful group strategy of boundary expansion? Indeed, some have argued that lighter-skinned Asians may be admitted to this 'club' in the near future, given rising rates of inter-racial marriage (Alba 1990; Gans 1994).

I am sceptical. The closer one looks at current trends, the more they show continuity with the shift towards liberal value change identified by writers like Daniel Bell (1980) and Ronald Inglehart (1990). Propelled by a university-educated 'New Class', vertical and horizontal cultural boundaries are dissipating. The boundaries of most American historic communities, whether religious or ethnic, are loosening.[4] Parallel rising rates of inter-ethnic, inter-racial and inter-religious marriage provide support for this. The rise of symbolic, voluntary and even 'post'-ethnicity reinforces the new trend. The appearance of white unity through intermarriage can be shown to be illusory by examining opinion polls on immigration and the results of popular anti-immigrant initiatives like California's Proposition 287 in which ideology and party identification are better predictors of attitudes than race. The true gainer from loosening boundaries is therefore not white dominant ethnicity, but trans-ethnic 'lifestyle' enclaves with their 'virtual' placelessness and temporal ephemerality.

Thus, one might better conceive of what is happening as a continuation of the narrative of dominant ethnic decline as whites and Protestants lose ground to others year after year. I theorise this as a shift from a *dominant ethnic* pattern – consisting of a 'vertical mosaic' of tightly bounded ethnic groups dominated by Anglo-Protestants – to a *liberal-egalitarian* pattern, in which ethnic hierarchies are largely flattened and ethnic boundaries considerably relaxed. Americans of British descent and Protestant religion still comprise almost 20 per cent of the population and continue to dominate the Oval Office to this day. But they are just one group among many, having lost the political, economic, demographic and cultural clout which seemed unassailable only yesterday.

The rise and fall of Canadian dominant ethnicity

The Canadian case sketches out many of the same social and political contours as the American. When we speak of Canadian dominant ethnicity, we really are referring to Anglo-Canadian Protestant ethnicity. French and Native (Aboriginal) Canadians were generally preoccupied with their own identity projects, while it was the English-speakers who spoke in the name of the Canadian nation. This was not always the case, for though New France had fallen to General Wolfe's forces on the Plains of Abraham in 1765, few English-speaking settlers joined the several hundred thousand French-speaking descendants of Colbert's early 1600s' colonisation effort. In fact, no less redoubtable a figure than Governor Guy Carleton of Quebec assumed that the British North American colonies 'must, to the end of time, be peopled by the [French] Canadian race, who have already taken such firm root, and got to so great a height, that any new [British] stock transplanted will be totally hid' (Wallace 1921: 4–5).

The equation of 'Canadian' with French-speakers soon changed with the arrival of 19,000 Americans loyal to the British Crown during the war of independence. These United Empire Loyalists were an incredibly disparate crew: they represented the most faithful component of the estimated one-third of the American population that remained loyal to Britain during the Revolution. Some generalisations can be drawn from the fact that New Englanders and Virginians were less likely than those in the Middle Atlantic states to be loyal. For the most part, though, motivation for Loyalism was largely ideological, hence social groups and even families tended to be divided on the issue (Nelson 1967).

The Loyalists gave Canada its American English dialect and Loyalist political philosophy as well as its Tory political culture and British institutions. They generally settled west, east or south of the established French population in the lower St. Lawrence valley. Continued American migration raised the strength of English-speakers, though they remained a minority as late as the 1820s. The successful British-Canadian rebuff of American expansionism during the War of 1812 helped to provide a narrative of Anglo-Canadian election, but otherwise this group remained strongly wedded to British myths and symbols.

The British connection was dramatically reinforced in the next half-century by a large wave of British immigrants, most of whom were Scottish or Irish Protestants. They helped create an English-speaking majority by 1830 and fortified the imperial link. Conflicts between Tories and Reformers in English Canada were severe, however, and involved not only differing political philosophies but distinct cultural identities. Tories tended to support the established church and the aristocratic 'family compact' elite as well as the British connection. Reformers, by contrast, stressed that Anglo-Canadian Protestantism was more dissenting and its culture more American than the Tories would allow. This chasm boiled over into the Rebellion of Upper Canada of 1837. The union of the Canadian colonies under the 1867 British North America Act led to a growth in Canadian self-awareness – but not at the expense of the British connection, which had been fully reaffirmed after the abortive rebellions of 1837 (Kaufmann 1997).

An important organisational form entered Canadian life at this time, notably the Orange Order. Stressing loyalty to the Crown and to Protestantism, this Irish import quickly transcended its ethnic base to appeal to a wide section of English-speaking Canadians. Between 1870 and 1920, close to a third of adult male Protestants in Ontario, the largest English-speaking province, were initiated into an Orange lodge. Orangeism provided Canada with several prime ministers (including the first, Sir John A. Macdonald), numerous mayors, premiers and members of parliament at all levels. It served as a bulwark of rural and working-class Toryism as late as the 1950s (Houston and Smyth 1980). The appeal of the British connection can also be gauged from popular participation in royal visits. The 1901 tour by the Duke of Cornwall (the future George V) drew 200,000–250,000 people in Toronto, a figure larger than the city's population. Similar enthusiasm was displayed throughout English Canada, in both cities and towns (Buckner 1998: 11).

British Canadians were energised by conflict with French Canadians, whose high birth rate and propensity to migrate made them an important demographic force in the English-speaking provinces of Ontario, New Brunswick and Manitoba. Orange pressure and high levels of British immigration led to the abolition of funding for Catholic schools in Manitoba in 1890 and was instrumental in suppressing the political aims of the French-speaking Métis (mixed-blood) population of the northwest in 1870 and 1885. British-Protestant dominant ethnicity also crystallised over the Crimean War (mid-1850s), Fenian raids (1866), the Boer War (1899–1901), conscription crises (the First and Second World Wars) and the flag debate (1964–5).

Dominant ethnic actors railed against non-British immigration, especially under Laurier's Liberal government from 1896 to 1904. The Orange Order, Imperial Order Daughters of the Empire (IODE) and other Loyalist associations were instrumental in hastening the exit of Clifford Sifton, Laurier's Minister for the Interior, who had encouraged German and Eastern European immigrants to settle in the prairie provinces (Anderson and Frideres 1981: 277). This led to a rebound in the proportion of British immigrants to nearly 60 per cent of the total by 1920. Nonetheless, the non-British immigration stream continued to gather pace after this date, reducing the British intake to just one-third of the total in 1930. However, once again, dominant ethnic pressure from prairie WASPs, largely Orange-led, resulted in the introduction of an Imperial Preference immigration policy in 1931. Though less rigid than the American National Origins quota system, it effectively laid down the basis for the maintenance of Canada's British-Protestant ethnic character.

The categories under the new dispensation included: (1) British subjects from the 'white' Dominions of Australia, New Zealand, South Africa, Ireland, Newfoundland or the UK; (2) US citizens; (3) relatives of Canadian male residents; and (4) 'Agriculturalists with sufficient means to farm in

Canada'. Combined with Oriental exclusion acts of 1923 and 1928, it is not surprising that this legislation reduced the non-British component in the immigrant stream from almost 70 per cent in 1930 to just 10 per cent by 1941. Synchronously, renewed efforts to Anglo-Canadianise the immigrants affected the school system and many sections of the public and private spheres (Palmer 1975).

The Anglo-Conformist philosophy was enunciated in 1928 by R.B. Bennett, Canada's Prime Minister from 1930 to 1935. 'We earnestly and sincerely believe that the civilization which we call the British civilization is the standard by which we must measure our own civilization,' thundered Bennett.

> We desire to assimilate those whom we bring to this country to that civilization … That is what we desire, rather than by the introduction of vast and overwhelming numbers of people from other countries to assimilate the British immigrants and the few Canadians who are left to some other civilization. That is what we are endeavouring to do, and that is the reason so much stress is laid upon the British settler.
>
> (quoted in Palmer 1975: 119)

Finally, while the French majority province of Quebec had a certain degree of federal autonomy, Quebec Anglo-Protestants controlled the province's economy and dominated its corporate sector. As in the American case, it seemed that the hegemony of the dominant WASP ethnic group had successfully been institutionalised

The decline of British Canada

In the United States dominant ethnicity lost some of its vitality due to its association with an unpopular, declining tradition – namely that of Prohibition. In Canada the dominant WASP group suffered as well since it had invested greatly in the symbolism of the British Empire since 1776. Thus the decline of the British Empire opened up space for criticism of the entire WASP Canada apparatus. To be fair, currents of anti-British, Canadian nationalism had their antecedents (among English-speakers) in the 1837 Rebellion of Upper Canada. Liberal supporters among dissenting Protestant sects like the Baptists were generally predisposed to this kind of sentiment. After Confederation in 1867, Canadian nationalism reappeared in the form of the Canada First movement. Though loyal to the Crown, it sought to establish a more independent sense of Canadian identity and steer loyalty towards Canadian interests over those of the mother country (Foster 1888).

A sense of disillusionment with empire and pride in Canada's contribution to the war effort contributed to a step-change in the popularity and stridency of Canadian nationalism after 1918. During the 1920s, Canadian

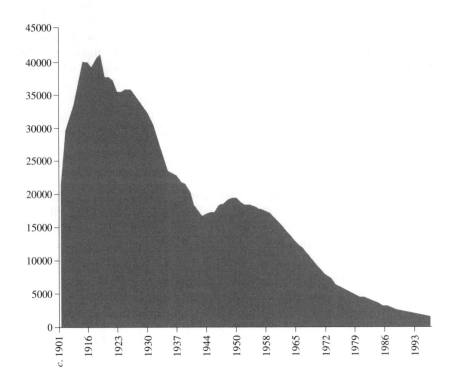

Figure 4.1 Orange Order membership, Ontario West (male), 1901–95

Source: Grand Orange Lodge of Ontario West annual reports

cultural nationalism took off – represented by bourgeois associations like the Native Sons of Canada (120,000 membership in that decade) and the Association of Canadian Clubs. The popularity of the Group of Seven landscape painters in the 1920s and 1930s owes much to this new spirit. Indeed, A.Y. Jackson, one of the leading Group members, produced one of the first Maple Leaf designs (1912) for what would become the new Canadian flag. Crucially, the Orange Order suffered a dramatic decline in membership after 1920 – even as the nation's population greatly expanded (Figure 4.1).

Between 1940 and the mid-1960s, new opinion polls found that British symbols were waning in popularity in competition with Canadian ones. Sentiment in favour of retaining the Union Jack as the national flag, for example, declined from 42 per cent in 1943 to 25 per cent in 1963, paving the way for the adoption of the new Maple Leaf flag in 1965 (Schwartz 1967: 119). The decline of British loyalty did not produce any immediate change in ethnic power relations in the country due to the entrenched position of WASPs at the pinnacle of what Canadian sociologist John Porter termed

Canada's 'Vertical Mosaic' (Porter 1965). Yet such changes loomed over the horizon. The rapid secularisation, or 'Quiet Revolution', of French Canada after 1960 irrupted the traditional social order and released secular-nationalist energies that burst forth in the rise of Quebec separatism. This new challenge, coupled with the disarray of English-Canadian identity in the face of imperial decline, opened up cracks in the WASP ethnocracy.

Developments in Canada show some similarities with the United States, though Canadian thought of the 'Liberal Progressive' variety came later and was a minor chord in the nation's intellectual and political life until the 1960s. The radical Cooperative Commonwealth Federation (CCF) movement – forerunner of today's left-wing NDP party – had its roots in agrarian prairie populism and thus shared a Social Gospel emphasis on organic social unity more characteristic of William Jennings Bryan and Teddy Roosevelt than John Dewey.[5]

An important counter-current of left-liberal thought did, however, emerge from the 1930s onwards, most clearly identifiable in the persona of Frank Underhill. An intellectual disciple of John Dewey and Walter Lippmann, Underhill enjoined his compatriots to study the new American thinking. It is also likely that he was influenced by the rise of anti-imperialist thought emanating from Britain's new internationalist historians of the Union of Democratic Control (UDC) (Kennedy 1977; Francis 1986). Though long a soldier in the wilderness, Underhill's moment finally arrived in 1966 in an opening statement he wrote for a book by the left-liberal University League for Social Reform.

Notice the use of the term 'WASP', which had been invented in the USA in the late 1950s and only popularised in the mid-1960s:

> Our authors ... abandon the concept of British North America as defining the Canadian identity ... Our new Maple Leaf flag will, one hopes, be taken by future generations as the epoch-making symbol marking the end of the era of the Wasp domination of Canadian society. At any rate, our authors are all post-Wasp in their outlook.
>
> (Underhill, quoted in Russell 1966: xvii)

A chrysalis for Underhill's rise was a renewed increase in non-British immigration after the Second World War as the Liberal Prime Minister Mackenzie-King allowed the Imperial Preference provisions to be interpreted more broadly to admit more non-British Europeans. By 1962, geographic preferences were abandoned – a measure executed with little fanfare, and which probably reflected the more prominent role played by federal bureaucrats in crafting such policy in Canada as compared with the USA (Veugelers 2000). Though polls are unclear on this, it is possible that post-war attitudes to European immigrants softened somewhat – as they did in the USA during 1945–65 (Simon and Alexander 1993). The expansion in the high-school and university-educated population in this decade may also

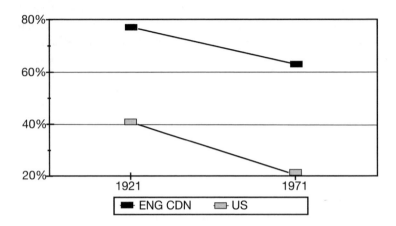

Figure 4.2 Proportion of English, Canadian and American populations of WASP origin in Canada, 1921 and 1971

Note: The Canadian figures refer to those of 'British' descent, including Irish Catholics, a far less significant population than in the United States. This partly reflects the fact that Irish Catholics were arguably closer to the WASP mainstream in Canada than Dutch and German Protestants – the reverse of the American situation. This may reflect the relative importance of Protestantism in American WASP identity as opposed to Britishness in the Canadian self-conception.

have exposed more Canadians to liberal social attitudes. In any event, the result was a continued erosion of the British demographic presence. Figure 4.2 shows the 'WASP' proportion of the population in both English Canada and the United States in 1921 and 1971. Canadian WASPs clearly experienced demographic decline in parallel with their American counterparts, though on a less steep tangent.

The Canadian government's Royal Bilingualism and Biculturalism Commission report of 1966 recommended the introduction of a more comprehensive bilingualism in the federal government, and drew attention to the economic disparity between English and French Canada. All this was facilitated by the almost unequivocal support provided to the Liberal government by French-Canadians and many Catholic immigrant groups. These communities made it much more difficult for British-Protestant Canada to elect Tory governments that might be more sympathetic to dominant ethnic hegemony. Yet this was nothing new. Accordingly, though Liberal governments were returned throughout the 1960s and 1970s under Lester Pearson and Pierre Trudeau, the key ingredient of change was that both were committed cosmopolitans.

Pearson's White Paper on immigration urged the country to accept as many immigrants as possible, and his government adopted an ethnically neutral 'points' system in 1966–67 which also embraced a strong humanitarian component.[6] Furthermore, the increased presence of so-called 'third-force' Canadians of neither French nor British descent infused itself into the increasingly heated debate over Canadian ethnic relations as Quebec nationalism's meteoric ascent began in the mid-1960s. The Royal Bi & Bi Commission thus made recommendations for accommodating the aspirations of third-force Canadians.

The Commission's report proved but the tip of an emerging iceberg of post-WASP Canadianism. Pierre Trudeau, the Liberals' new charismatic leader, was instrumental in pushing forth this agenda. Due to his part-French background, he had always been sympathetic to the aspirations of this underprivileged segment of Canadian society. Yet Trudeau broke with his left-wing Quebec nationalist colleagues in the influential *Cité Libre* magazine *cénacle* in which he was involved. Spurning what he took to be the 'narrow' premises of Quebec nationalism, he instead favoured a cosmopolitan, post-WASP Canadianism based on the model of a bilingual and multicultural Canada (Trudeau 1968). Some writers suggest that this was Trudeau's personal response to his own ontological crisis as a British–French, bilingual Canadian cosmopolitan – a response that ultimately stoked Quebec nationalism and alienated many unilingual English Canadians (McRoberts 1997).

Trudeau's long reign as Liberal Prime Minister between 1968 and 1984 helped to institutionalise his vision. Multiculturalism and bilingualism became official policies with the former even engraving itself on Canada's constitution. Meanwhile, the decline of British Canada's demographic preponderance gathered force with the immigration reforms of the 1960s. As in the United States, most post-1970 immigrants were non-Europeans, mostly from Asia, and this new wave bolstered the rise of a more self-confident multiculturalist movement. As in the United States, this is one of the few policy areas in which the Left has scored important successes. The notion of Anglo-Saxon and now 'white' decline tends to be viewed as a positive development by most within the (largely white) cultural elite and is perceived as an indicator of progress towards a new type of civilisation. Reaction against this reigning posture has been intermittent, but has achieved little discursive or policy success.

Conclusion

The timing of the rise and decline of dominant ethnicity in both English Canada and the United States is striking in its similarity: Anglo-Protestant groups in both nations asserted their political power through important ethno-nationalist movements in civil society. In Canada, the Orange Order and other pro-imperial societies played this role, whereas in the United States a diverse series of 'Native American' Protestant mass movements held sway. Immigration was an important battleground. The Protestant working class, which dominated both Canadian Orangeism and American

Nativism, was instrumental in restricting non-British immigration. On the other hand, the commercial elite – represented by figures like Clifford Sifton in Canada or President Taft in the United States – pushed for more open borders.

Non-British ethnic groups, notably Catholic immigrants and their descendants in the USA and both French and 'third-force' Canadians ,played their part in engineering WASP decline. Yet the minorities' struggle against oppression is more of a universal phenomenon and cannot account for key policy and identity shifts. Therefore, a far more important factor were *intra-ethnic* divisions. The shift in the sensibility of the WASP cultural elite in both countries thereby becomes crucial. In the USA, left-wing Anglo-Protestant intellectuals of both secular and religious stripe gradually abandoned the organic Protestant reform crusades of the early Social Gospel Movement in favour of Liberal Progressivism. Pluralism and ecumenism thereby displaced ethnic homogeneity in the leftist vision of the nation.

Here is where we come to an important difference between the two societies in question. The rise of American Liberal Progressivism took place between 1905 and 1917, well before analogous Canadian developments. Only in the 1930s did mavericks like Frank Underhill introduce these ideas to the Canadian context. This delay can partly be explained by the smaller proportion of 'non-founding' groups in Canada, but also by the more conservative and cautious nature of English-Canadian intellectual life in this period. This difference aside, if we look at the broader sweep of policy and identity change, we see a pattern of pre-1939 dominant ethnic hegemony slowly giving way to greater openness in the 1940s and 1950s, followed by collapse in the 1960s.

In the United States, the expansion of the university education system and national media helped to transmit Liberal Progressive and Modernist ideas to a wider section of the population. The Supreme Court – again, a reflection of elite-driven change within WASPdom – helped pave the way for dominant ethnic decline by ordering reapportionment of the legislature between polyglot cities and WASP-dominated rural areas. This helped to repeal the National Origins quota immigration scheme and introduce new civil rights legislation under the Johnson Democrats during 1964–65. In Canada, the federal bureaucracy served as the engine of liberal change, abetted by the post-1945 success of the Liberal Party, with its strong Catholic support base. A reorientation of Canada's geographic preference-based immigration policy towards a system grounded in merit and international compassion followed in 1962 and 1966–67.

Some see a resurgence of dominant ethnicity in the rise of far-right political activity and the emergence of a more race-conscious white population shorn of internal ethnic and religious differences. However, far-right activity has generally been muted in comparison to both the North American past and to European movements. 'White flight' is a significant social feature of the North American landscape but political resistance to demographic change or multiculturalism remains but a shadow of its 1920s' ancestor. The historiography, public discourse and political institutionalisation of post-ethnicity, whether in its civic nationalist or multiculturalist guise, appear to have attained an almost unassailable position.

Similar processes are noticeable in Quebec and Britain, as Danielle Juteau and Steve Bruce suggest in their chapters in this volume, as well as in a number of European societies. It is true that resistance to dominant ethnic decline appears stronger in Europe than in North America, something borne out by the rise of anti-immigration politics in several European societies. Yet this may only be loosely related to higher levels of North American tolerance or the greater legitimacy of 'civic nationalist' traditions. Instead, it is probably explicable in terms of the more favourable (for ethno-nationalists) political opportunity structure offered by Europe's many proportional representation electoral systems as well as the more limited potential for 'white flight' caused by lower labour mobility. The greatest difference in dominant ethnic legitimacy thus remains between Enlightenment/New Left-influenced Western societies, with North America at the forefront, and the non-Western world in which norms of liberal-cosmopolitan 'correctness' have had far less socio-political impact.

Notes

1 Antebellum Southern writers tried to stress their Norman, as opposed to Anglo-Saxon, inheritance. A century later, however, it is interesting that Southern segregationists like George Wallace were among the last to speak of themselves as the 'Anglo-Saxon people' (Wallace [1963] 2002; Horsman 1981).
2 In 1890, just 8 per cent of 'native' whites lived in cities of over 100,000 people. By contrast, fully a third of the foreign-born did so (Easterlin 1982).
3 This theme continued after the war, as is evident in Tennessee Williams's post-war play, *A Streetcar Named Desire*.
4 Black males and certain Asian and Hispanic groups with large components of recent immigration represent an obvious exception to this rule. Otherwise, the broader pattern holds quite well.
5 CCF leader J.S. Woodsworth, for instance, penned the influential *Strangers Within Our Gates* (1909), a tome which echoed some of the same left-wing ethnic nationalist themes as Josiah Strong's *Our Country* (1885) had in the United States.
6 'History of Canada's Immigration Policy', http://www.canadiangeographic.ca/Magazine/JF01/culture_acts.html

References

Abrahams, E. (1986) *The Lyrical Left: Randolph Bourne, Alfred Stieglitz and the Origins of Cultural Radicalism in America*, Charlottesville, VA: University Press of Virginia.

Alba, R.D. (1990) *Ethnic Identity: The Transformation of White America*, New Haven, CT: Yale University Press.

Anderson, A.B. and Frideres, J.S. (1981) *Ethnicity in Canada: Theoretical Perspectives*, Toronto: Butterworth and Co.

Anderson, C.H. (1970) *White Protestant Americans: From National Origins to Religious Group*, Englewood Cliffs, NJ: Prentice Hall.

Bell, D. (1980) *The Winding Passage: Essays and Sociological Journeys, 1960–1980*, Cambridge, MA: ABT Books.

Billington, R.A. (1938) *The Protestant Crusade, 1800–1860: A Study of the Origins of American Nativism*, New York: Macmillan.

Buckner, P. (1998) 'Migration and national identity in Canadian history', paper delivered at the British Association for Canadian Studies (BACS) meetings, Swansea.

Burkey, R.M. (1978) *Ethnic and Racial Groups: The Dynamics of Dominance*, Menlo Park, NJ: Cummings.

Cavert, S.M. (1968) *The American Churches in the Ecumenical Movement: 1900–1968*, New York: Association Press.

Christopher, R.C. (1989) *Crashing the Gates: The De-WASPing of America's Power Elite*, New York: Simon & Schuster.

Colley, L. (1992) *Britons: Forging the Nation 1707–1837*, New Haven, CT: Yale University Press.

Easterlin, R.A. (1982) 'Economic and social characteristics of the immigrants', in R.A. Easterlin, D. Ward, W. Bernard and R. Ueda (eds) *Immigration*, Cambridge, MA: Belknap Press, pp. 1–34.

Erikson, R.S. (1972) 'Malapportionment, gerrymandering, and party fortunes in congressional elections', *American Political Science Review*, 66: 1234–45.

Fischer, D.H. (1989) *Albion's Seed: Four British Folkways in America*, New York: Oxford University Press.

FitzGerald, F. (1979) *America Revised: History Schoolbooks in the Twentieth Century*, Boston: Little, Brown & Company.

Fitzgerald, K.A. (1987) 'Immigration, the state and national identity: the development of United States immigration policy, 1880–1965', unpublished PhD thesis, Indiana University.

Foner, E. (1970) *Free Soil, Free Labor, Free Men: The Ideology of the Republican Party before the Civil War*, New York: Oxford University Press.

Foster, W.A. (1888) *Canada First: An Address* [microform], Toronto.

Francis, D.R. (1986) *Frank H. Underhill: Intellectual Provocateur*, Toronto: University of Toronto Press.

Frantzen, A.J. and Niles, J.D. (eds) (1997) *Anglo-Saxonism and the Construction of Social Identity*, Gainesville, FL: University Press of Florida.

Frey, W.H. (1996) 'Immigration, domestic migration, and demographic Balkanization in America: new evidence for the 1990s', *Population and Development Review*, 22(4): 741–63.

Gallagher, C.A. (1997) 'White racial formation: into the twenty-first century', in R. Delgado and J. Stefancic (eds) *Critical White Studies: Looking behind the Mirror*, Philadelphia: Temple University Press, pp. 6–11.

Gans, H.J. (1994) 'Symbolic ethnicity and symbolic religiosity: towards a comparison of ethnic and religious acculturation', *Ethnic and Racial Studies*, 17(4): 577–92.

Gossett, T.F. (1953) 'The idea of Anglo-Saxon superiority in American thought, 1865–1915', unpublished doctoral dissertation, University of Minnesota.

—— (1963) *Race: The History of an Idea in America*, Dallas, TX: Southern Methodist University Press.

Greenfeld, L. (1992) *Nationalism: Five Roads to Modernity*, Cambridge, MA: Harvard University Press.

Gyory, A. (1998) *Closing the Gate: Race, Politics, and the Chinese Exclusion Act*, Chapel Hill, NC: University of North Carolina Press.

Hamilton, A. ([1768–78] 1961) *The Papers of Alexander Hamilton*, vol. 1, ed. H.C. Syrett, New York: Columbia University Press.

Haseler, S. (1996) *The English Tribe*, Basingstoke: Macmillan.

Herberg, W. (1955) *Protestant, Catholic, Jew: An Essay in American Religious Sociology*, Garden City, NY: Country Life Press.

Higham, J. ([1955] 1986) *Strangers in the Land: Patterns of American Nativism, 1860–1925*, 2nd edn, New Brunswick, NJ: Rutgers University Press.

Horsman, R. (1981) *Race and Manifest Destiny: The Origins of American Racial Anglo-Saxonism*, Cambridge, MA: Harvard University Press.

Houston, C.J. and Smyth, W.J. (1980) *The Sash Canada Wore: A Historical Geography of the Orange Order in Canada*, Toronto: University of Toronto Press.

Inglehart, R. (1990) *Culture Shift in Advanced Industrial Society*, Princeton, NJ: Princeton University Press.

Jackson, K.T. (1967) *The Ku Klux Klan in the City, 1915–1930*, New York: Oxford University Press.

Kaufmann, E.P. (1997) 'Condemned to rootlessness: the Loyalist origins of Canada's identity crisis', *Nationalism and Ethnic Politics*, 3(1): 110–35.

—— (2002) 'The ethnic origins of the American nation', *Geopolitics*, 7(2): 99–120.

—— (forthcoming 2004a) Book review of Carol M. Swain's 'The New White Nationalism in America', *Nations and Nationalism*, 9 (4): 641–2.

—— (forthcoming 2004b) *The Rise and Fall of Anglo-America: The Decline of Dominant Ethnicity in the United States*, Cambridge, MA: Harvard University Press.

Kennedy, P.M. (1977) 'The decline of nationalistic history in the West, 1900–1970', *Journal of Contemporary History*, 8: 77–100.

King, D. (2000) *Making Americans: Immigration, Race and the Origins of the Diverse Democracy*, Cambridge, MA: Harvard University Press.

Leinenweber, C. (1984) 'Socialism and ethnicity', in J.H.M. Laslett and S.M. Lipset (eds) *Failure of a Dream? Essays in the History of American Socialism*, Berkeley, CA: University of California Press.

Lind, M. (1995) *The Next American Nation: The New Nationalism and the Fourth American Revolution*, New York: Free Press.

Lipset, S.M. (1996) *American Exceptionalism: A Double-Edged Sword*, New York: W.W. Norton & Co.

Lissak, R.S. (1989) *Pluralism and Progressives: Hull House and the New Immigrants, 1890–1919*, Chicago: University of Chicago Press.

McClosky, H. and Zaller, J. (1984) *The American Ethos: Public Attitudes toward Capitalism and Democracy*, Cambridge, MA: Harvard University Press.

McRoberts, K. (1997) *Misconceiving Canada: The Struggle for National Unity*, Toronto: Oxford University Press.

Mayer, W.G. (1992) *The Changing American Mind: How and Why American Public Opinion Changed between 1960 and 1988*, Ann Arbor, MI: University of Michigan Press.

Nelson, W.H. (1967) 'The Loyalist rank and file', in L.F.S. Upton (ed.) *The United Empire Loyalists: Men and Myths*, Toronto: Copp Clark.

Palmer, H. (ed.) (1975) *Immigration and the Rise of Multiculturalism*, Toronto: Copp Clark.

Porter, J. (1965) *The Vertical Mosaic: An Analysis of Social Class and Power in Canada*, Toronto: University of Toronto Press.

Putnam, R.D. (2000) *Bowling Alone: The Decline and Revival of American Community*, New York: Simon & Schuster.

Roof, W.C. and McKinney, W. (1987) *American Mainline Religion: Its Changing Shape and Future*, New Brunswick, NJ: Rutgers University Press.

Roosevelt, T. (1889) *The Winning of the West*, vol. 1, New York: G.P. Putnam & Sons.

Ross, D. (1984) 'Historical consciousness in nineteenth century America', *American Historical Review*, 89(4): 909–28.

Russell, P. (ed.) (1966) *Nationalism in Canada*, Toronto: McGraw-Hill.

Savage, B.D. (1999) *Broadcasting Freedom: Radio, War and the Politics of Race 1938–1948*, Chapel Hill, NC: University of North Carolina Press.

Schrag, P. (1973) *The Decline of the WASP*, New York: Simon & Schuster.

Schwab, L.M. (1988) *The Impact of Congressional Reapportionment and Redistricting*, Lanham, MD: University Press of America.

Schwartz, M.A. (1967) *Public Opinion and Canadian Identity*, Berkeley, CA: University of California Press.

Silbey, J.H. (1985) *The Partisan Imperative: The Dynamics of American Politics before the Civil War*, New York: Oxford University Press.

Simon, R.J. and Alexander, S.H. (1993) *The Ambivalent Welcome: Print Media, Public Opinion and Immigration*, Westport, CT: Praeger.

Smith, A.D. (1986) *The Ethnic Origins of Nations*, Oxford: Blackwell.

—— (1991) *National Identity*, London: Penguin.

Smith, H.N. (1950) *Virgin Land: The American West as Symbol and Myth*, Cambridge, MA: Harvard University Press.

Smith, R.M. (1995) 'American conceptions of citizenship and national service', in A. Etzioni (ed.) *New Communitarian Thinking*, Charlottesville, VA: University Press of Virginia.

—— (1997) *Civic Ideals: Conflicting Visions of Citizenship in US History*, New Haven, CT: Yale University Press.

Strayer, M. (1958) *The DAR: An Informal History*, Washington, DC: Public Affairs Press.

Swain, C.M. (2002) *The New White Nationalism in America: Its Challenge to Integration*, Cambridge: Cambridge University Press.

Trudeau, P. (1968) *Federalism and the French Canadians*, Toronto: Macmillan.

Veugelers, J. (2000) 'State–society relations in the making of Canadian immigration policy', *Canadian Review of Sociology and Anthropology*, 37(1): 95–110.

Wallace, G. ([1963] 2002) Inaugural address, Alabama Department of Archives and History, http://www.archives.state.al.us/govs_list/inauguralspeech.html (accessed 2002).

Wallace, W.S. (1921) *The United Empire Loyalists: The Beginnings of British Canada*, Toronto: Glasgow, Brook and Co.

Wimmer, A. (2002) *Nationalist Exclusion and Ethnic Conflict*, Cambridge: Cambridge University Press.

Wright, T.P., Jr. (1980) 'The identity and changing status of former elite minorities: the contrasting cases of North Indian Muslims and American Wasps', in J. Ross and A. Baker (eds) *The Mobilization of Collective Identity: Comparative Perspectives*, Lanham, MD: University Press of America, pp. 279–96.

Zelinsky, W. (1988) *Nation into State: The Shifting Symbolic Foundations of American Nationalism*, Chapel Hill, NC: University of North Carolina Press.

5 'Pures laines' Québécois

The concealed ethnicity of dominant majorities

Danielle Juteau

Introduction

This chapter on the *pures laines Québécois*[1] probes the intricate relation between a now dominant majority, the nation it constituted, and the state. It tells more precisely the story of a subordinate ethnic group that became dominant – at least within Quebec – while transforming itself, with the help of 'its' state, into a national community.

The passage from subordinate to dominant majority[2] cannot be examined outside the quest for nationhood, an ongoing project that began with the Quiet Revolution in the early 1960s. While nation-building first involved the definition of a dominant and relatively autonomous ethno-national community, the *Québécois*, whose boundaries were to coincide with those of the state, the second and current stage entails the tentative extension of the bounded collectivity. My analysis centres on this transition, usually depicted as the passage from an ethnic to a civic nation, and explores its still ambiguous relation to ethnicity.

As the collectivity that had presented itself as national was pressured[3] into differentiating its boundaries from an enlarged and somewhat more inclusive national community, it had to redefine itself in narrower terms. This process remains unfinished, I contend, because the now dominant majority fails to recognise, and often shuns, its ethnic status, a position associated with the equation that is made in the political arena – and recently still in scientific discourses – between an ethnic status and a subordinate one. Consequently, it seems incapable of finding a suitable appellation and remains nameless.

Concluding remarks re-examine the link between the social relations that constitute ethnic majorities and minorities, and the differential assignation of an ethnic label to these socially constructed groups.

From French Canadian to *Québécois*: a subordinate majority becomes dominant

The transformation from subordinate French Canadians to dominant *Québécois* can best be understood in terms of the relation between this collectivity and the rest of Canada, a country where ethno-national congruence has been challenged from the very beginning. It entails a change in boundaries, ethnic and national, in techniques of boundary-maintenance, as well as a shift in communal narratives, in political goals and practices, all of which will now be examined.

The 'conquest' of the French, the first European colonisers, by the British or, as some prefer, the cession of New France by France to the British,[4] was soon to be followed by a series of social, political, and legal measures that recognised the significance of ethnic diversity in Canada and institutionalised structural pluralism.[5] While French–English dualism[6] represents a democratic form of institutional pluralism, the status of Native Peoples as fixed by the Indian Act of 1876 constitutes a non-democratic form. Until the early 1960s, both modes of structural pluralism were associated at the ideological level with assimilation, which presented itself here under the guise of Anglo-Conformity.[7]

After World War II, in many parts of the world and for different reasons,[8] assimilation was strongly contested and rejected as part and parcel of domination. In Canada, the liberalisation and de-racialisation of immigration policies in 1962 and 1967, the Statement of the Government of Canada on Indian Policy in 1969 (the White Paper), the adoption of the Official Languages Act in 1969 and of the Policy on Multiculturalism in 1971 were vital in setting up a 'just' society, where equality met pluralism (Juteau 2002).

These measures, however, did not alter significantly the democratic forms of structural pluralism in Canada, which remained a federal system with ten provinces exercising jurisdiction over areas such as education, health, and social services. More specifically, the thesis of two nations advocated by French Canadian elites was rejected, as was the proposal that the two 'founding' peoples share power equally at the federal level. In other words, binationalism, the project of setting up a binational state, was replaced by bilingualism. What was recognised was the presence of two languages, anchored in two collectivities composed of individuals possessing linguistic rights. The policy is about individual rights, although it can be viewed as having a *portée collective*. For the *Québécois*, this meant remaining a minority in Canada, a numerical minority of course, but also a social one, since they could not share power equally with the British in a renewed federal structure. As colonisers who were colonised, French Canadians held a double status in Canada: *vis-à-vis* Aboriginals and later immigrants, they were dominant, while they constituted a subordinate group in relation to the British, both in Quebec and in Canada. In this sense, it is impossible to categorise the emerging *Québécois* collectivity as a dominant ethnic minority. In Canada, this numerical minority remains one province among others, a minority whose language is official nonetheless and whose status has considerably improved in the past decades.[9]

But the transition from subordinate to dominant majority could be, and was, achieved in Quebec. I hesitate to write that the subordinate ethnicity became a dominant *ethnie*, because the term dominant ethnicity remains problematic in this context. This transformation involves new boundaries and identities; it is embodied in the passage from French Canadians, a community often described as an ethnic group[10] with a minority status in Quebec and in Canada as a whole, to *Québécois*, a nationally defined community striving towards economic, political, and cultural sovereignty, which many consider to require self-government and statehood (Juteau 1993). An equation is made between French Canadian, being a numerical minority in Canada, and subordination, on the one hand, and *Québécois*, being a numerical majority, and dominant status, on the other. In one case, a subordinate ethnic group, in the other, a dominant national collectivity.

Numerical majorities are thought of as being dominant because they are more numerous, and numerical majorities, it is believed, should be dominant. What is implicit here is that a numerical majority should be a sociological one, and that it is 'normal' for a numerical minority to be subordinate. Not surprisingly, then, the position of Anglo-Quebecers, who for many years represented a dominant minority in Quebec, controlling its economy and thus making English the means of communication and social mobility in the business world (Levine 1990), was often viewed as illegitimate – one remembers the expression white Rhodesians used by Premier René Lévesque – precisely because they are a numerical minority.[11]

Not only is the slippage between the two meanings, numerical and sociological, most confusing, the inherent link made between the two is pernicious. That is why I strongly endorse using the terms minority and majority solely in relation to power, reserving the term majority for dominant groups and minority for subordinate groups, irrespective of size.[12] The difficulty in establishing this usage[13] is related, I would suggest, to a generalised adhesion to the idea, which remains implicit, that in a democracy it is the numerical majority that has legitimate control over a society's functioning. It might also be associated with colonial situations, where domination by a numerical minority was illegitimate.

I am arguing that in Quebec, in the course of a process that began after World War II, and accelerated during the 1960s and 1970s, the numerical majority became the dominant group. This transition involved material and ideal dimensions that are interconnected. French Canadians gradually gained greater control over their collectivity by using the state, which in turn redefined the boundaries of the collectivity, now presented exclusively in national terms. The replacement of the term French Canadian by *Québécois* embodies this transition from subordinate to dominant majority. The community became dominant as it became national, discarding its ethnic status as it shed its subordinate position. This is why the term dominant ethnicity rarely appears in scientific analyses or in everyday discourse. It is seen by most analysts as a contradiction in terms, and, in some cases, as a political statement against sovereignty.[14] But as Weber wrote (1971: 426): 'I am not doing sociology for the sake of doing sociology' (my translation), and I will now use the sociologically correct term, for this group is an ethnic one, in the sense that it represents a collectivity that defines itself in terms of a subjective belief in a community of origin, real or putative, sharing a common historical trajectory (migration and colonisation), a common language, culture, and organisational structures.[15]

The numerical majority was mesmerised by the nationalist project, by which it transformed itself into a dominant group. The boundaries of the emerging *Québécois* national community narrowed, excluding French Canadians who live outside Quebec and consequently were not under the jurisdiction of the government of Quebec, as well as residents of other ethnic origins, such as English, Irish, Italian, Greek, immigrant groups and Aboriginals. In the early 1960s, *Québécois* clearly refers to French Canadians living in Quebec, and the struggle for equality centres mainly on the rights of this *ethnie*. While in some cases the term *Québécois* is defined as encompassing all residents of Quebec, as in the report of the Gendron Commission in 1972, it is most often used to designate the '*pures laines*', an expression that resurfaces in the 1970s to qualify the *Québécois*. Although it can be used to differentiate the unnamed *Québécois* of French-Canadian ethnicity from other *Québécois*, it can denote a strong nationalist and xenophobic feeling, coupled with the fear of minoritisation in the face of perceived increasing immigration.

The first stage of this process extends from 1960 to 1980, and focuses on economic, political and cultural equality. Since the 1980s, however, demands voiced by Aboriginal groups and cultural communities as well as an effort to rally them to the independence cause have brought on a second phase, characterised by debates over the redefinition and extension of the boundaries of the national community. Paradoxically, the very project of becoming a nation-state, which first excluded others, this time around requires their inclusion within a renewed national community. The former overlap between dominant ethnicity, ethnic nationalism, and state nationalism is contested, as is the ethnic component of *Québécois* state nationalism. State elites will articulate a civic nationalism, proposing a more pluralist conception of the national collectivity. Embracing all residents of Quebec, it no longer coincides with the boundaries of the French-Canadian collectivity. It is this very movement that drives a wedge between the dominant *ethnie* and the national community. The political manifestation of the dominant *ethnie* is precisely the elaboration of a nationalist project that goes from ethnic to civic, from pluralist to republican, in an effort to achieve its goal of independence.

I will now turn to these two stages, first comparing the new and modern *Québécois* nationalism to the former and traditional French-Canadian one, and then examining the debate over the extension of the boundaries of the national community

Ethnic nationalism, from traditional to modern

While the following comparison between a Church-oriented French-Canadian nationalism and a state-defined *Québécois* nationalism, usually depicted as ethnic and civic, focuses mainly on their differences, it also establishes their continuity.

Portrayed as conservative, traditional, and past-oriented, French-Canadian nationalism has constructed a narrative I will summarise and over-simplify. French Canadians viewed themselves as descendants of the 10,000 French who settled in New France between 1608 and 1760 and numbered 60,000 by the conquest, a historical event which remains a founding myth central to their identity. Abandoned by their elites, and by France, so the story continues, their heroic clergy ensured their survival by negotiating arrangements with the British.[16] Common ancestors, a common historical trajectory and values constituted and characterise a group originally called *Canadiens*. They often emphasise that, as the first arrivals, they, unlike later immigrants, potentially constitute a national community. Of course, Aboriginals proceeded to set them straight and contested this conception of an empty land where they settled. Of interest here is that descendants of other immigrant groups, such as Jews, Blacks, Italians, were also quick to point out the early arrival of their ancestors, all of which indicates that the concept of autochthony is used here to defend various forms of recognition and/or special status (Roosens 2000).

My own view is that, from a sociological perspective, temporality, although invoked as part of the legitimation process, is not the determining factor in understanding specific political demands. More important are the relations underlying contemporary ethnic interactions, what Schermerhorn (1970) calls the sequence of interaction, colonialism, migration – from slavery to 'free' – and annexation. Therefore, demands articulated by Aboriginals (doubly colonised) and by ethnic French Canadians and *Québécois* (colonised colonisers) differ from those who arrived without a colonial project.

In the decade preceding the British North America Act (1867), the term Canadian was gradually enlarged, so as to include descendants of the British settlers in Canada. This was eventually followed by the terms French and English Canadian, so as to differentiate the two communities. *Canadiens* was replaced by *Canadiens français*, although those born before World War II sometimes utilised it. According to the *Dictionnaire du français québécois* (Poirier 1985), the expression '*pures laines*' was utilised at the beginning of the twentieth century (1912) to qualify the noun *Canadiens*, so as to distinguish the latter from English Canadians. This expression can literally be translated by Pure Wool, or Virgin Wool. In line with an essentialist conception of ethnicity, '*Pures laines*' are the real Canadians, the original and authentic ones. Although this term was used later by Premier Maurice Duplessis, it is not required when talking about French Canadians who by definition are '*pures laines*'.

French-Canadian and *Québécois* nationalisms can be effectively differentiated by their relation to boundary-maintenance. For French Canadians, boundary-maintenance is equated with pattern-maintenance and past-orientation. Survival was to be achieved by closing societal boundaries and effectuating monopolistic closure, by adopting an autarkic *petit paysan* mode of production and maintaining socio-economic isolation for as long as possible, by displaying high fertility rates and opposing immigration[17] – and by ensuring that religion and language be duly transmitted.

Québécois nationalism, characterised as modern, secular, future-oriented, and self-affirming, relates boundary-maintenance to self-sufficiency, and emphasises control over the economic, political, and cultural institutions of the society, as well as over its environment.[18] The now dominant majority increased its power *vis-à-vis* the federal government as attested by the creation of a Department of Immigration in 1968 and the signature of four ententes between 1971 and 1990, at the end of which Quebec controlled the selection of immigrants and programmes of integration (Juteau 1999).

Political and bureaucratic elites, along with intellectuals and artists, fashioned a collectivity possessing new boundaries and a new identity. But they did so by using an existing substratum, what Otto Bauer called the *indestructible* community of destiny. Consequently, as previously mentioned, the *Québécois* national community corresponded at the time to the French Canadians of Quebec. While the subordinate *ethnie* had become dominant, it clung to the same myth of origin and the same narrative regarding the conquest, its domination by the British, its endangered language and culture, and its right to self-determination.[19] During the 1960s and 1970s, *Québécois* nationalism was defined by the state and state nationalism is ethnic, and they both overlap with the dominant *ethnie*, which designates itself as national.

As the territorial base of the collectivity narrowed from Canada to Quebec, the attitudes of the *Québécois* towards ethnic minorities were multifaceted. Relations with the French-Canadian diaspora were tense, with pain and anger on the part of the French Canadians and a dismissive attitude on the part of the *Québécois* who see them as doomed.[20] As for Anglo-Quebecers, the adoption by the Liberal Party of Bill 22 in 1974, making French the official language of Quebec, was seen as treason and abandonment. With the passage of Bill 101, the status of Anglo-Quebecers definitely tilted towards a minority position.

As state-oriented and secular elites replaced clerical ones, religion lost its centrality and cultural markers were modified. Language turned into the principal *enjeu*, and linguistic boundaries became salient, a process I will examine in the next section. I will mention in passing that language and culture are sometimes differentiated, in the sense that Francophone and Anglophone collectivities include diverse ethnicities, but they also overlap, when, for example, it is said that to be a *Québécois* is to be a Francophone.

A final point must be made, concerning the opinion of the dominant majority toward its 'ethnic' status. The *Québécois* national identity, a dominant one, was opposed to the former French-Canadian ethnic identity, which entailed subordination and traditionalism. For analysts such as sociologist

Marcel Rioux (1969), French Canadian corresponds to an ethnic status and to a subordinate position. The dynamics at work are most instructive. An equation is made between national status, modernity, and dominance, on the one hand, and ethnic status, traditionalism, and subordination, on the other. This is not unlike what characterises scientific discourses, where ethnicity was, until most recently, viewed as an attribute of subordinate groups, and in some cases as an attribute to be discarded because it is non-modern, essentialising, and hazardous (Juteau 1996). The process by which ethnicity is confounded with minority status leads groups to erase their ethnicity, hindering their capacity to recognise their socio-cultural and historical specificity. I will return to this point in my conclusion. In this particular case, this process conceals the fact that the state-defined *Québécois* national identity constitutes an ethnicised national identity.

I have shown in this section that the passage from subordinate to dominant majority was accomplished by implementing a strong national identity and by disclaiming its ethnic status. But I have also indicated that the new modern and secular *Québécois* nationalism remains ethnic after all, as it refers to a bounded collectivity that continues to be defined in terms of shared ancestry and common historical trajectory.

The national community of citizens: pluralist and homogeneous?

I now turn to the present scene and examine how factors internal and external to Quebec dynamics called into question the boundaries of the national community, perceived as too narrow, excluding *Québécois* who are not *pures laines*. The ensuing implementation of a national model closer to the civic mode, that would encompass all residents of Quebec irrespective of ethnic origin, occurred in two successive phases, the first characterised by the pluralist option (1980–95), and the second, since 1995, marked by a shift towards the definition of a specifically *Québécois* citizenship that would 'unite all citizens over and above their differences'. I will argue that the choice of a thick republican-type model of citizenship serves once more to conceal ethnicity, not only of the dominant *ethnie* but also of all constituent parts of the community.

Taking pluralism into account

The victory of the NO side in the Quebec Referendum, 1980 made the elites of the dominant majority reconsider their strategy. They recognised the need to bridge the gap with minority groups in Quebec, and doubtless hoped to convince them to support their project. How does a dominant majority take minorities into account? Canada was to provide a weighty example. It is a well-known fact that *Québécois* elites had scorned multiculturalism, a policy they interpreted as a rejection of biculturalism and as a negation of

Quebec's special status in Canada. Such a view centres on the *Québécois*, and not on the situation of non-coloniser ethnic groups who could benefit from the policy. By the end of the 1970s, multiculturalism as ideology and policy had acquired greater clout, as it had positively affected the ideal interests of minorities. Not only did it offer a welcome alternative to assimilation, it contributed to the deconstruction of the former Canadian identity built on Anglo-Conformity, ushering in a renewed and enlarged conception of the national community. Multiple identities were no longer seen as conflicting, but as multiple and embedded. The multicultural policy adopted by Canada, and the rise of multiculturalism internationally, influenced future developments in Quebec.

The dominant majority chose pluralism, first of all by recognising the significant presence of others in Quebec, and by setting up related organisational structures: the creation of the *Ministère des Communautés culturelles et de l'Immigration* (MCCI) and the *Conseil des Communautés culturelles* (CCC) in 1981, elaboration of the *Programme d'action à l'intention des Communautés culturelles* (PACC) and its *Comité d'implantation* (CIPACC), soon to be followed by anti-discrimination legislation in 1986. The pluralist ideology was called interculturalism, and was touted as less static, less ghettoising, and more interactive than multiculturalism, less historically blind because it recognises the centrality of a dominant majority towards which others necessarily converge.

My examination of this process (Juteau 2002) has indicated that the pluralist conception was first applied to the territory, and later to the collectivity. While the document *Autant de façons d'être Québécois* for example recognises the presence of 'Others' in Quebec, it continues to differentiate between *Québécois* and members of cultural communities. This indicates that the term *Québécois* still refers to the dominant *ethnie*. During the period that followed, the term *Québécois* is sometimes qualified, by adding '*de souche*' and '*pures laines*'. But many analysts are uneasy with this expression, which they consider pejorative and restrictive. This led three social scientists (Bouchard *et al.* 1991) to propose a more inclusive name, *les Francophones québécois*, which comprises those whose ancestors arrived before the conquest, those who joined the French-Canadian collectivity through assimilation, and those Francophones whose ancestors do not come from France. As I will later indicate, this still does not provide a distinctive name for the dominant *ethnie*. Furthermore, in a bizarre twist, the authors discard the use of *Québécois* so as not to offend those whose mother tongue is not French. Bizarre, because it somewhat implies that the latter cannot feel *Québécois*!

In the 1980s, cultural communities, sometimes united as Anglophones, formed pressure groups such as Alliance Quebec and a political party *Parti Égalité* to defend their rights and achieve equality. Their mobilisation brought amendments to Bill 101, the development of intercultural practices in schools, health services, and police training, anti-discrimination legislation, etc. When the fourth agreement concerning immigration was signed between the provincial and federal governments in 1990, Quebec received important subsidies to implement measures of integration. The Liberal Party published at the time its statement on immigration and integration, *L'Énoncé de politique en matière d'immigration et d'intégration* (1990), which stated, for the first time, that all residents of Quebec are *Québécois* as it refers to *Québécois des communautés culturelles*.

Interculturalism provided an ideological framework guiding social practices in various institutional realms, as the multiculturalism of the national collectivity was gradually recognised. But another process, which is usually overlooked, is also at work. As the state's role increased, ethnic collectivities were losing their institutional completeness (Laferrière 1983), and their elites were becoming brokers interacting with the dominant *ethnie*. There was, in addition, a strong impetus to direct minorities towards the institutions of the dominant *Québécois* majority, rather than those of the Anglophone minority.[21]

By the end of the officially pluralist period, ambiguity concerning the dominant majority remained unresolved. The *Québécois* civic nation comprised many ethnic groups, including a dominant collectivity that refused to be designated as ethnic. Regarding itself as neither a dominant *ethnie* nor an ethnic nation, it insisted on defining itself as civic: so we are confronted with a civic nation inside a civic nation(!), an equivocal situation associated surely with its namelessness.

The narrow defeat of the YES side (50.4 per cent vs 49.6 per cent) in the referendum on sovereignty held in 1995, with a majority (60 per cent) of '*pures laines*' voting in favour, was to provide an opportunity to break this impasse.

Articulating a specifically Québécois citizenship

The 'failure' of the second referendum was interpreted as a failure to win the ethnic vote, as then Premier Jacques Parizeau blamed 'ethnics' for this defeat. Ethnic differences were now seen as divisive, and were to be minimised to create overarching bonds that would link groups beyond their specificities. It was thought that a fresh approach, bridging the former separation between cultural communities and the host society, would prove more successful in developing an inclusive society.[22]

This goal was to be achieved through the articulation of a specifically *Québécois* citizenship, a process linked in part to a broader movement observed in the national and international arenas (Kymlicka and Norman 1995).[23] Debates over citizenship centred on the implementation of full equality for all members of the bounded collectivity that is differentiated, in addition to class, along sexualised and ethnic-racialised categories. Equality was now conceived in terms of the extension of the boundaries of the national collectivity and the institutionalisation of cultural rights, associated with the politics of recognition (Taylor 1992). But the move towards a multicultural citizenship was not followed everywhere, and countries such as France preferred to maintain a citizenship centred on the existence of a homogeneously defined national subject. In this conception, all citizens are the same, equality means equal treatment, and differentiated treatment creates inequalities. In examining the articulation of a specifically *Québécois* citizenship, I will be arguing that the dominant majority's will more closely follows a thick republican model. The erasure of its own ethnicity is carried over to the community of citizens, which is imagined as transcending ethnic differences.

Speeches made by then Premier Lucien Bouchard and André Boisclair, Minister of the newly minted MRCI (*Ministère des Relations avec les Citoyens et de l'Immigration*), emphasise the need to strengthen a sense of belonging to Quebec through the development of civic links which would unite all citizens above their differences.[24] The *Conseil des Relations interculturelles* (CRI) – whose name had also been changed to leave out cultural communities – was perturbed by this emphasis on citizenship alone and the deletion of the term cultural community (CRI 1997: 15). It pointed out that newcomers had specific needs and that some ethnic or racialised groups (ibid.: 16) remained unequal, and that consequently equality required taking the diversity of situations into consideration. It made additional recommendations concerning the symbolic realm, insisting that ethnocentric connotations should be expunged from the term *Québécois* so as to include others than French Canadians. It stressed the need to recognise multiple forms of belonging, and proposed that citizenship combine civic inclusion and pluralism (ibid.: 16). Its recommendation that the *Semaine interculturelle* (National Intercultural Week) be replaced by *la semaine de la citoyenneté et des relations interculturelles* (Citizenship and Intercultural Relations Week) was not taken up by a government intent on uniting citizens over and above their ethnic differences. In Quebec, the community of citizens was to be de-ethnicised.

The much-contested document prepared for the *Forum national sur la citoyenneté,* held in the fall of 2000, presents *la citoyenneté québécoise* and the *peuple québécois* as indivisible. The citizenship that is proposed incorporates a set of rights – the fundamental one being the political right to self-determination (MRCI 2000: 15) – and a heritage that involves a common language, sharing essential cultural references which are identity references, and participating in the institutions of the dominant majority.

The publication of the *Rapport des États Généraux sur la situation et l'avenir de la langue française* (2002) is noteworthy, because it serves to further explain the common citizenship that 'unites us beyond our differences'. Language, citizenship, and culture are placed on a single axis, forming a chain where each element reinforces the other:

> French is described as the means of accessing the civic heritage, values, rights, obligations, and institutions common to all, which constitute

> the foundation of their citizenship. Mastering French is essential to exercising citizenship, because it impacts on the participation in civic and democratic life. Language is also presented as the means of entering into the common culture of Quebec and participating in its *épanouissement*.
>
> (Juteau 2002: 13)

As the bearer of a culture and a history that would unite all *Québécois* culturally and historically, the centrality of language is reaffirmed. Learning French is to acquire a common culture and history, a common good to be defended by all. Of interest here is that the commission offers a more encompassing narrative than the conquest, since now all residents of Quebec can unite in defending a shared attribute. The recommendation to formally recognise an original citizenship in North America, and to organise a distinct ceremony following the reception of Canadian citizenship further testifies to some of the measures to be carried out by the dominant *ethnie*.

The construction of a strong and shared *Québécois* citizenship was to be achieved through the homogenisation of the national subject, the participation in, and assimilation to, the dominant majority's language, all of which entails the subordination of ethnic identities which are now seen as particularising and divisive. What is proposed is a cultural definition of the community, a republican-like conception of thick citizenship, which, according to Bourque *et al.* (1996), more closely follows the French model that stresses integration to a common culture, than it does the Canadian one that proposes a multicultural and liberal conception of citizenship emphasising individual rights in a pluralist context. Furthermore, the 'post-ethnic' model of citizenship that is introduced resembles more, I contend, the national model described by Soysal (1994) than the post-national one. In the national model, nations have the right to possess their state, citizenship is anchored in a territorialised notion of cultural belonging, national citizenship commands belonging to the political community (ibid.: 3); membership and identity that exist within the territory are thought of as homogeneous.[25]

Therefore, what unites all *Québécois* is the French language that delimits the core identity of the citizens of Quebec. By being Francophone, the latter share a common culture, and also a common project, to defend and protect the French language, 'our' common good, in the face of globalisation and its pressures to Anglicise. The current situation, I submit, is somewhat different. Language links groups that remain hierarchical and a still unnamed core occupies centre space, surrounded by a national, ethnic, and immigrant periphery.

Since we are all to be Francophones, at least in the public sphere, the expression Francophone *Québécois* proposed by Bouchard *et al.* seems to fit. It allows for the discarding of the controversial '*pures laines*' rejected by Premier Landry in the late 1990s, when he stated that such a term did not represent the tolerance and overture of Quebec society, where exclusion on the basis of ancestry was out of the question. The term Francophone *Québécois* does in fact comprise a large proportion of Quebec residents, because it includes those who have assimilated linguistically, those who speak French and come from other countries such as Haiti and Morocco, and because French now represents the maternal language of 81.2 per cent of the population.[26] But I am quick to add that Francophone is a linguistic category that encompasses in principle many *ethnies*, so this term does not solve the problem of naming the dominant majority. Or else, it is used to designate principally French Canadians, thus excluding others. In either case, the dominant majority yet again dodges its ethnic status. The term *Québécois d'ethnicité canadienne-française* remains taboo.

I will now turn in my conclusion to the elucidation of the phenomenon observed in this chapter, the denial, concealment, erasure by the dominant majority of its ethnic status, an attitude shared by many dominant *ethnies*, as pointed out in the different chapters of this book.

Thinking through the concealment of ethnicity

I have been arguing that since the Quiet Revolution, the dominant majority has endeavoured to discard and to transcend ethnicity – both its own and that of the enlarged community for citizens. Probing into these two events will help us gain additional insights into the dynamics of ethnicity. In the first case, a now dominant majority rejects the label formerly attached to the group when it was subordinate. It refuses to consider itself ethnic, because that would denote a subordinate position, the adoption of an attribute that was associated with subordination.

This attitude is shared by other minorities who also reject their ethnic status. In Canada, this is the case for Aboriginals who claim a national status, and of Official Languages minorities (Anglophones in Quebec and Francophones in the other provinces) who demand total control over educational institutions. Nobody, it seems, wants to be labelled ethnic, which is construed as being 'less than'. This might partially explain why, in Canada, the term multicultural was chosen over multi-ethnic, although it clearly designates solely those cultural groups that are ethnic. This position is easy enough to understand, for equating an ethnic status with a subordinate one is a fallacy shared until recently by social scientists. But my point is that while ethnicity involves domination, it is more than domination. This is why the introduction (Smith 1991) of the term dominant *ethnie* is a powerful tool, allowing us to disengage ethnicity from subordinate status.[27] It opens up space for the study of ethnic groups who are dominant, allowing social scientists to discover the other factors underlying their dynamics, and to explain why the ethnic label is assigned to some – subordinate – groups.

I have been brought in my own work (Juteau 1996) to theorise the construction of ethnicity in terms of a double relation, to others and to one's specific historical trajectory and culture. As a result, I argue that ethnic boundaries comprise two dimensions, external and internal, which are not mutually reducible. While ethnic groups are constituted through relations to others, they cannot be reduced to that dimension, as the internal side of the boundary, which is mobilised through unequal relations, pre-exists domination.[28] Finally, to ignore the internal boundary is to strip ethnic minorities of their historicity, of their memory, to deprive them of the trajectory that impacts on, and gives meaning to, their present social conditions.

In the second situation, that is, the elaboration of a broader community of citizens, ethnicity is rejected as a barrier to strong civic bonds and full equality. Ethnicity has indeed often been used to exclude and to subjugate the 'others', to expel and even to murder them. Since ethnicity has been linked to domination, equality would then necessitate, so it seems, its erasure. In France, for example, ethnicity is played down in the public sphere precisely because it is considered to be an obstacle to material and symbolic integration.

My point is that doing away with ethnic labels conceals their foundation. Furthermore, it mistakes the effect for the cause. By diverting the observers' gaze and preventing them from perceiving the specific and unequal social relations – colonialism, annexation, migration – constitutive of ethnic and racialised groups, it masks what Guillaumin (1972) calls the ideological and discursive aspect of domination, namely the process by which dominant groups assign an ethnic label to subordinate ones. For while ethnicity and domination are related, the argument must be turned back on its head.

There is a further problem associated with the failure to observe the internal side of the boundary. When dominant groups reject ethnic labelling, even with the best of intentions in the name of equality, they are involuntarily hiding their own ethnicity from themselves. This allows them to define their organisations, their culture, their nation as non-ethnic, and to impose their ethnicity on to others, often under the guise of universalism. Furthermore, this omission masks the very process through which majorities conceal their ethnicity.

What's in a name?

As the subordinate majority became dominant, it shunned its own ethnicity, and eventually engaged in the process of constructing a citizenship that would also transcend ethnicity.[29] Although one could argue that this erasure is related to the goal of fostering equality, I contend that in both instances the dominant *ethnie* behaved precisely like a dominant group. First, it cast off its own ethnicity, viewed as an attribute of subordination, as it became dominant. In building a community of citizens, it also adopted the traditional ethnically blind perspective of dominant groups, which leads them to impose their own ethnicity on to others. In fact, ethnicity is only superficially discarded, as it remains operative on the ground level, as part and parcel of hierarchical social relations.

The dominant *ethnie* could instead choose to recognise ethnicities, both subordinate and dominant. It would then be in a better position to establish a more egalitarian society. In addition, *Québécois* of French-Canadian ethnicity would no longer dilute their own specificity under the covering term Francophone *Québécois* and no longer deprive themselves of a name designating their own distinct and mobile[30] identity within the *Québécois* community of citizens.

Acknowledgements

I would like to thank Eric Kaufmann for his insightful questions and for his comments on a first version, as well as Sébastien Arcand and Didier Berry, graduate students in the Department of Sociology at the Université de Montréal, for their research and other help on this chapter, for which I assume full responsibility.

Notes

1 I will shortly discuss this contested term.
2 I am here using the term majority in its statistical sense, but will comment on this problematic usage in the course of the chapter.
3 These pressures are partially attributable to the impact of the federal policy of multiculturalism (1971), demands for self-determination formulated by Aboriginal groups, and the need to rally cultural groups to the sovereignist project.
4 John Ralston Saul (1997) has recently challenged this interpretation, claiming that the Treaty of Paris in 1763 resembled more a cession than a conquest.
5 I am following Schermerhorn's (1970) usage of the term pluralism and adopting his well-known distinction between cultural, structural, and normative pluralism. While the latter concerns what is desirable, structural pluralism involves institutional duplication, the establishment of separate, analogous, and parallel institutional spheres. The Act of Quebec (1774) and the Constitutional Act (1791) which created Upper and Lower Canada, each with their Legislative Assemblies, represent two examples of institutional pluralism.
6 The British North America Act (1867) recognises provincial jurisdiction over areas such as education, health, and social welfare, as well as the right to be educated in Catholic or Protestant schools.
7 For an enlightening discussion on Anglo-Conformity, see Raymond Breton (1984).
8 For example: the international flow of labour and capital, the break-up of colonial empires, the delegitimation of ideologies central to colonialism, the critique of Eurocentrism, of Jacobinism, and of assimilation, accompanied by the rejection of economic, political and cultural forms of domination.
9 Since the 1960s, Canadian Prime Ministers have come mainly from Quebec, they speak French and English, the civil service has become bilingual, and, more recently, ententes have been signed between the federal and provincial government increasing Quebec's control over labour market training, forestry, mining, and recreation, food inspection, environmental management, social housing, tourism, and freshwater fish habitat (McRoberts, cited in Juteau 2002: 446). But across Canada as a whole, English remains the dominant language and medium of communication, the nexus of cultural production for many immigrants.

10 Depending on the enunciators, French Canadians were designated as an ethnic group or as a national community. Looking into this question is the subject matter of another article.

11 It has often been presented, even outside Quebec, as the best treated minority in the world, a privilege they owe to the generosity of the majority. The passage of Anglo-Quebecers from a dominant to a subordinate group within Quebec remains an instructive example of a process of minoritization (Stein 1982).

12 Guillaumin (1972) and Simon (1995) indicate how to be *minoritaire* is to be *mineur* and *sous tutelle*.

13 Schermerhorn, for example, does not, but he admits mass subjects is an awkward term (1970: 13).

14 My usage of the term *Québécois* of French-Canadian ethnicity is rarely taken up, and most often criticised. By using the term ethnic, one is perceived as negating the legitimate right of a national community to self-determination.

15 My definition of ethnicity borrows from Weber's constructivist approach and emphasises the process of communalization (Juteau-Lee 1979).

16 The *Acte de Québec* ensured the protection of religion and language and maintained the French civil code.

17 The attitude of the majority towards immigration is closely related to its conception of boundary-maintenance. It evolves from a rejection of immigration, the famous '*cheval de Troie*' position, to a vigorous stance, controlling both immigration and integration policies outlined in *Énoncé de politique en matière d'immigration et d'intégration* (MCCI 1990).

18 Since the Quiet Revolution, the economic, political, and cultural interests of the majority have been enhanced through the creation namely of the Hydro-Québec, Société générale de financement, Caisse de dépôt, Charte de la langue française, etc.

19 This is most striking in Marcel Rioux's book (1969). The dominant ethnie will later come to recognise the anterior presence of Native Peoples as well as their national status.

20 Today, most support for the Francophone communities living outside Quebec comes from the federal government.

21 When the new *Ministère des Relations internationales, de l'Immigration et des Communautés culturelles* was announced in 1993, it presented the integration of immigrants solely within the institutions of the Francophone majority (Juteau *et al.* 1998).

22 This sentence indicates that cultural communities are still not considered a part of the society; furthermore, as Sayad writes (1999), if the society is a host, then immigrants remain guests.

23 Other factors were at work, namely geopolitical forces such as the critique by Native groups of Quebec's plans to build other dams in the North, the remaining irritants of Bill 101, the absence of non-French Canadians in the civil service and their strong under-representation in provincial political parties, the documented presence of racism and discrimination.

24 For a more detailed analysis of this process, see Juteau (2002).

25 In the emergent post-national model, she argues that citizens are no longer national: they possess multiple memberships and are not necessarily attached to a national collectivity (Soysal 1994: 141).

26 Source: http://www.tlfq.ulaval.ca

27 As did Hughes and Hughes (1952).

28 My position differs from Isajiw's (1980), who distinguishes internal and external boundaries in terms of the groups involved.

29 In Quebec the current project defended by the dominant *ethnie* is a civic republican model of nationalism, which aims at including all *Québécois* who would

hopefully adhere to a political project originally fuelled by ethnic nationalism. Although heuristically useful, the dichotomised ideal types ethnic–civic do not grasp the totality of nationalism. The latter can oscillate from one variant to another, and both can be present at any given time (for example, right-wing parties in European liberal democracies). In addition, they often mesh, and a state could well articulate an ethnic nationalism while the dominant ethnie uses the state to develop an inclusive one. Furthermore, civic nationalism can be pluralist or emphasise cultural homogeneity. Keeping in mind these differences allows us to further deconstruct the opposition between an ethnic and exclusive nationalism, on the one hand, and inclusive state nationalism, on the other, and to pursue critical reflection on dominant nationalisms, such as French and Canadian. Often portrayed as inclusive (Schnapper 1991), the state nationalism of France has strongly opposed pluralism to implement assimilation to a strong core culture. But to whose culture? State nationalisms do not always transcend ethnicity and, when they do, they are not necessarily inclusive (Sayad 1999)! By the same token, a dominant *ethnie* could in principle articulate a pluralist civic nationalism, as in Australia and perhaps in Canada.

30 An analysis of the new *Québécois* French-Canadian cultural identity would explore, for example, the passage from artists, writers, song-writers and poets committed to independence, to international stars such as Céline Dion and Robert Lepage whose repertoire has little to do with Quebec, as well as the world success of film-maker Denys Arcand and the ground-breaking *Cirque du Soleil*. It would explore musician Yves Desrosier's work of translating and singing the compositions of Russian composer and singer Vladimir Vissotsky; it would note that the Francophone connection remains important, as songwriters and singers alike are most successful in France, while their repertoire is neither 'nationalist' nor always specifically *Québécois*.

References

Bouchard, G., Rocher, F. and Rocher, G. (1991) *Les Francophones québécois*, Montréal: Conseil scolaire de l'Ile de Montréal.

Bourque, G., Duchastel, J. and Armany, V. (1996) *L'identité fragmentée: Nation et citoyenneté dans les débats constitutionnels canadiens, 1941–1992*, Montréal: Fides.

Breton, R. (1984) 'The production and allocation of symbolic resources: analysis of the linguistic and ethnocultural fields in Canada', *Canadian Review of Sociology and Anthropology*, 21(2): 123–44.

Guillaumin, C. (1972) *L'Idéologie raciste: Genèse et langage actuel*, Paris: Mouton.

Hughes, E. and Hughes, H. (1952) *Where Peoples Meet: Racial and Ethnic Frontiers*, Glencoe, IL: Free Press.

Isajiw, W.W. ([1970] 1980) 'Definitions of ethnicity', in R.M. Bienvenue and J.E. Goldstein (eds) *Ethnicity and Ethnic Relations in Canada*, Toronto: Butterworths.

Juteau, D. (1993) 'The production of the Québécois nation', *Humboldt Journal of Social Relations* (special issue, 'Race, Gender and Ethnicity: Global Perspective'), 19(2): 79–108.

—— (1996) 'Theorizing ethnicity and ethnic communalisations at the margins: from Quebec to the world system', *Nations and Nationalism*, 2(1): 45–66.

—— (1999) *L'ethnicité et ses frontières*, Montréal: Presses de l'Université de Montréal.

—— (2002) 'The citizen makes an entrée: redefining the national community in Quebec', *Citizenship Studies*, 6(4): 441–58.

Juteau, D., MacAndrew, M. and Pietrantonio, L. (1998) 'Multiculturalism à la Canadian and intégration à la Québécoise: transcending their limits', in R. Bauböck and J. Rundell (eds) *Blurred Boundaries: Migration, Ethnicity, Citizenship* (*Public Policy and Social Welfare* series, vol. 23), Aldershot: Ashgate.

Juteau-Lee, D. (1979) 'La sociologie des frontières ethniques en devenir', in D. Juteau-Lee (ed.) with L. Laforge *Frontières ethniques en devenir/Emerging Ethnic Boundaries*, Ottawa: Éditions de l'Université d'Ottawa.

Kymlicka, W. and Norman, W. (1995) 'Return of the citizen: a survey of recent work on citizenship theory', in R. Beiner (ed.) *Theorizing Citizenship*, Albany, NY: State University of New York Press.

Laferrière, M. (1983) 'L'éducation des enfants des groupes minoritaires au Québec: de la définition des problèmes par les groupes eux-mêmes à l'intervention de l'état', *Sociologie et Sociétés*, 15(2): 117–33.

Levine, M.V. (1990) *The Reconquest of Montreal: Language Policy and Social Change in a Bilingual City*, Philadelphia, PA: Temple University Press.

McRoberts, K. (1997) *Misconceiving Canada: The Struggle for National Unity*, Toronto: Oxford University Press.

Poirier, C. (ed.) (1985) *Dictionnaire du français québécois, Volume de présentation*, Sainte-Foy: Presses de l'Université Laval.

Rioux, M. (1969) *La Question du Québec*, Paris: Seghers.

Roosens, E. (2000) 'National identity, social order and political system in western Europe: primodial autochthony', in E.K. Sceuch and D. Sciulli (eds) *Annals of the International Institute of Sociology*, vol. 7: *Societies, Corporations and the Nation State*, Leiden: Brill.

Saul, J.R. (1997) *Reflections of a Siamese Twin: Canada at the End of the Twentieth Century*, Toronto: Viking.

Sayad, A. (1999) 'Immigration et pensée d'État', *Actes de la recherche en sciences socials*, 129: 5–14.

Schermerhorn, R.A. (1970) *Comparative Ethnic Relations*, New York: Random House.

Schnapper, D. (1991) *La France de l'intégration: Sociologie de la nation en 1990*, Paris: Gallimard.

Simon, P.J. (1995) 'Minorités', *Pluriel recherches: Vocabulaire historique et critique des relations interethniques*, vol. 3, Paris: L'Harmattan.

Smith, A.D. (1991) *National Identity*, London: Penguin.

Soysal, Y.N. (1994) *Limits of Citizenship: Migrants and Postnational Membership in Europe*, Chicago: University of Chicago Press.

Stein, M. (1982) 'Changing Anglo-Quebecer self-consciousness', in G. Caldwell and E. Waddell (eds) *The English of Quebec: From Majority to Minority Status*, Québec: Institut de recherche sur la culture.

Taylor, C. (1992) 'The politics of recognition', in A. Gutmann (ed.) *Multiculturalism and 'The Politics of Recognition'*, Princeton, NJ: Princeton University Press.

Weber, M. ([1921–2] 1971) *Économie et société*, vol. 1 (trans. by J. Freund *et al.* of *Wirtschaft und Gesellschaft, Grundriss der verstehenden Soziologie*, 4th German edn, ed. J. Winckelmann, Tübingen: J.C.B. Mohr (P. Siebeck) 1956), Paris: Plon.

Official documents and government reports

Commission d'enquête sur la situation de langue française et sur les droits linguistiques (Commission Gendron) (1972) *Les groupes ethniques et l'épanouissement du français*, Québec: Éditeur officiel, Livre III.

Commission des États généraux pour la situation et l'avenir de la langue française au Québec (2001) www.etatsgeneraux.gouv.qc.ca (in English: summary and final report).

CRI (Conseil des Relations interculturelles) (1997) *Un Québec pour tous ses citoyens: Les défis actuels d'une démocratie pluraliste*, Québec: Bibliothèque nationale du Québec.

MCCI (Ministère des Communautés culturelles et de l'Immigration) (1981) *Autant de façons d'être Québécois: Plan d'action du gouvernement du Québec à l'intention des communautés culturelles*, Montréal: Gouvernement du Québec.

MCCI (Ministère des Communautés culturelles et de l'Immigration) (1990) *Au Québec pour bâtir ensemble: Énoncé de politique en matière d'immigration et d'intégration*, Montréal: Gouvernement du Québec, Direction des Communications.

MRCI (Ministère des Relations avec les Citoyens et de l'Immigration) (2000) *Forum national sur la citoyenneté et l'intégration*, Montréal: Gouvernement du Québec/ MRCI.

6   The concept of 'dominant ethnicity' in the case of France

Dominique Schnapper

The concept of *dominant ethnicity* proposed by Eric Kaufmann is paradoxical in the case of France. The concept is certainly fruitful if applied to the founders (WASP) of the 'political project' (Schnapper 1994: 36) of the United States or, as in the case of Israel, of the Jews of Central and Balkan Europe with their political project to build an independent Jewish State. It helps to analyse the conditions of *nation-building* in many states which emerged from colonisation in Africa or in some Asian countries, whose national borders were arbitrarily determined by colonial powers and their 'divide and rule' policy. In countries formed of different ethnic groups, possibly hostile to each other, nation-building was often realised by a dominant ethnic group for its own benefit (possibly by two or three ethnic groups). Similarly, the concept of dominant ethnicity is a fruitful one in the case of the Balkans, where for centuries the mixing of peoples conscious of their historical and cultural specificity within the empires led, at the time of the dissolution of the Austro-Hungarian and Turkish empires in 1919, the newly settled nations to create national minorities: Slovaks in Hungary, Germans or Hungarians in Czechoslovakia, Hungarians in Romania, for example, or, as in Yugoslavia, where state-formation brought together different ethnic groups (i.e. Slovenians, Serbs, Croats, Bosnians) within the same nation-state.

On the other hand, the concept becomes problematic when we talk about the most ancient nations settled in Europe, such as the ones that have appeared since the Congress of Constance in 1414: France, England, Germany, Italy and Spain. In their cases, the ruling power made age-old efforts to make the so-called dominant ethnie coincide with political organisation. This process far preceded the blossoming of nationalism in the nineteenth century and the ambition proclaimed by nationalist militants to make the ethnic group coincide with the nation: 'Nationalism is primarily a political principle, which holds that the political and the national unit should be congruent' (Gellner 1983: 1). Policies which followed in the course of the centuries in the old European nations aimed to delete the entire notion of ethnic group in order to make it coincide with the *national*. The concept of dominant ethnicity has heuristic value for the analysis of a distinction that policies managed for centuries by the ancient European nations aimed precisely to erase. It is true in the case of many countries of Western and also Eastern Europe, e.g. the case of Poland; it is in any case true in France.

The entire history of nation-building in France consisted of denying the idea that a dominant ethnie existed. The national mythology, whose elaboration is indissolubly linked with nation-building, denied the existence of ethnic groups and claimed that only one nation existed. In other words, according to the expression of Eric Kaufmann, in Western European nations the policy of nation-building consisted of 'an attempt to render Western states ethnically neutral'.

This policy rested on a piece of reality that the French state has helped to create, even though it always had limits. But at the present time this policy presents stronger limits, as the development of *providential democracy* (Schnapper 2002) tends to legitimate all particularisms, including the ethnic ones. Does the progressive recognition of ethnic dimensions in the public life lead to the creation of dominant ethnicity?

History of France

A historical detour is necessary to understand the problematic character of dominant ethnicity in the case of France. The nation was progressively formed from the eleventh century by the kings of France, successors of Hugues Capet, who struggled to establish the power of the king against the great feudal lords. The original royal estate in 987, when the dynasty of *Capétiens* (from King Capet) was founded, consisted of just a few territories scattered in what we now call 'Ile-de-France' or the Parisian region. For a century, the policy of the Capétien kings was to unify those small territories so as to settle a compact royal domain. From the twelfth century, they progressively annexed other provinces to this initial territory through a clever policy of military conquests, purchases and exchanges of territories, negotiations and marriages (Mirot 1930). This policy continued for centuries. Some important stages include: the annexation of Languedoc, Champagne, Brie, and Artois in the thirteenth century, Navarre and Guyenne in the aftermath of the Hundred Years War, and Dauphiné, Provence, Bourgogne and Bretagne between the fourteenth and fifteenth centuries.

In 1610, when Henri IV died, 'all France was in the domain of the king' (ibid.: 106). From this date, the royal policy aimed to extend its borders toward the north and east. Alsace was conquered in the seventeenth century (later to be annexed to the German Reich between 1870 and 1914 and between 1940 and 1944, before being given back to France in 1919 and 1945). The same occurred with Franche-Comté, Lorraine, Artois and Flandre, in the aftermath of different treaties that set the European order as defined by the congress of Westphalia in 1648. The purchase of Corsica from Genoa in 1768 increased the national territory outside the hexagon.

The ambition of Napoleon briefly extended the borders of the French Empire very far towards the east but the defeat of 1815 restored the boundaries that pre-existed the Revolution. The annexation of Nice and Savoy, sold to the French government by King Victor-Emmanuel II in 1860 in recognition of the French contribution to the unification of Italy, was the last stage of this slow formation of national territory.

The constitution of the territory accompanied its political organisation. Philippe Le Bel, who ruled from 1285 to 1314, created the first elements of the state. According to the famous expression of Bernard Guénée, in France the state preceded and created the nation. In France, as elsewhere in England and Spain, state institutions slowly emerged from the Middle Ages, created by the need to maintain an army that imposed a heavy burden on its population. Agents of the king had to collect taxes, to recruit men, to requisition goods. The income from taxes, first gathered for military purposes, later permitted the state to consolidate the royal territory, to centralise the administration, to differentiate tools of control of the state. 'War made the state and the state made war' (Tilly 1975: 42). Against both the power of lords and popular revolts, civil servants, lawyers and soldiers of the king progressively built the state, in narrow symbiosis with the nation.

The French state-nation which emerged from this age-old process existed in its monarchical form well before the nationalist idea of the right of peoples to self-determination. It was formulated long before the political emergence of nationalism and the wars that came with it, long before the mass migrations of the end of the nineteenth century. The monarchy enmeshed itself so well with the nation that when France transformed itself into a republic, the nation remained: 'this great French kingship had been so highly national that in the aftermath of its fall, the nation could last without it' (Renan [1882] 1947: 894). French history paralleled the rise of the national idea more generally. It also followed the French development of political and state structures – the latter were, within relatively stable borders, the incarnation of the unity of the nation and symbolised it.

The process of political unification was reinforced by the religious policy of the monarchy. Religious unity of population around the monarchy and the Roman Catholic Church, tightly linked to each other, was realised through the expulsion of the Jews in the course of the fourteenth century and the revocation of the Edict of Nantes in 1685 that led to the exodus of Protestants. Protestants, chased from Catholic France, took refuge in Protestant Europe: Germany, the United Kingdom, and Sweden. The dynastic principle and the religious one, narrowly overlapping, intensified their integrative effects: religious unity reinforced royal power.

On the model of the dual nature of Christ, human and mystical, the doctrine of the King's Two Bodies was a real Royal Christology. By elaborating the fiction of a mystic royal body, distinct from the natural body of the king but united to him in a mysterious way, English lawyers had formed the abstract idea of a kingship whose existence transcended the person of the king. The king, image and instrument of God on earth, tended to be the head of the religious organisation of his realm. 'The state tended more and more to become almost a church or a rationalised version of a mystic corporation' (Kantorowicz [1957] 1989: 146). Particularly in France, the very Christian king, image and instrument of God on earth, who had chased Jews and Protestants from the kingdom was the symbol of divine law. This maintained a privileged place between the kingship and the Catholic Church. France was 'the elder daughter of the church'.[1] The old motto of the French monarchy summarised the principle and legitimacy of political organisation: 'one faith, one law, one king'.

By annexing provinces to the kingdom of France one after the other, monarchs successively increased the cultural diversity of the population. The policy that aimed to homogenise the cultures of the king's subjects is similarly ancient. François I imposed French as the official language of the kingdom in 1539 through the famous order of Villers-Cotteret. The French Academy was created and declared guardian of the language in the seventeenth century. The progress of the common language at the expense of local languages followed the rising education level. As early as the seventeenth century, literacy was largely acquired: most people could read and write in French (Furet and Ozouf 1977).

In what sense can we then speak of a dominant ethnicity? The French population was progressively united in the course of centuries in political, religious and linguistic terms. In fact, according to recent historical research, we find the first expressions of a national feeling, beyond the identification with a particular province, as early as the thirteenth century (Beaune 1985). The national idea was progressively born, in France as in England, from the Hundred Years War between the two. Only provinces on the geographic margins, i.e. Alsace, Corsica and the Basque country, kept an ethnic consciousness that did not fully melt into the national feeling. Breton advocates of political independence, on the other hand, always remained marginal because of their small number of members and limited political weight. The attempt by the Germans to revive them during the military occupation in the Second World War was a failure.

The question of the national identity of Alsatians was more narrowly linked to wars that set Germans against French – as they fought sometimes for the German side and other times for the French one – and to the annexation of the province by the Reich rather than to relations between Alsatians and the 'French from inside', as they used to say in Alsace. Regions of 'Langue d'Oc', that is Languedoc and Provence, kept in a marginal way the feeling of having been 'annexed' to regions of 'Langue d'Oil', following the wars of the kings of France from the north against local lords. But the dominant ethnie was so widely dominant that it thought of itself in national terms. In what sense could the French from Ile-de-France and Paris be considered a dominant ethnie? Social and regional inequalities existed, but they were not considered in ethnic terms. The opposition between Parisians, some among them could be close to the court and power, and the 'Provincials' – the notion itself of 'provincials' demonstrates the existence of the contrast – was more significant than the reality and feelings that could be described as ethnic. On the other hand, inhabitants of all provinces participated, without invoking any form of 'ethnic' identification, in 'national' wars conducted by the armies of the Revolution, of the Napoleonic Empire, and in all the wars of the nineteenth and twentieth centuries.

The 'nationalisation' of French society by the Republicans

In this field as in others, the Revolution prolonged the centralising and homogenising action of the *Ancien Régime*. Revolutionaries, just crowned as the source of political legitimacy, tried to impose the learning of the national language on all citizens. They were convinced that it was necessary to eliminate local languages or *'patois'* that prevented new citizens from gaining access to 'lights' (i.e. Enlightenment) and being 'regenerated', according to the term of the time (Certeau *et al.* 1975). If the usage of the king's language was limited to the social elite and scientists, command of the national language now became a right and a duty for all citizens.

Fin-de-siècle 'Republicans' (1880–90) again utilised the essential tools of national integration created by the kings. I will now refer to the role of the Republican school and army, as they were consciously created and organised by the Republicans in the 1880s in order to build a modern nation and make France a republic; but we must not forget that they were drawing on a very ancient tradition and that other institutions did their job to achieve national integration – i.e. the Church, the state and its vast institutions, political parties and unions.

Revolutionaries of 1789 replaced the old terms of schoolteacher, regent and *'recteur'* (i.e. chief administrative officer of an education authority) with *'instituteur'* (i.e. primary school teacher), because the latter had the new task of 'instituting' the nation. From now on, school was the school of *citizens*. The 'Republican school' was the privileged instrument of the 'republican model', i.e. the model of national integration. By establishing the foundations of the public school, Republicans of the 1880s considered themselves sons of the Revolution and heirs to its eighteenth-century philosophy. According to this philosophy, it was important to prise the *individual* away from his distinctive religious and ethnic features; education and 'secularism' (i.e. *laïcité*) could provide freedom, they were tools of freedom and reason, of autonomy of judgement against the tyranny of traditions and ethnic identities.

These latter, which we can call 'ethnic' – i.e. infra-national – were classified alongside fanaticism and religious fundamentalism. Only education was likely to form free men, i.e. citizens. From this philosophical conception, the school was put in charge of spreading a political culture whose 'secularity' was a fundamental element, even though – as Peguy has stressed – the republican moral philosophy, inspired by the teaching of the church, was the Christian one without God. The exclusive learning of a national common language was becoming an instrument for the freedom of men. The teaching of history had to arouse the feeling of historical community and was a privileged way to spread a completely national education among all future citizens. The story of past events, scientifically established, would permit the nation to assert its collective identity and encourage contemporaries, consecrated as the heirs of this glorious history, to prolong this heritage and to carry on common activity. We know that somehow, in every country, historians invented nations. 'Republican historians', Ernest Lavisse being the most perfect example of this, did not depart from the rule.

Beyond the content of teaching, school, for Republicans, was an imaginary space modelled on the political society, where pupils, just like citizens, had to be equally treated, regardless of their familial, social and, especially, 'ethnic' characteristics. It was a place, both in a material and abstract sense, that was set against historical or religious identities, against real inequalities of social life, to resist movements in civil society. The order of the school, like the one of citizenship, was impersonal and formal. The abstraction of school society had to train the child to understand and master the one of political society. That is why the same curriculum was imposed on everybody – same content, same methods, same timetable, teachers recruited through competitive national examinations – even to the most distant of the 36,000 towns of France. It consisted of educating all children in national citizenship. What we now call 'interculturalism', i.e. to consider in some way ethnic differences, was unimaginable for the Republican school. The idea of considering the national origins of immigrants' children was unknown to Republicans, as was recognising '*patois*' or regional and local languages. Like all children, those of foreigners had the vocation to participate in national life. They could not belong to a particular group. Otherwise they would have called into question the social functions, the moral and political justifications, values and ambitions of a school that pretended to be the school of the citizen.

The Republic also aimed to emancipate people and to ensure the promotion of the best. To provide education to everyone meant to give equal chances of promotion to future citizens, and, consequently, to fight ignorance and, with it, the principal sources of poverty, injustice and class struggle. School had the mission to ensure the promotion of the most deserving among the children of the people or, in modern terms, to fight against inequality, to permit social mobility and favour equality of opportunities. Scholarships had the essential role, symbolic more than real, of allowing the most talented pupils to benefit from promotion, regardless of their social, national or 'ethnic' origins.

The army reinforced the effort of the school where often schoolteachers continued schooling recruits and spreading patriotism. The myth of the armed nation, the soldier-citizen, and the civic role attributed to the army, belonged to the national tradition. Due to rivalries among European countries, national service was generalised to everybody in 1873 (in actual fact it became universal only in 1905) and it was perceived to be a way to spread education. Military training was inseparable from the education and formation of the citizen. The army contributed to the nationalisation and modernisation of its recruits. The army mixed children of immigrants of all origins, all French regions and social classes; it was an occasion for travelling, the first contact with material comfort, the first meeting with other nationals from different backgrounds and regions. Schoolteachers became non-commissioned officers and had to continue a double mission: to teach the recruits to read and write and to make them patriots. Civic and patriotic education was part of military training. After their national service, young recruits were to consider themselves the heirs of the armed *Grande Nation*, the one of 1793, an integral part of revolutionary and patriotic mythology. The enthusiastic departure of young Frenchmen for war in 1914, a 'divine surprise', demonstrated that the army was effective from this point of view. That is why conscription was abolished in France only in 1996, long after its abolition in England and United States. Even though people continued to accept it without enthusiasm, they did not revolt – even in the middle of the 1968 movements – and did not ask for its abolition.

If regional differences did not lead to the constitution of ethnic groups, mass immigration in the course of the nineteenth and twentieth centuries could have promoted them, on the model of the 'ethnic groups' typical in American society. France experienced, more than a century before other European countries, a demographic revolution that made it a mass immigration destination in the course of the nineteenth and twentieth centuries (Noiriel 1988). France was the only major country of immigration in Europe until after World War II. Unique in Europe, France 'imported' men, while other countries 'exported' them. From the Restoration onwards, France experienced the settlement of British and German engineers, Belgian labourers, and Swiss soldiers. In the second half of the century, waves of Italians and Poles, Jewish refugees from Tsarist Russia, Russians after the 1917 Revolution, Ukrainians and people from the colonial empire, among others, arrived. Low fertility since the beginning of nineteenth century, national ambitions and traditional confusion between historical and political unity can explain French policy *vis-à-vis* immigrants. The aim was to make them French citizens or, in any case, their children. Contrary to the USA, which considered immigration an essential dimension of its national identity, France did not integrate immigration in its national myth. France considered itself a land of settlement (i.e. taking root).

The integration of immigrants into the whole, from which they could not be separated, was a political project, rooted in values strongly linked to the ideals of the Revolution: the idea of individual citizenship and the refusal to accept the role of intermediating special communities in the integration of individuals (Schnapper 1991). This policy, formerly called 'assimilation' and now known as 'integration', did not imply the suppression of people's identities. It implied that all those identities had to be maintained in the private sphere and that individuals had to conform to the French logic in the public sphere. There was no space to publicly recognise the particular 'communities' that came from immigration. The so-called policy of assimilation never prohibited multiculturalism in personal and social life, provided immigrants did not express it in the public sphere. It rested on the Hegelian distinction between the specificity of private man and the universalism of the citizen.

The logic of this policy was to easily accord French nationality, and thus citizenship, if not to immigrants themselves, at least to their children. The right to nationality in France was guaranteed for longer than in other European countries because of the national ideology but also because it was meant to satisfy the demographic and military ambitions of France. Only Argentina and the United States, countries of immigration as well, are more liberal than France, as in those countries nationality is awarded to any individual born in the country. France, according to Article 44 of the Nationality Code, automatically issues nationality to children of immigrants who were born in France and have resided there for five years before the age of 18 (unless they formally give up this right) or to children of foreign parents provided one of them was born in France, and, according to Article 23, to people born in France who have at least one parent also born in France. To demonstrate the effects of this legislation, still in force today, we can compare France with Germany. Every year 40,000 children of Turkish parents are born in Germany and, until 1999, only 1,000 had become Germans, while in France only 2,000 out of 30,000 children of foreign parentage do *not* become French by the age of 18.

We cannot conclude that the integration of immigrants in France was a quiet process. As long as the dominant ethnie tended to view itself as the *nation*, oppositions and conflicts emerged against the *foreigners*. For instance, in Aiguemortes, in 1893, a genuine slaughter of Italians took place. Prejudices and hostilities against Italians at that time were violent. Towards the end of the nineteenth century, feelings of hostility against Germans, British and Italians at a time of competing nationalism were widespread. They concentrated particularly, in the course of the 1880s, on xenophobia *vis-à-vis* the Jews, foreigners *par excellence*. The inexplicable defeat of the French army in 1870 could only be explained by the action of 'enemies from inside', assimilated to foreigners: stateless persons, cosmopolites, Jews manipulated by foreign countries were considered betrayers. Jews became the archetype of the foreigner. Maurice Barrès said that he was 'at war' at the time of the Dreyfus Affair. At the beginning of the twentieth century, the international situation became explosive and struggle against enemies from abroad became a priority. But the Jew continued to be 'outside' as 'he remains a stranger in all countries where he lives and he doesn't adopt the fatherland that provides refuge to him. This people that could not be assimilated were a great threat to the "French Nation"' (Sternhell 1978).

Hostility towards immigrants and Jews was part of a counter-revolutionary intellectual trend, nostalgic for the *Ancien Régime*, that died out only with the Vichy Regime. Even Jean Marie Le Pen's *Front National* today uses a discourse invoking citizenship, the legitimacy of elections and unions (Schnapper 1996). The entire history of nineteenth-century France was a conflict of legitimacy between two Frances, the one that referred to the *Ancien Régime*, and the one that invoked Revolutionary values and glory.

Institutions of the Republic proved to be effective in integrating the children of immigrants, as shown by the tragic experience of the First World War. Children of immigrants, or immigrants themselves who became French citizens, fought like the others (Ponty 1988). It is in the name of individual citizenship and thanks to the action of the school and other national institutions that the foreign population formed the French one as a whole: today more than 18 million French have at least one grandparent born abroad.

Of course, linguistic and cultural homogenisation has its limits; it is a process that never ends and can still maintain identities of all types. On the other hand, the education policy of the Third Republic relied on local and regional cultures and identities, as recent works have proved (Chanet 1996; Thiesse 1997). When the Republican school organised by Jules Ferry in the 1880s imposed on all children the same secular, free and compulsory teaching, French was still a foreign language to half the pupils. In 1914, even prior to Alsace's return to France, seven languages were spoken in the national territory excluding the languages of immigrants (Weber 1976). Bretons died in the First World War because they did not understand orders assigned in French by officers. Priests preached in Breton until the 1960s. At the same time, in Provence and Languedoc, languages close to Occitan were spoken by elders of small villages. Neither Alsatian, a Germanic language, nor Corsican, close to Italian, nor Basque, nor Occitan were totally erased by political domination until after World War II. But those languages were spoken within families and local communities, while French – whose learning increased with the spreading of national education – was the language that permitted participation in collective life. It is astonishing that after so many centuries of effort to homogenise the population 'regional identities gave up only recently' (Mendras 2002: 215). Nevertheless, can we say that those regional and social differences are 'ethnic', as one and all felt they belonged to the same people?

The denial of ethnic identity that characterised nation-building in France was not a description of the reality but a principle of integration and a political ideal directly linked to the national mythology. It asserted that every person, despite his/her origins and beliefs, was likely to be integrated as a citizen in the political society, as long as he or she had received a national education through which different individuals, members of 'small fatherlands', could become French citizens. Supporters of the *Ancien Régime* and counter-revolutionary thinkers alike have, for decades, invoked local and historical identities, ethnic identities and cultural 'roots' in order to argue that they contravene the ideals of national citizenship and that a child of immigrants or Jews would always be unable to understand Racine or other great French writers, regardless of his/her education.

'Providential democracy'

Today, people like to imagine a culturally unified France of the past, as opposed to a new French society that wants to be multi-cultural, multi-ethnic and multi-confessional. But the idea of unity in the past was more a 'voluntarist' policy than a reality. Also the actual multiculturalism is one of degree, as the population is not more diverse now than in the past. Nevertheless, it is true that national institutions, the project of a centralised state and the value accorded to unity/homogeneity of population in the name of a philosophical conception of universality are now criticised and called into question.

To analyse this evolution it is important to bear in mind the inevitable tension that afflicts democratic societies (Schnapper 2002). By according civil, legal and political rights to all citizens, modern democratic society sets out a principle of transcendence of economic and social differences. This tension between the civil, legal and political equality of all citizens and the perpetuation of their economic and social inequalities was immediately perceived at the time of the French Revolution. It was one of the subjects of the first debates of the National Assembly in 1789. 'Once political equality will be established, poor people will soon understand that it is weakened by inequalities of fortunes, and they will ask for equality of fortunes' (Rabaut Saint-Etienne, quoted in Gauchet 1989: 212). Tension between equality of rights and the reality of economic inequalities was the topic of critics, whether of social Catholic, Marxist or the Socialist bent.

Acceptance of this critique led to the policies of the 'providential state' (or welfare state). In modern terms, equality of political rights has promoted the claim to economic equality by individuals. This claim led to the implementation of policies that aimed to make living conditions less unequal. Such policies were both the condition and the consequence of the principle of citizenship. In fact, below a certain standard of living, citizenship becomes merely formal, as the citizen's dignity is not respected. The Republic, i.e. the political regime organised by the principles and institutions of citizenship, irresistibly leads not only to 'formal' equality, i.e. civil, legal and political, but also to 'real' equality, to borrow from the Marxist lexicon.

This is why there is increasing intervention by the state in order to satisfy the social, educational, cultural, sport, and identity (or ethnic) needs of individuals. Interventionist policies increase in order to ensure the well-being and the equality of everybody. A part of the society becomes 'providential', i.e. linked to interventions of the welfare state and its inevitable bureaucratisation.

The political and military state was based on the idea and value of individual citizenship, representative political institutions and large national institutions organised by the state. The welfare state moves away from universalism to different forms of categorisations, always finer and distinctive. The state action takes the diversity of individual cases and social dimensions that we can call 'ethnic' more and more into account

Republican centralism in France adapted itself to the needs of a differentiated society. The policy of the providential state is like a huge mechanism of social transfers aimed to complete and correct the insufficiencies of universal policies. Republicans have joined with the critics of republican universalism and think that marginalised individuals have the right to receive more than the others in the name of national solidarity. The logic of intervention is less and less the one of the Republican state (ideally neutral, rational and an arbitrator), and has now been replaced by a state in charge of ensuring the well-being of everybody. The modern democratic state tends to move from the informal to the individual, from the universal to the particular. The French state progressively adopts more and more 'particular' policies, including in the ethnic sphere.

Ethnicisation of social life

Urban policies, for instance, in the past twenty years have been granting financial aid to ethnic associations, as they are perceived to favour the integration of the children of immigrants. Many jobs promoted by the state help to recruit social workers, called 'big brothers', in order to train and guide young people of the same ethnic origin in the suburbs of big cities. This breaks with the republican tradition, according to which ethnic origin is not to be taken into account in recruitment. Police agents of the same ethnic origin of suburban teenagers have been recruited to guide their behaviour: they are supposed to be better able to understand the situation, their authority is supposed to be stronger, and they are claimed to be role-models for their 'younger brothers'. More generally, social workers increasingly take into account the 'cultural' traditions of populations with whom they work: multicultural sensitivity is critical. Housing administrators distribute – even though informally, as it is illegal – people according to their origin in order to avoid the formation of 'ghettos'.

The 'ethnicisation' of social and also political policy continues to spread. France refuses to adopt a multicultural policy – as Canada and Australia officially do – by invoking the 'republican model', but there are other forms of providential state that we may call 'ethnic', in Anglo-Saxon terms. Public resources are given to groups to allow them to maintain distinctive cultures. Libraries, cultural associations, Jewish or Armenian schools, for instance, benefit from public funding. There are radio stations for Jews or French of North African origin that express themselves in the public space. In the name of social work and integration policy – that is the official policy since the end of the 1980s – associations founded by French originally from North Africa benefit from particular financial aid. Mosques play an increasing social role among Muslim people. The expression of ambiguous and contradictory identities (Jewish, Muslim ...) no longer raises suspicions, as it did during the time of the triumphant nation-state. Rather, they become a source of prestige. Legal recognition of the Armenian genocide by the National Assembly in 1998 is an example of this symbolic 'ethnicisation' of political life. The Premier every year addresses the Jewish Community of France (CRIF), even though the idea of a Jewish community is contradictory to the traditional model of national integration. The Ministry of Culture is increasingly sensitive to cultural groups, with more awareness of the ethnic element, and makes reference to the 'plural' origins of the population.

With such developments, the national education is responding more and more to special requests. More than 300,000 children study 'regional' languages in public schools (Occitan, Corsican, Breton, Alsatian). At 'A-level', students have a huge choice of foreign languages to take exams in. Stemming from a European proposal, the teaching of native languages to immigrants has been in place in the public education system since 1975.

The so-called 'assimilation' policy of the central state seems to be less and less compatible with authenticity and the value placed on the freedom of the individual. French people wonder if their traditional policy of assimilation – which does not consider immigrant distinctiveness – is still worthwhile. In the 1970s, regionalist militants said the central state was an 'ethnic group killer'. They likened their movement to those struggling for independence from colonial powers. Expressions like 'the right to difference' and 'multicultural and plural France' emerged in scientific publications and speeches. The Ministry of Culture encouraged the teaching of 'native languages and cultures' and in 1982 founded a National Committee of Regional Languages and Cultures. According to a government report which follows EU guidelines for the protection of regional and marginal languages, twenty-seven languages should be protected (Cerquiglini 1999).

On the other hand, since the 1980s, the debate between multicultural militants and supporters of traditional integration policies has been limited. No one called into question the principal instruments by which the children of immigrants have become French citizens since the nineteenth century (i.e. the right to nationality, education, etc.). The proposal to teach Corsican in Corsica as a compulsory language in the primary school shocked most French people, who are still attached to the 'language of the Republic' which is inscribed in the Constitution.

Difficulties of the national state in managing 'particularisms' – whose legitimacy is now fully recognised – are increasingly criticised. Home secretaries have long tried to build a representative organisation of Muslims that could meet the expectations of people (halal meat, Muslim feasts, etc.). The present Home Secretary, Nicolas Sarkozy, managed to set up an elected representative assembly of French Muslims at the beginning of 2003. Nobody publicly disputes the right of Muslims to have places of worship, but the social settlement of Islam within the French 'landscape' continues to raise opposition from local people. During the Gulf War in 1991, passions were controlled by the Jewish and Muslim moral and religious authorities, but the situation was very different in 2003, highlighting the extended 'ethnicisation' of social life in France. Meanwhile, this 'ethnicisation' meets resistance, e.g. the wearing of the veil by young Muslim girls. A national committee was founded in July 2003 to rethink the principles and the adaptation of secularism (i.e. *laïcité*), as it is inscribed in the Constitution.

Is the policy of recognising 'particularisms' – one that breaks with the secular policy of rejecting the claims of ethnic groups – unintentionally leading towards dominant ethnicity? Is this policy, typical of 'providential democracy', leading to the constitution of minority ethnic groups and also one (or several) dominant ethnies? It is a question with no answer. But one question we have to ask: is there a risk that public recognition of 'particularisms' will consecrate the existence of those 'particularisms' and, by extension, that of a dominant ethnie? Ethnic identities and social statuses, like nations, are not data or essences; they are created by history and social conditions.

Conclusion

The concept of dominant ethnicity can have a heuristic value in the two historical moments that we have distinguished. It is, however, not useful in the analysis of the age-old history of French nation-building. This fact is itself significant as it illuminates the case-specificity of the nation-building process. The idea and the reality of the nation were born in Western Europe, but the process of each European nation is specific.

As concerns the present, the concept of dominant ethnicity allows us to probe the transformation of social links brought about by the rise of 'providential democracy'. The potential birth of a dominant ethnie exists if, in the future, the process of progressive 'ethnicisation' of social life continues to speak in the name of democratic values and of the right of each citizen to be fully 'recognised' in the public space, according to Charles Taylor (1994).

It is important to bear in mind that concepts have no value in themselves and that they are not inscribed in the social world. They are tools of research, more or less useful, effective or fruitful in understanding the evolution of society. If the traditional policy of denying the expression of ethnic groups within the ancient nations is progressively replaced, in an ever more providential society, by a policy of recognising intra-national or transnational ethnic identities, the concept of dominant ethnicity will find its full heuristic value, accounting for the evolution of contemporary democracies.

Note

1 Catholic kings of Spain had equally based their political legitimacy on the religious unity of their kingdom.

References

Beaune, C. (1985) *Naissance de la nation France*, Paris: Gallimard.

Cerquiglini, B. (1999) *Les langues de la France* (Rapport au Ministre de l'Education nationale, de la recherche et de la technologie et à la Ministre de la culture et de la communication), Paris: Délégation générale à la langue française.

Certeau, de M., Julia, D. and Revel J. (1975) *Une politique de la langue: La Révolution française et les patois*, Paris: Gallimard.

Chanet, J.-F. (1996) *L'Ecole républicaine et les petites patries*, Paris: Aubier.

Furet, F. and Ozouf, J. (1977) *Lire et écrire: L'alphabétisation des Français de Calvin à Jules Ferry*, Paris: Minuit.

Gauchet, M. (1989) *La révolution des droits de l'homme*, Paris: Gallimard.

Gellner, E. (1983) *Nations and Nationalism*, Oxford: Blackwell.

Kantorowicz, E. ([1957] 1989) *Les Deux corps du Roi*, Paris: Gallimard.

Mendras, H. (2002) *La France que je vois*, Paris: Autrement.

Mirot, L. (1930) *Manuel de géographie historique de la France*, Paris: Auguste Picard.

Noiriel, G. (1988) *Le Creuset français*, Paris: Seuil.

Ponty, J. (1988) *Polonais méconnus*, Paris: Publications de la Sorbonne.

Renan, E. ([1882] 1947) *Œuvres complètes*, vol. 1, Paris: Calmann-Lévy.

Schnapper, D. (1991) *La France de l'intégration: Sociologie de la nation en 1990*, Paris: Gallimard.

—— (1994) *La communauté des citoyens: Sur l'idée moderne de nation*, Paris: Gallimard. (English translation, *Community of Citizens: On the Modern Idea of Nationality*, Transaction, 1998.)

—— (1996) 'Le discours du Front National', *Commentaire*, 75: 667–72.

—— (2002) *La Démocratie providentielle: Essai sur l'égalité contemporaine*, Paris: Gallimard.

Sternhell, Z. (1978) *La droite révolutionnaire, 1885–1914: Les origines françaises du fascisme*, Paris: Seuil.

Taylor, C. (1994) 'Politics of recognition', in A. Gutman (ed.) *Multiculturalism: Examining the 'Politics' of Recognition*, Princeton, NJ: Princeton University Press.

Thiesse, A.-M. (1997) *Ils apprenaient la France: L'exaltation des régions dans le discours patriotique*, Paris: Editions de la maison des sciences de l'homme.

Tilly, C. (ed.) (1975) *The Formation of National States in Western Europe*, Princeton, NJ: Princeton University Press.

Weber, E. (1976) *Peasants into Frenchmen: The Modernization of Rural France 1870–1914*, Stanford, CA: Stanford University Press.

7 The strange death of Protestant Britain

Steve Bruce

Introduction

There are two ways in which a dominant ethnic group can lose its position: the rulers may be displaced or they may mutate. In the cases of the Afrikaners in South Africa and the Protestants of Northern Ireland (who feature on the margins of this chapter), an identifiable people lost its position of supremacy: power passes sideways. The alternative is for a people to remain dominant but to abandon what once defined them: power continues to pass down through the generations but what was once a core characteristic is lost. It is this second sort of change that is examined in this chapter.

My aim is to describe and explain what, after George Dangerfield's classic *The Strange Death of Liberal England*, we may think of as the strange death of Protestant Britain. Though the two things go hand-in-hand, I am not initially concerned with the decline of religion as such. Rather, I am interested in the complete disappearance of the Protestant faith from the centre of British politics and from British national identity.

The use of the term 'British' in that last sentence is both deliberate and awkward. It is deliberate in the sense that I wish to concentrate on England, Scotland and Wales: 'Great Britain'. Northern Ireland will feature as an independent rather than a dependent variable. It is awkward in that it glosses over what must be an important part of the explanation: the composite nature of Britain. Of course all social identities are in some sense artefacts. Only the most partisan and uncritical nationalist will maintain that a nation (or any such grouping) has an unchanging essence which may be apparent or submerged but retains its nature regardless. Shared identities are always to some extent problematic and require social engineering. Nonetheless, even if we begin with Ernest Gellner's well-known position that nationalists create the nation, rather than the other way round, it is still reasonable, as Anthony Smith has done, to point out that some identities require more constructing than others (Gellner 1965, 1983, 1997; Smith 1986; O'Leary 1998). We can see the point if we contrast the Poles with the inhabitants of the United Kingdom of Great Britain and Ireland (or even its smaller Eire-less version). Despite being frequently divided between Sweden,

Germany and Russia, Poland has retained a considerable degree of homogeneity. Its people are united by a common language and religion and, despite having a variety of foreign masters, its core territory has not been much populated with strangers. In contrast, the people of the UK have belonged to four nations, had at least that number of religions and almost as many languages.

Before considering in detail the collapse of a religiously informed sense of ethnic identity, I will briefly consider the other side of the coin: the reasons why religion so often plays a part in ethnic and national identity.[1] We can begin with the obvious historical point: religion was usually there first. Whether we assign the rise of modern European nationalism to 1792 (the French Revolution), 1815 (the Congress of Vienna), or 1919 (the break-up of the Ottoman and Austro-Hungarian empires), the date will be centuries after the peoples who formed putative 'nations' acquired their religion. The Serbs were Orthodox Christians long before they were Serbs. As they were already in place, religious belief systems and institutions were always likely to be implicated in evolving modern identities and social institutions. But religions typically have some features that make them fit well with nationalism.

One is the dual characteristic of dividing without and uniting within. Most religions create a clear divide between those who adhere to the true faith and the heathen, the infidel and the pagan. More often than not, they also create suspicion, animosity and resentment. There is no God but Allah. My God is a jealous God. Confessional loyalty is almost always turned into a rule for close association. Adults marry only those of the same religion or insist that spouses convert. People may teach their children two languages but they do not teach them two religions. But as well as dividing one people from another, religion unites within its reach. All religions periodically throw up radical sects that allow membership only to those who meet exacting standards, the religious virtuosi, but generally religions seek to encompass an entire people. They will not tolerate rebellion but they will accept considerable laxity in ritual performance and moral life. Almost all religions confer membership at birth: hence baptism and the analogous rituals that incorporate babies and children into the community of the faith. Furthermore, most major religions at least pay lip-service to the notion of equality. Together those characteristics fit well the shape of the world according to nationalism: a theoretical comradeship within the community and abrupt divisions between this community and the aliens, us and them.

The primacy of religion also owes much to functions more mundane than identity-creation. Before the rise of the modern bureaucratic nation-state, a religion's network of officials often formed what little there was by way of social organisation beyond the local feudal estate. Monasteries and cathedrals provided the embryonic framework for national administration and the religious institution provided the main source of trained literate officials. The Church educated the nobility and provided secretarial services for the government. Most European countries had senior clergymen holding high office. Cardinal Wolsey ruled England from 1515 to 1529 as Henry VIII's Lord Chancellor; Cardinal Richelieu ruled France from 1621 to 1642.

The stability and continuity of the religious institution meant that churches were often keepers of records and artefacts. For centuries monastery and cathedral annalists had added notes to the margins of the calendars that were used to keep track of the round of religious offices. Although the gradual extension of secular education eventually produced cadres of secular intellectuals, well into the nineteenth century in most European countries clergy played important roles in producing histories of their people that could be turned to nationalist purposes.

One virtue of religion is its durability. It generally outlasts regimes. It might have been possible for the fifth generation of a ruling family to talk of the divine right of kings but such continuity is extremely rare. The mundane origin of kingship was all too obvious in the German states in the seventeenth century or the Balkans in the early nineteenth century, where local notables argued about whom they might invite to be the first occupant of the thrones of their new formed kingdoms. Of course, the earthly representatives of God also change. Anyone who lived in England between 1534 and 1558 and paid much attention to church affairs changed allegiance three times: from Catholic to Protestant to Catholic and back to Protestant. In the Balkans church authorities manoeuvred for autonomy from the Greek Orthodox leadership in Constantinople as much as the local notables tried to free themselves of Ottoman rule. But many of the rituals remained stable, as did many of the beliefs. Both as a world-view and as a structure, religion generally enjoyed far greater permanence than the more obviously human affairs of politics and hence could serve as the basis for a sense of shared identity better than mundane creations. The Orthodox Church leaders who celebrated a thousand years of Russian Christianity in 1988 might have hoped but they could not know that Soviet communism was shortly to collapse. The commissars lasted a mere seventy years.

Religion also provides ideological justification for arrangements in this world. Rulers have always sought divine justification and support. For many centuries European monarchs sought the blessing of the Pope. In their disputes over the independence of the Scottish throne from England, both English and Scottish monarchs petitioned the Pope for his approval. The Catholic Church in France was so firmly associated with the aristocracy that its influence was radically reduced by the French Revolution and the subsequent development of a strong national consciousness was secular-led. But in other countries the Church found it relatively easy to shift from supporting and legitimating monarchs to the new democratic task of sponsoring national identity.[2]

Anthony Smith (1999) has drawn attention to one particular device for promoting national identity that is uniquely in the gift of religious institutions: the myth of election. We are glorious because God chose us. We do not need to be too cynical to appreciate the value of exalting base interests.

On 16 December 1838, white Afrikaners circled their sixty-eight wagons beside the Ncome river and awaited the onslaught of thousands of Zulu warriors. The Afrikaners prayed and made a pact with God that if they were spared they would keep the day holy and build a monument on the site. In the event some 3,000 Zulus and only three Afrikaners died. The Battle of Blood River (as it was aptly renamed) became a central theme of Afrikaner ideology: proof that God would preserve his people. One of the political virtues of religious myths of election is that they allow assertions of moral superiority: in the minds of the Afrikaners they triumphed not because they had rifles but because they had God's divine approval.

The religious complexion of the British Isles

The Christian Church in England officially 'Reformed' in 1529 when, for reasons that had little to do with the new theology of the Protestants, Henry VIII declared himself supreme head and separated the Church from Rome. It was further nationalised with the dissolution of the monasteries between 1536 and 1539. Gradually Protestant ideas became well embedded but the church never entirely reformed. It remained episcopalian in organisation and much of its liturgy remained capable of bearing a Roman interpretation. The preferences of the clergy and of the laity ranged from high Catholic to low Protestant and in many times and places did not match. Which ethos dominated the national church depended on the preferences of the country's political rulers and hence changed; at times, such as during the English Civil War period, quite dramatically. Periodically internal dissent developed into outright 'nonconformity' and schism. The competing sects (and the denominations into which some sects evolved) grew so that by the time of the 1851 Census of Religious Worship more than half of those who attended church did so with some organisation other than the state church.

The Reformation in Scotland was both more popular and more effective. The lowlands, containing the largest part of the population, became Presbyterian; the Highlands and islands, long untouched by economic and political modernisation, remained Roman Catholic or Episcopalian Protestant. The Reformation eventually reached the Highlands in the late eighteenth and early nineteenth centuries but it failed to create a unified Scottish culture because at the same time as the Highlanders converted to a conservative and evangelical variety of Protestantism, the lowlands were becoming increasingly liberal or secular. The religious culture was further fragmented by a Presbyterian fondness for schism that meant that, in the late nineteenth century, the state Church of Scotland was challenged by two large nationally distributed Presbyterian alternatives, an Episcopalian remnant, a number of smaller Presbyterian alternatives and outposts of many English dissenting movements. Migration from Ireland in the nineteenth century further increased the variety of Scottish religion by creating significant Catholic populations in the industrial lowlands. Not all the Irish migrants were Catholic; about a third were Ulster Protestants, who added a strongly anti-Catholic tone to elements of lowland Scottish Protestantism.

Wales differed from England only in that the dissenting movements of the late eighteenth and early nineteenth centuries were proportionately more popular and, once well established, the Baptist, Congregationalist and Methodist chapels became closely associated with a distinctive Welsh (and usually anti-English) ethos. In the 1890s Welsh Members of Parliament campaigned for the disestablishment of the Church of Wales (which by then enjoyed only minority support) and succeeded in 1914.

Despite (or because of) the best British efforts to impose the Protestant faith on the Christian Church in Ireland, the majority of the Irish people remained Catholic. Hence at the start of the nineteenth century Ireland had an Episcopalian Protestant Church established by law and supported by the British state but this sister to the Church of England was supported only by the descendants of English settlers and was disestablished in 1869. In the north-east (what later became Northern Ireland) there was a significant population of Presbyterians, close in every sense to the Scots. And there was the Roman Catholic majority.

Unity in diversity

The internal variegation of British religious life was at times glossed over by a common popular Protestantism. For all their theological and ecclesiastical differences, the Scots Presbyterians, Welsh Baptists and Methodists, English Methodists and half the Church of England could find common ground in Low Church evangelicalism. In the 1820s the young William Gladstone at Oxford used to forward *The Record*, an Anglican evangelical magazine, to a Miss Bethune, an evangelical Presbyterian Scot in Dingwall (Bebbington 1982: 501). As we will see, the Protestant flavour to British identity was particularly strong when events focused attention on the neighbouring Catholic powers.

It is a foundational principle of Christianity that the promises made to the Jews by the God of the Old Testament were generalised to all of God's creation by his sacrifice of his son Jesus Christ. That metaphorical relationship with the Old Testament explains why Christians the world over periodically refer to themselves as 'The Children of Israel'. In the nineteenth century a number of British Christians began to argue that the British were not just metaphorically the descendants of the Jews but were actually descended from the ten northern Israelite tribes that disappeared from recorded history in the sixth century BC (Wilson 1967). Not surprisingly, the popularity of this claim to be God's chosen people rose with the expansion of the British Empire (surely a sign of divine approval) and fell with its decline but it was never terribly popular.[3] An obvious obstacle to such a notion becoming widely accepted among the small part of the population that was interested in ethnic histories was the fact that it clashed with previously popular ethnic genealogies that had been developed in each component part of the United Kingdom. Antiquarian-minded Scots, Welsh and English already had their own separate accounts (Kidd 1999).

More important than the specific ethnic history offered by British Israelism was a general sense of superiority and a set of matched contrasts. The British were hard-working and diligent, independent of spirit but loyal once persuaded of a cause, literate but never artistic or intellectual, reliable and sober, democratic but not revolutionary. Foreigners, especially such close ones as the French and the Irish, were slothful and feckless, dishonest and treacherous, drunken and illiterate and priest-ridden; unless they were rich in which case they were foppish dilettantes. The assumed explanation for each side of this contrast was religion. The British possessed the social virtues (and the empire which such virtues had created and justified) because they were Bible-believing Protestants; Johnny Foreigner lacked the virtues precisely because he lacked the true religion.

Such stereotypes were encouraged by such internal conflicts as the Reformation struggles and the English Civil War but they derived their greatest power from Britain's foreign wars. That the principal enemies of the British state – the Spanish, the Irish and the French – were Roman Catholic encouraged a British identity in which Protestantism created social virtue. The stereotypes were also reinforced by nineteenth-century conflict between Irish migrants and the native British in the areas where the Irish settled in large numbers: the western lowlands of Scotland (McFarland 1990) and the north-west of England (Waller 1981; Neal 1987; MacRaild 1998). Here the Orange Lodges – local voluntary associations that combined the benefits of fraternal organisation with an ideology of Protestant superiority – became popular. Orangeism always occupied an uneasy position in British political and cultural life. Some religious enthusiasts supported it as a vehicle for maintaining a connection between serious religion and the unchurched elements of the working class. Some politicians saw it as a vehicle for mobilising a working-class Conservative vote. But it was always suspect because it was a loose cannon: difficult to control and prone to periodic violence. Hence the attraction of more malleable vehicles such as the Liverpool Working Men's Conservative Association, which was formed in 1867 by Conservatives who wanted to mobilise the Orange vote without being beholden to the Orange Institution; at its peak it had over 7,000 members and exercised considerable influence on Liverpool's municipal politics.

While the Orange Institution and its local competitors were influential in those places and for those people where economic competition with Irish migrants was pressing, much more important in the ideological work of promoting a popular association of evangelical Protestantism and British identity were the Christian churches, a vast array of religiously inspired voluntary associations, and a variety of public rituals. In the middle of the nineteenth century at least half the adult population of Britain attended church (almost all of them Protestant churches) and a larger proportion of the children had some sort of Sunday school connection. Beyond the churches was a considerable penumbra of social, educational and reforming 'good works' which, with varying degrees of heavy-handedness, promoted an association between the right religion, patriotism and social improvement. And, as Wolffe (1994) ably documents, the second half of the nineteenth century saw a boom in national state ceremonies (often repeated in local communities) that ritually linked Protestantism, the monarchy and the nation.

Popular Protestantism peaked with the Empire; the great red swathes on the globe giving the most concrete proof of divine approval. Its zenith was somewhere between the coronation of Victoria as Empress of India in 1876 and the onset of the Great War in 1914. But for those who cared to notice there were important counter-trends.

The secularisation of identity

The decline of Protestantism could be illustrated from any number of fields but given its centrality I will concentrate on the evolution of the British Conservative Party. The great challenge of the nineteenth century was to manage democratisation. The Conservative Party's main organisational response to the expansion of the franchise was the Primrose League (so named after Benjamin Disraeli's favourite flower):

> The League sponsored a great array of social activities that were easily accessible to ordinary people, in this way successfully embedding the Conservative cause in the routine social life of many communities. It proved enormously successful in convincing large numbers of middle and working-class people to identify a common interest with the ruling parliamentary elite as members of a British patriotic nation increasingly under threat from outside and to regard their political opponents ... as, at best, feeble friends of Britain's enemies or, at worst, traitors.
>
> (Pugh, in Loughlin 1995: 39)

What is remarkable is that the League went out of its way to avoid militant Protestantism – the Orange Order was very deliberately shunned – and to add nonconformists, Catholics and Jews to the patria; an important signal was sent by the involvement of the Duke of Norfolk, England's leading Catholic. In an attempt to rise above the more recent religious and political divisions and to imply an ancient and enduring British unity, the League adopted archaic language. Its members were known as 'Dames' and 'Knights' and its branches were 'Habitations'.

Andrew Bonar Law, who succeeded Arthur Balfour as Tory Party leader in 1911 and was briefly Prime Minister in the early 1920s, was probably the last Conservative leader who had any sort of sentimental or romantic attachment to the idea of the Union as a political unit defined by its religio-ethnic identity and it is significant that he was not English. He was born and raised in New Brunswick, Canada, and spent his early adult years in Glasgow, both settings where Presbyterian culture was strong and where the notion that the Empire was justified by its religiously based social virtues was more appealing than some narrow English nationalism. As we run through the list of subsequent Conservative leaders – Chamberlain, Churchill, Macmillan, Douglas-Home and Heath – we see a clear decline in commitment to evangelical Protestantism, Imperialism and 'Britishness'. The Conservative leader in the late 1970s, Margaret Thatcher, may have had a Little Englander's suspicion of closer ties with Europe but her hostility to the continent was not augmented by any romantic attachment to the British hinterland. She despised the Scots and the Welsh for their reluctance to embrace her attacks on the state and she was perfectly happy to give the Irish Republic a greater say in the management of the Northern Ireland problem.

Thatcher and her heirs were economic liberals and secular social conservatives whose 'national' identity, so far as they had one, was based on white anti-European Englishness largely derived from borrowing in a minor key from Enoch Powell and the racist right. Thatcher had no particular Christian faith and her closest ally, Norman Tebbitt, was a professed atheist. When Thatcher's successor John Major struggled to explain what England meant to him, his only mention of religion was a rather tongue-in-cheek reference to a phrase of George Orwell's (Orwell, in Davison *et al.* 1998: 392) that was itself rather mocking and seems to have been chosen for its piquant and dated flavour. Major told fellow Conservatives in 1993:

> Fifty years from now Britain will still be the country of long shadows on county grounds, warm beer, invincible green suburbs, dog lovers and [betting] pools fillers and – as George Orwell said – 'old maids bicycling to Holy Communion through the morning mist'.

Other recent expressions of British nationalist sentiment are equally devoid of religion. Sir James Goldsmith, the millionaire founder of the UK Referendum Party, launched to contest the 1997 general election on a platform of demanding a referendum on membership of the European Union, was Jewish by birth but was not known to have any particular faith. His daughter, Jemima, married a famous Pakistan cricketer and converted to Islam. Although the Referendum Party attracted the support of 'English nationalists', religion never featured in any of its policy statements. The racist British National Party also very deliberately avoids religion. According to its web-site manifesto in 2003:

> The BNP takes no particular religious position. The BNP would protect the British tradition of separating church and state. The dangers facing the race are so great that it would be crass criminality to allow our

people and country to be divided along religious lines. We have to save our country first.

Perhaps more surprising, religion is also absent from the identities promoted by nationalist parties in the two parts of the United Kingdom which for most of the twentieth century were more (and more consensually) religious than England: Wales and Scotland. Although there was a Welsh nationalist colouring to the 1890s' campaign to disestablish the Episcopalian Church in Wales, the relation has not been maintained in the other direction. Religion was not central to Welsh or Scottish nationalism. Insofar as Welsh and Scottish church leaders were involved in promoting devolution in the 1980s, it was not in the spirit of asserting historic religio-ethnic identities. Kenyon Wright, one of the leading figures in the finally successful campaign for Scottish devolution, was a canon of the Episcopalian Church in Scotland but the substance of his religion gave him no particular standing in the cause and he did not claim divine approval for his politics. His church office was impor- tant because it allowed him to be seen as an honest broker, outside and above the party disputes that threatened to wreck the campaign. It gave a certain *gravitas* to what otherwise might be dismissed as low politicking.

The one part of the United Kingdom where religion remained an essen- tial component of ethnic identity was, of course, Northern Ireland. Arguably evangelicalism became more, not less, important to Ulster Unionists over the twentieth century as their situation within the United Kingdom became ever more precarious. Granting independence to three- quarters of Ireland, attempting to give the rest away in return for Eire joining the Allies in the 1939–45 war, closing down the devolved Stormont Parliament in 1972, and in the 1980s giving the Irish Republic a say in running the North, all threatened Ulster's claim to be British. Although a minority of liberal unionists have tried to construct a secular defence of their Unionism, it is the Reverend Ian Paisley, the leader of the evangelical Free Presbyterian Church of Ulster, who dominates unionist politics at the start of the twenty-first century. The significance of that fact for British judgements of the role of religion in politics will be discussed below.

The explanation

Historians of particular periods will have found the above very brief review synoptic to the point of pastiche but I cannot imagine any scholar denying the central point of the survey: popular Protestantism was once a major part of British identity and it is no longer. Clearly a major part of that is the general decline of religion. A secular society cannot sustain a religio-ethnic identity; when few believe in any God, then those who wish to create a posi- tive image of their people can hardly invoke divine approval. However, the secularisation of British identity has an interesting relationship to the general decline in the popularity of religious ideas and institutions: it slightly precedes it! Of course it is a function of general secularisation but it can more accurately be regarded as an early warning of the general collapse of religion. Protestantism as a central part of British identity is the coalminer's canary. The death of religion-in-ethnic-identity was the first sign of the firedamp that would eventually poison the British churches.

Secularisation is a complex social process that takes a variety of forms and there is no scope here to explain it in detail (see Bruce 2002). Here I can only assert that religion declined in social significance and popularity in stable affluent liberal democratic societies because a plurality of religions combined with an essentially individualistic and egalitarian ethos to erode state, public and elite support for any particular religion and weaken the conviction with which individual believers could hold their faith. From being a consensually held shared world-view deeply embedded in the life of the community, religion shrank to being a matter of individual preference with no implications beyond the family hearth. In most western societies people either gave up religion altogether or retained a connection only to the most liberal and least demanding forms of it.

Any sensible discussion of secularisation will immediately follow the above with a string of vital qualifications. One way of expressing many of mine is to note the string of adjectives attached to settings which become secular: stable, affluent, liberal democratic, religiously diverse, individualistic, egalitarian. These suggest that the circumstances that encourage secularisation are rare and that is indeed so. Most of the world is not like Western Europe.

Religion remains vital and popular when it forms a major component of national identity and it is likely to do that whenever a people united by a common religion is opposed by another people of a different religion or none. The archetypal example is the place of Catholicism in the self-consciousness of peoples such as the Poles and Lithuanians who faced frequent pressure from Orthodox Russia before the vastly more effective imperialism of Stalin's communism.

Cultural defence and diversity

Clearly Catholicism could only play such a role because almost all Poles and Lithuanians are Catholics and have been for a very long time. Here we need to go back to my brief sketch of the religious composition of Great Britain. Although some common ground could be found in a popularised evangelicalism, the British did not share a common religion. England and Scotland each had a state church but it was only the same one for two months in the middle of the seventeenth century. Oliver Cromwell's Parliament called together the leading Protestant divines from around the United Kingdom to create common standards for the church. In a remarkable cooperative intellectual effort, the Westminster Assembly between 1643 and 1648 produced a Confession of Faith, two versions of a catechism to teach the basic beliefs (one long and one short), a model for church government, and an agreed liturgy. All items were ratified by the General Assembly of the Church of Scotland; all were ignored by almost everyone in the Church of England. The Puritans rejected the Assembly's work because it favoured Presbyterianism rather than their Independent version of Protestantism (which we would now call Congregationalism). The Cavaliers rejected it because it was too Protestant. With the Restoration of the monarchy under Charles II in 1660, the Independents were suppressed in England and the Church of England went back to being semi-Catholic.

Two features of modernisation made the lack of a shared religious identity problematic: increasing egalitarianism and the expansion of the state. Pressure to extend a variety of rights called into question the principle of excluding people who refused to conform to the state religion. The desire of the state to improve the population (for example, by creating a national network of schools) challenged the position of the two state churches as the main provider of social services. Arguments between competing Protestant churches were bitter enough but the growth of the Catholic population of Britain with migration from Ireland added an additional charge.

Social harmony

Put schematically, the nation-state has two choices when confronted with increasing religious diversity. It can either continue to privilege the dominant religion or it can marginalise religion. In the late seventeenth and early eighteenth centuries Britain tried the former but when initial attempts at repression failed to stem the tide of nonconformity, most elements of the ruling classes gave up attempting to preserve the hegemony of the state churches of England and Scotland. The extension of the franchise in the Reform Act of 1832 and again in 1867 created a large nonconformist electorate and broke the power of the state churches.

The acceptance of non-state church Protestants into the body politic and into civil society made possible the creation of a popular British Protestant identity and it briefly flourished in tandem with the growth of the Empire. But it was a thin sense of identity easily ruptured here and there by specific disputes. For example, in an 1837 campaign against the ending of specifically Anglican religious education in corporation schools, the Liverpool Protestant Association not only attacked the Catholic population of the city but also turned against the Quakers, Unitarians and other nonconformists. In Scotland, the schismatic formation of the Free Church in 1843 triggered decades of bitter legal argument about the ownership of church property. In Wales, church and chapel fought over the rights of the established church. And to all those quarrels within the Protestant family we need to add the arguments over the steadily increasing number of Catholics.

Some illustrations of the behaviour of Protestant elites, when faced with the choice between preserving the ethnic honour of the dominant ethnie and promoting social harmony, can be given from the case of lowland Scotland, where the concentration of Catholics and militant Protestants made the choice particularly stark. In the 1920s two leading figures in the Church of Scotland – John White and Duncan Cameron – tried to build an anti-Catholic campaign, arguing for the repatriation of the Irish and selective employment policies to benefit Scots Protestants. Although he was himself a member of the Orange Order and an honorary member of Grand Lodge, Sir John Gilmour, the Secretary of State for Scotland, politely heard the case, considered it and then politely but firmly rejected it. He gave two reasons for declining to act. First, he concluded that the number of Irish migrants had been greatly exaggerated. Second, and this is a remarkable argument for an Orangeman, Gilmour pointed out that the Irish Free State was a dominion within the British Empire and as such could hardly be treated as 'foreign'. In May 1930 White led another delegation, this time to a Labour Secretary of State. William Adamson, himself an evangelical Baptist, gave similarly short shrift to White's schemes. Sir Charles Cleland was a leading Orangeman and Unionist elected to the Glasgow School Board. Once in a position of having to manage the public provision of schooling, he proved himself entirely rational, utilitarian and even-handed and was recognised as such by the Catholic representatives on the Board.[4]

In the early 1930s two militantly anti-Catholic parties enjoyed brief electoral success in Glasgow and Edinburgh (Bruce 1985). Alexander Ratcliffe's Scottish Protestant League (SPL) won its first seat on the Glasgow council in 1931, peaked with seven seats in 1933 and had lost them all by 1937. John Cormack's Protestant Action (PA) had a similarly rapid rise and fall in Edinburgh's municipal politics. Neither party enjoyed any significant elite support. Lord Scone, Ratcliffe's only elite supporter, abandoned him quickly. Even evangelical Church of Scotland ministers who were members of the Orange Order refused to support Ratcliffe and Cormack. When Ratcliffe was denied the use of Dunoon town hall for a meeting, he wrote to all five local Protestant ministers asking for support. None replied. What little clerical support Ratcliffe and Cormack did enjoy (and it was trivial) came from maverick independent clergy (Bruce 1986; Rosie 2001). The Orange Order declined to support the SPL and PA and played a major part in Ratcliffe's demise. When Ratcliffe came up for re-election, the Glasgow council conservatives persuaded Matthew Armstrong, a popular JP and former councillor, to come out of retirement. Armstrong had Orange credentials and was a church elder but he was also on good terms with local Catholic groups. The two left-wing parties declined to field candidates. The best-selling Glasgow newspaper came out against Ratcliffe and in a straight fight Ratcliffe lost his seat.

Cormack was similarly friendless in Edinburgh. The Orange Order, the business elites and the Protestant churches all declined to support him and only the postponement of the 1939 elections (because of the war) prevented Cormack following the rest of his tiny party into oblivion.[5]

A good indicator of the attitude of Scottish Unionist MPs to anti-Catholicism is the behaviour of Sir Thomas Moore, the member for Ayr, who on the same day in 1933 opened a Catholic bazaar in the Town Hall and addressed 4,000 Orangemen at a parade in Maybole.

A further example of Scottish elites putting social harmony ahead of a narrowly evangelical religio-ethnic identity was the easy acceptance of the state funding of Catholic schools. The Scottish Presbyterian churches had handed their schools to the state under the terms of an 1872 act. The small Episcopalian Church and the much larger Catholic Church declined to hand over their schools because they feared losing control. Their concerns were eventually answered with the 1918 Munro Act that saw local education boards adopt Catholic schools and pay their costs while leaving the Church in charge of staffing and curriculum matters. That this effectively created a biased labour market, where Catholics could teach in both sectors but non-Catholics could teach only in state schools, gave anti-Catholic bigots one of their most popular (the term is relative) issues. What is significant is that the Scottish Presbyterian churches accepted the Munro Act and refused to support militant Protestants such as Ratcliffe who tried to make political capital out of 'Rome on the Rates'. It is particularly significant that the only education board that petitioned for a reconsideration of the 1918 act was Caithness, where there were no Catholic schools to be transferred. In Caithness anti-Catholicism was entirely theoretical: a theological dislike for Romanism was not tempered by any significant social contact with Catholics or with any public policy need to accommodate. Boards in those parts of Scotland that had significant Catholic populations accepted the Munro Act. The Association of Education Boards in Scotland did not discuss the religion clauses of the act once in the eleven years of its life from 1919 to 1930.[6]

What religion?

Elsewhere I have explored in some considerable detail the differences between major religions in their potential for becoming entangled with ethnic and national identities (Bruce 2003). Here I want to make a few brief points about the capacity of Protestantism to serve as a guarantor of ethnic identity.

The first observation has already been implied. Reformed Christianity has trouble sustaining a dominant ethnicity because it is essentially fissiparous. Its stress on the equality of all believers and its rejection of the value of an authoritarian hierarchy ensures that it constantly fragments as groups develop their own particular interpretation of what God requires and the religion offers no accepted mechanism for settling such disputes. In contrast, Catholicism, Orthodoxy and the Lutheran strand of Protestantism, because they lay great stress on the church as an institution, fragment little and thus permit the continued elision of the religious community of the church and the political community of the nation.

The second point (and it is closely related) is that Protestantism has at its heart a principle that undermines all group identities: individualism. The individualism of the Reformers was initially one-sided in that it concerned only responsibility: we were each severally (rather than jointly) answerable to God. Religious merit could not be transferred from the Godly to the ungodly by such rituals as saying mass for the dead. But once one asserts the primacy of the individual over the community in one sphere, it is very hard to prevent that idea being generalised. Individual responsibilities gradually became the grounds for arguing for individual rights. That individualism was eventually to have profound political effects in that it stimulated the rise of liberal democracy but in the shorter term it had the effect of making religious affiliation a voluntary matter.

Of course, groups of Protestants managed to find many good reasons for not following their own voluntaristic logic to its inevitable conclusion. When dissenters argued for their own liberties against the power of the state church, they usually argued that they and a few others very like them should be tolerated but that some other group of dissenters should continue to be harried. Such temporising positions never held long. Individuals within the camp broke ranks (as Thomas Chalmers, one of the founders of the Free Church of Scotland, did when he argued in favour of Catholic Emancipation) and outsiders enthusiastically pointed out the hypocrisy.

If Protestants are true to their stated principles, then they must accept the right of others to disagree with them. If such others become a majority, then, with the appropriate safeguards for the rights of individuals, the Protestants must accept defeat. I once heard a leading Scots Orangeman responding with umbrage to a journalist who suggested the organisation was bigoted. He fumed: 'We are an inclusive organisation. We are a democratic organisation. We will accept anyone regardless of colour, class or ...'. He was obviously about to list the third item of that well-known list – 'creed' – when he realised that the Orange Order was by definition a sectarian organisation: that was the whole point!

If you accept the principle of individual liberty in matters of religion, the grounds for campaigning against some other religion are narrowed to two. You could argue that a particular religion should not be tolerated because it is socially harmful. Or you could argue that, irrespective of its general character, a particular religion should not be tolerated because, if it gains power, it will deny such toleration to others. Both cases were made by Protestants. They pressed for legislation on convent inspection because they believed that ascetic monasticism was a cover for sexual exploitation. And they pointed to the Catholic Church's deliberate rejection of the principles of democracy. Neither argument was for long persuasive in the British context. The vice case could be addressed by distinguishing the religion from the offending behaviour. The British state was strong enough to punish Catholics who did bad things; it did not have to prevent people being Catholics. The second argument fell again on the strength of the

British state but also on Catholic numbers. It was quite true that the Vatican was anti-democratic but there were so few Catholics in Britain that most Protestants could not see Catholicism as a plausible threat to British political freedoms and institutions.

Accelerating secularisation

There is no scientific formula for identifying this point but there is a watershed in the secularisation of politics. Religion as a key element in national identity does not decline gradually; rather, for various constituencies, there are switching points at which a dramatic change in interpretation occurs. At a certain point, people lost interest in distinguishing between religions so that they were no longer judged separately and what the protagonists wanted to portray as the vices of a particular creed became seen by everyone else as 'what happens when people take religion too seriously'. We see some of this in the first quarter of the twentieth century when British mainland Conservatives start to disparage Ulster Unionism as 'sectarian' and as alien to 'the British way of life', which by then was being stripped of its Protestant heritage and being recast as inclusive and tolerant (Loughlin 1995: 226). It became even more apparent in the 1970s when the vast majority of people in Britain (even regular churchgoers) interpreted the violence in Northern Ireland as proof of the evils of mixing religion and politics. Pastor Jack Glass, a militant anti-Catholic preacher in Glasgow in the 1970s, had a vastly harder furrow to plough than Ian Paisley not just because there were far fewer evangelicals in Scotland than in Northern Ireland but because the basic terms for assessing religion had changed. For Scots the Ulster Troubles proved that religion was properly a private family matter that should have no public consequences and should not be part of social identities.

Diversity, threat and unity

Although it makes it sound rather trite, the above could be summarised as saying that religion cannot convincingly or for long play a part in an ethnic or national identity when the putative people do not share a common religion. Religious diversity undermines religio-ethnic identity, especially in a modern liberal democracy where the preferences of ordinary people can no longer be ignored and hence where there is a high price to be paid in social conflict if the state is to continue to privilege one religion over another.

It should be obvious but it is worth stressing that the social consequences of diversity cannot be 'read off' without some attention to circumstances. Identity is almost always a matter of social choice in that we have available to us a large number of sources of identity. Family, clan, occupation, region, ethnicity, religion, nationality and even hobby all offer different identities; which is given priority will depend on what most presses on us at any time and on what options for action are available. As people can choose to over-look differences, we cannot treat diversity in isolation as a fixed property. It may be more or less significant depending on the options. An illustration will make the point. In almost every Protestant culture, sects have divided over the propriety of baptising infants and over the likely end of the world. Yet Ian Paisley's Free Presbyterian Church of Ulster has permitted its minis-ters and congregations liberty of conscience on these two often bitterly disputed questions for thirty years and it has not divided over them. The explanation is that Paisley's Free Presbyterians feel themselves so threatened by the twin forces of Catholicism and liberal Protestantism that they believe maintaining a coherent Bible witness means they must set aside quarrels which, in more propitious times, would split them.

I raise this point to make sense of where we started. Protestantism is essentially fissiparous. Its individualism, egalitarianism and rejection of hierarchical models of divine inspiration give it a very strong tendency to fragment. However, that can be retarded. Or, to put it in individual terms, Protestants can choose to concentrate on what unites rather than what divides them. To return to where this chapter began, the majority of British Protestants did manage for some time to find something of a common reli-giously inspired identity when faced with serious threats; from within in the struggles over the Catholic Stuart monarchy and from without when at war with France, Spain or Ireland. For a brief period a common Protestantism was given additional salience by the Empire. The Empire needed an honourable justification and spreading the benefits of Protestant civilisation was more attractive than stealing other people's wealth. That many of the heroes of the Empire (General Gordon, for example) were evangelical Christians and that many Christian missionaries died in taking the gospel to the four corners of the earth gave added plausibility to the view that the imperial race was made great by its shared faith. But the Empire was short-lived and in its detailed workings had too many shortcomings to allow the pious Christians to mourn its passing.

The decline of the Empire undermined the unity of Great Britain (McCrone 1997). So long as there was a vast external Empire, the national components of Britain could subordinate both their internal differences and the differences between them in sustaining the core of the Empire. A cultural illustration of the complexities involved in glossing over the internal divi-sions and proof that, for a time, such glossing was effective can be found in the careers of Scottish novelists Walter Scott and John Buchan, who were immensely popular throughout Britain during its imperial period. Scott first came to prominence in the 1820s; Buchan was still widely read in the 1940s. Both were lowlanders who were proud of their country, its Scots (not Gaelic) language and its traditions; but both were Unionists who wrote in English. Both were Presbyterians who saw the independent democratic ethos of Protestantism as essential to progress but both romanticised the wild spirit of the highlanders. Scott in particular stimulated the English Victorian fondness for highland holidays, sporting estates, and tartan. Buchan became a Unionist MP and ended his career as Governor-General of Canada. With a vast empire to rule jointly, the relative sizes and interests of the component parts of Great Britain could be overlooked. When it lost its empire, Britain also lost much of its purpose. Tom Nairn's celebrated *The Break-Up of Britain* (1977) may have been a little premature but only a little.

It is worth repeating the point that the regional nationalist movements that are both benefiting from and encouraging the break-up of Britain have not reintroduced religion as an integral component of the national identity they seek to promote. Even in the first half of the twentieth century, when the shrinkage of the church-going population was less apparent than it is now, the leaders of Welsh and Scottish nationalism were prevented from mobilising around religion because they were themselves divided by it (Hughes 2002), as were the electorates to which they had to appeal.

Conclusion

There is one final element to add to this explanation of the death of Protestant Britain: the stability of the state. We can divide in two the grounds that states, governments and rulers present as reasons to be supported: utility and sentiment. It is no accident that a large number of new nation-states of the twentieth century began with a clearly secular ethos but in the last quarter of the twentieth century started to look for religious legitimation. In Tunisia, Algeria, India, Pakistan, Egypt and a host of other states, ruling parties sought religious legitimation after a period of secular rule failed to deliver the twin promises of government: peace and prosperity. Britain (and here I am deliberately excluding Ireland) has enjoyed an extraordinarily long run of stable and effective government. From 1690 to the present there have been no serious challenges to the monarchy or major rebellions; despite their modern role in promoting Scottish tourism, the two Jacobite excursions of 1715 and 1745 were not major threats. There has been no foreign invasion. The transition from feudal monarchy to parliamentary democracy has been smooth; no revolutions, no *coup d'état*, no uprisings, no police state.

A stable and effective state earns its legitimacy by its actions. It may seek the additional approval that flows from successfully laying claim to ideological legitimation. The myths of divine election and regular renewals of divine approval will be welcomed but there is less need for them.

Protestantism played two major roles in its own demise as part of British national identity: it created a problem and it helped shape an environment which allowed the problem to be solved with very little pain. The problem has been mentioned frequently: Protestantism fragmented the religious culture. In replying to Linda Colley's bold assertion of the importance of religion in British identity, Hempton (1996: 174) notes:

Even in its shared Protestantism eighteenth- and nineteenth-century Britain was deeply divided over matters of religion: divisions between the orthodox and the heterodox, between Episcopalians and Presbyterians, between Churchmen and dissenters, between evangelicals and High Churchmen, between clergymen and anti-clericals … even within a single denomination such as Methodism a vigorous Protestantism and anti-Catholicism [were] not sufficient to maintain internal discipline … Protestantism certainly offered an important organising principle for the expression of identity, but it did not always deliver on its own propaganda. Its limitations as well as its power need to be recognised.

Protestant dissent flourished, Irish migration boosted the Catholic population, and the extension of the franchise forced the state to choose between permitting liberty and promoting one religiously exclusive (and minority) brand of religio-ethnic identity. That is the problem created by the fissiparous nature of Protestantism. But reformed religion also provided the solution.

The case can only be asserted in this brief space: Protestantism played a major part in creating the conditions that allowed a stable society to develop that did not depend on a shared religio-ethnic identity for cohesion. Religion could be dumped because those who argued that the first tentative steps towards public secularity (such the repeal of the Test Acts) would create anarchy were proved wrong. Britain was sufficiently prosperous and strong in its civil society to survive the ditching of religious tests of loyalty.

Notes

1   This subject is discussed at greater length in Bruce (2003: Chapter 3).
2   There is one particular way in which a church enjoys an unusual advantage over other social institutions in a society threatened by an external alien force: if the aliens are of a different religion, they cannot infiltrate the church. In Yugoslavia the more powerful and numerous Serbs increasingly settled in Croatia and they enjoyed privileged access to positions of power and influence. Although they made up only some 15 per cent of the population of Croatia in the 1980s, they were 40 per cent of the police force (more in the senior positions) and a disproportionate part of the ruling Communist Party. But being Orthodox Christians, they could not take over the Catholic Church, which was left in the hands of Croats. The Soviet policy of exporting Russians to neighbouring republics meant that the churches of Orthodox countries could be officered by aliens but the Catholic and Lutheran churches of the Baltic states could not be so manipulated. Likewise the English and Scots settlers in Ireland: they might take the best land and dominate the magistracy and the polity but they could not displace the natives from the Church.
3   Just who constitutes the missing tribes varies with time, place and ideological function: in some versions, the English-speaking peoples; in others, all northern Europeans. British Israelism is now to be found mainly in sections of the 'Christian patriot' movement in the USA.

4 For further illustrations of the unwillingness of Scottish Unionists to support anti-Catholic campaigns, see Seawright (1999) and the essays in Macdonald (1998).
5 Militant Protestantism in Liverpool in the twentieth century was similarly reliant on independent pastors. George Wise, who sat for the council ward of Kirkdale, founded his Protestant Reformers Church in 1903. His successor, H.D. Longbottom, founded the Liverpool Protestant Party in the 1960s. In the early 1980s the congregation was taken into Paisley's Free Presbyterian Church.
6 Stirlingshire joined Caithness in putting two motions to the Association of Education Authorities. Both were heavily defeated. The explanation for Stirlingshire's interest was that the Revd Donald Ross, who had been a member of a school board in Caithness, moved to the area. That the entire opposition in Scotland actually came from one individual is a mark of how clearly the rest of Scotland saw the relative balance of ideological rectitude and social harmony.

References

Bebbington, D. (1982) 'Religion and national feeling in nineteenth-century Wales and Scotland', in S. Mews (ed.) *Religion and National Identity*, Oxford: Blackwell, pp. 489–503.

Bruce, S. (1985) *No Pope of Rome: Militant Protestantism in Modern Scotland*, Edinburgh: Mainstream.

—— (1986) 'Militants and the margins: British political Protestantism', *Sociological Review*, 34(3): 797–811.

—— (2002) *God is Dead: The Secularisation of the West*, Oxford: Blackwell.

—— (2003) *Politics and Religion*, Cambridge: Polity.

Davison, P. (ed.), with Angus, I. and Davison, S. (1998) *A Patriot After All: 1940–41* (vol. 12 of *The Complete Works of George Orwell*). London: Secker and Warburg, p. 362.

Gallagher, T. (1987) *Glasgow: The Uneasy Peace*, Manchester: Manchester University Press.

Gellner, E. (1965) *Thought and Change*, London: Weidenfeld and Nicolson.

—— (1983) *Nations and Nationalism*, Oxford: Basil Blackwell.

—— (1997) *Nationalism*, London: Weidenfeld and Nicolson.

Hempton, D. (1996) *Religion and Political Culture in Britain and Ireland: From the Glorious Revolution to the Decline of Religion*, Cambridge: Cambridge University Press.

Hughes, T.O. (2002) 'An uneasy alliance? Welsh Nationalism and Roman Catholicism', *North American Journal of Welsh Studies*, 2(2): 1–6.

Kidd, C. (1999) *British Identities before Nationalism: Ethnicity and Nationhood in the Atlantic World 1600–1800*, Cambridge: Cambridge University Press.

Loughlin, J. (1995) *Ulster Unionism and British National Identity since 1885*, London: Pinter.

McCrone, D. (1997) 'Unmasking British identity: the rise and fall of British national identity', *Nations and Nationalism*, 3: 579–96.

Macdonald, C.M.M. (1998) *Unionist Scotland 1800–1997*, Edinburgh: John Donald.

McFarland, E.W. (1990) *Protestants First: Orangeism in Nineteenth-Century Scotland*, Edinburgh: Edinburgh University Press.

MacRaild, D.M. (1998) *Culture, Conflict and Migration: The Irish in Victorian Cumbria*, Liverpool: Liverpool University Press.

Nairn, T. (1977) *The Break-Up of Britain*, London: Verso.

Neal, F. (1987) *Sectarian Violence: The Liverpool Experience 1819–1914: An Aspect of Anglo-Irish History*, Manchester: Manchester University Press.

O'Leary, B. (1998) 'Ernest Gellner's diagnoses of nationalism ...', in J.A. Hall (ed.) *The State of the Nation: Ernest Gellner and the Theory of Nationalism*, Cambridge: Cambridge University Press, pp. 40–88.

Rosie, M. (2001) 'Religion and sectarianism in modern Scotland', unpublished PhD thesis, University of Edinburgh.

Seawright, D. (1999) *An Important Matter of Principle: The Decline of the Scottish Conservative and Unionist Party*, Aldershot: Ashgate.

Smith, A.D. (1986) *The Ethnic Origins of Nations*, Oxford: Blackwell.

—— (1999) 'Ethnic election and national destiny: some religious origins of nationalist ideals', *Nations and Nationalism*, 5: 331–55.

Waller, P.J. (1981) *Democracy and Sectarianism: A Political and Social History of Liverpool 1868–1939*, Liverpool: Liverpool University Press.

Wilson, J. (1967) 'British Israelism: the ideological restraints on sect organisation', in B.R. Wilson (ed.) *Patterns of Sectarianism*, London: Heinemann, pp. 345–76.

Wolffe, J. (1994) *God and Greater Britain: Religion and National Life in Britain and Ireland 1843–1945*, London: Routledge.

8 Russians as a dominant ethnie

Geoffrey Hosking

There is a real puzzle about the Russians. For most of the twentieth century, they looked like the dominant nation in the world's largest territorial empire, the core element of a great army which won the Second World War, pioneers in the exploration of space, a nation of great scientists, writers and musicians. Yet they spent much of that same twentieth century poverty-stricken, uprooted, the helpless victims of tyrannical and ruthless rulers; and at the end of it, they were divested of much of 'their' empire and subjected to economic doctrines brought to them from outside. In the early 1990s the politician Vladimir Zhirinovskii articulated the public mood in a way which obviously attracted a favourable response, since it netted him a good many votes:

> For most of the twentieth century, our nation has been in transit. We travelled in carts, rattling over potholes in country roads. We smashed the Germans and sent men into space, but in the process destroyed families and lost our sense of history ... We mutilated our country. We turned it into a backward place, compelling the Russian nation, which at one time had occupied the vanguard, to retreat. We drove the population underground by economic, legal and psychological pressure. And today we're being told we cannot manage without the help of foreigners.
> (Zhirinovskii 1996: 15, 17)

This is a real paradox, not just Zhirinovskian rhetoric, and its background lies far back in history. Because of its geo-political situation on the immense open north Eurasian plains, Muscovy as early as the sixteenth and seventeenth centuries expanded to become a huge multi-ethnic empire long before Russia had been constituted as a nation. From the outset the Russian sense of community articulated itself not through the institutions of an emerging nation-state, but rather through the symbols and structures of an empire which included many other peoples. The ruling class of that empire consisted of the elites of the major nationalities, though Russian was the state language. The ruling class was defined by inherited social status, not by ethnic origin. The other strata, of all nationalities including Russian, were of inferior status. As a result, Russians have usually thought of themselves neither as 'ethnicity' nor as a people dominating others.

Since Russia had no political institutions not shared with other ethnies, being Russian was defined rather by language, culture and religion. But empire inflicted strains on these too. It generated a considerable divide between Russian imperial (*rossiiskii*) and Russian ethnic (*russkii*) cultures. From the eighteenth century onwards Russia's culture was split between the numerous local *russkii* folk cultures of the peasantry, among which Ukrainian and Belorussian may be counted, on the one hand, and, on the other, the internationally oriented European culture of the elites and increasingly of the urban population in general. The Russian Empire (*Rossiiskaia Imperiia*) had only an indirect relationship to Russian (*russkaia*) culture (Hosking 1997). One might have expected that the Orthodox Church, a central institution for both imperial and ethnic cultures, would have been able to act as a bridge between the two, and to ease the transition between them for individuals rising in the social scale. However, in the interests of empire, the Tsars fostered for Russia's elites a post-Renaissance European culture which was largely secular in orientation and which left the Church marginalised and impoverished. Suffice it to say that in the nineteenth century not one Russian university had a theological faculty: the Church's leaders went through an education entirely segregated from the secular one, and were poorly placed to respond to the needs of Russia's fast-growing towns (Hosking 1997: Chapter 4).

The split between urban and rural culture, between peasants and elites, between the religious and the secular, was a major preoccupation of Russia's greatest nineteenth-century writers, notably Gogol, Tolstoi and Dostoevskii. But they examined that split as a purely Russian affair. They did not see non-Russians as affecting the issue or as posing any threat to the integrity of the state. Most nineteenth-century intellectuals simply took it for granted that Russia was a nation-state parallel to Britain, France or (from 1871) Germany. (Although the word 'empire' was used as the official designation of the Russian state, intellectuals and statesmen seldom used the term: they referred more often to the *gosudarstvo* or 'state', a term which could equally be used to designate a nation-state.) The implication was that ethnic distinctions within Russia had no political significance. How to treat the non-Russians living on their territory Russians considered a purely internal affair, on which other nations had no right to comment. A celebrated early articulation of this sentiment was Pushkin's poem *Klevetnikam Rossii* (To the Slanderers of Russia), written in 1831 in response to European powers' protests against Russian suppression of the Polish rebellion:

> What are you clamouring about, bards of the peoples?
> Why do you threaten Russia with your anathema?
> What has angered you? The disturbances in Lithuania?
> Leave all that alone: it is a quarrel of Slavs among themselves,

> An old domestic quarrel already weighed up by Fate,
> A problem you will never solve.
>
> (Pushkin, adapted from Fennel 1964: 69)

Russians often asserted that the peoples of Siberia, the Baltic, the Caucasus and so on had gravitated voluntarily and peacefully to the Russian state, and had not been forcibly annexed, as other European nations had done to their colonies. An authoritative expression of this view came from the leading nineteenth-century Russian historian Sergei Solov'ev (1960: 647–8), according to whom the territory of Russia in the Middle Ages was 'a huge virgin country, awaiting its population and awaiting its history: hence ancient Russian history is the history of a country colonising itself'. Note the 'itself': Solov'ev briefly mentions 'Finnish hunters', but otherwise offers no hint that any other peoples populated the territory (see also Tolz 2001: 162, 170–1).

This 'self-colonising' empire was extremely successful from the mid-seventeenth to the mid-nineteenth century, during which period it expanded right across northern Eurasia, and also advanced westwards to establish itself indisputably as a European great power. However, when from the mid-nineteenth century European nation-states became the dominant model of great power status, Russian statesmen became uncertain and divided over how to re-articulate their sense of community in a fashion appropriate to the modern world. One possible way was to look back to Muscovy of the late-fifteenth to mid-seventeenth century, which had been a more compact and ethnically homogeneous Russian state than its successors; it had also felt a sense of national mission, to spread the one true form of Christianity, Orthodoxy, throughout Christendom, overcoming heresy and apostasy. Nicholas II (1894–1917) took Muscovy as his model, idealising especially the revival of the Russian state which expressed itself in the foundation of the Romanov dynasty in 1613. He named his long-awaited heir Aleksei (after the seventeenth-century Tsar), celebrated the bicentenary of St Petersburg incongruously with a ball in Muscovite costume, and heeded the advice of the bogus starets Rasputin in preference to his western-educated ministers or even the more homespun politicians in that 'constitutional' body the State Duma (Dixon 1996: 51–2). He even belatedly renewed the Orthodox messianism of Muscovy when he concluded in 1915 the secret treaties with Britain and France, providing for Russian occupation of the 'Second Rome', Constantinople, in the event of a victorious war.

Some early twentieth-century Russian political movements proposed re-classifying 'Russia' as an ethnic or even racial category and claiming superior rights for Russians in their 'own' empire: 'Russia for the Russians!' Since ethnic movements usually require a hostile 'other' to function effectively, these proto-fascist 'Black Hundreds' directed their attacks against the Jews: 'Beat up the Jews and save Russia!' was their battle cry (Rogger 1986: Chapters 7–8).

Nicholas II's flirtation with these elements was one of his gravest mistakes, not just for moral reasons, but also because it weakened the fabric of the empire. His Prime Minister, Sergei Vitte, warned him against it, and his reflections on the subject in his memoirs are worth quoting at length:

> The whole mistake of our decades-old policy is that we still have not realised that since the time of Peter the Great and Catherine the Great there has been no such thing as 'Russia'. What we have is the Russian Empire. Since 35 per cent of the population consists of aliens (*inorodtsy*) and the Russians are divided into Great Russians, Little Russians and White Russians, we cannot in the nineteenth and twentieth centuries conduct a policy which ignores that cardinal fact, which ignores the peculiarities of the other nationalities belonging to the Russian Empire – their religion, their language, and so on. The watchword of such an empire cannot be 'Let us turn everyone into genuine Russians.' Such an ideal cannot be shared by all the subjects of the Russian Emperor, cannot unite the entire population and generate a single political will. Perhaps it would be better for us Russians if 'Russia' did exist and we were just Russians and not the sons of a Russian Empire common to all the subjects of the Tsar. In that case we should renounce the borderlands, which cannot accept such a political ideal. But that our Tsars have not wished to do, and our present Emperor least of all.
>
> (1960: 273–4)

Note the word 'borderlands'. Even Vitte underestimated the problem: many Russians lived in the 'borderlands', and many non-Russians lived in what by implication Vitte considered the 'heartland'.

The project of a Russian ethnocracy failed without ever being properly launched. Protagonists of empire like Vitte were opposed to it because it would disrupt the delicate ethnic balance, while most Russian workers and peasants before 1914 remained indifferent to it: they saw their grievances in class terms and had only a weak and diffuse sense of national identity. Pondering the collapse of the monarchy in 1917, the historian I.V. Got'e reflected in his diary on how weak nationalist support for it had proved to be:

> The absence of Russian patriotism in general and of Great Russian patriotism in particular is an extraordinary ugly phenomenon. There are all kinds of patriotism in the Russian realm – Armenian, Georgian, Tatar, Ukrainian, Belorussian – their name is legion. Only general Russian (*obshcherossiiskii*) patriotism is lacking; and the Great Russians lack it as well.
>
> (Got'e, in Emmons 1988: 36)

The 1917 Revolution launched exactly the opposite solution to Russia's nationality problem from that sponsored by Nicholas II. The victorious Bolsheviks believed that Russia should offer an integrative model, not just for other nationalities within the Russian Empire, but for the peoples of the world. After the 1917 Revolution the ultimate aim of the Communist Party was the creation of an 'international proletarian state', which in principle would cover the entire planet. In the meantime, as an intermediate stage, the Soviet Union would construct from its diverse ethnies a 'single Soviet people' (*edinyi sovetskii narod*). Russia thus became an even more internationalist state than before 1917, and the interests of the Russian ethnos were downgraded even more than before.

Since both the Russian state and the Russian people had suffered so heavily, Russians felt a powerful sense of loss. Aleksandr Blok, probably Russia's foremost poet of the time, noted in January 1918 that around him everyone was saying 'Russia is finished; Russia no longer exists; let Russia rest in peace' (Blok 1962).

As we shall see below, Blok himself did not entirely accept these gloomy prophecies, but the first ten years of the new Soviet state seemed amply to bear them out. Lenin and Stalin had their differences on nationality policy, but they both shared the anti-Russian feeling of which Got'e wrote, and they agreed that non-Russian national sentiment could and should be encouraged at the expense of Russians. They believed that in the short term it was a useful tool for mobilising the population, and that in the long term nationalism was a passing phase, which would not obstruct the building of the international proletarian state. Meanwhile the Soviet republics would be 'national in form, but socialist in content'.

The question remained of how that national form should be institutionalised. The Austro-Marxist theorists Otto Bauer and Karl Renner, who had ample experience of ethnic problems in the Habsburg Monarchy, considered that membership of a nationality and the associated civil rights should be determined by the language, culture and identity of the individual. Such a solution would have suited Russian realities quite well, with ethnic groups living closely intermingled among one another. Lenin and Stalin, however, took the view that ethnic rights and the 'national form' should be collective and territorial rather than individual and cultural, that is, that the Soviet Union should be made up of ethno-territorial entities, nominally self-governing, though in fact bound indissolubly to the rest of the Union by the Communist Party and by the economic planning system. They rejected the Austro-Marxist view, first, because it implied that nationalities were permanent formations, not destined to disappear in the course of social evolution, and, second, because it took for granted a concept of individual rights which Bolsheviks had always rejected as sham (Kappeler 1992: 300–2; Slezkine 1994). The trouble was, their concept shackled the Soviet Union with ethno-territorial boundaries which corresponded poorly to demographic realities.

To give real content to these initially rather arbitrarily created non-Russian republics the Bolsheviks pursued in them a policy of *korenizatsiia*, or indigenisation. Non-Russian languages were used for the liquidation of illiteracy, in the mass media, and as the vehicle of instruction in schools, so that, for instance, in the Ukrainian Republic all primary school children were taught in Ukrainian, including Russians, Greeks, Jews, etc. This policy was often resented by Russians and other non-Ukrainians, who objected to having their children taught in what they considered a 'farmyard dialect'. Those non-Russians who showed promise at school were favoured in higher education and then promoted to become officials and specialists in their own republic (Martin 2001).

More even than that: the Soviet state promoted what one might call 'ethnic engineering', constructing nations out of raw ethnic material. Ethnographers and linguists were sent out into the non-Russian regions to collect data on language, religion, customs, economy, tribal allegiances and other factors. They found evidence of the existence of some 190 'nationalities' on the basis of this data, and the fact was duly recorded in the first Soviet census of 1926. Their accumulated material was used to compile dictionaries and grammar books for hitherto non-literary languages, and also to draw the boundaries of new nominally autonomous ethnically named territories. The list was later pared down and reordered in hierarchical categories, so that by the census of 1939 only 99 nationalities were enumerated. The resultant complex hierarchy was tightly governed from Moscow, but still gave quite small and undeveloped ethnies the external symbols of statehood (Slezkine 1994; Tishkov 1997: 15–21, 131).

There was just one exception to the rule that national cultures should be fostered and nationalities taught self-government: that of course was the Russians. The early Bolsheviks were determined to make no concessions to Russians' national feelings, which they regarded as 'great-power chauvinism'. The new Soviet state, the Union of Soviet Socialist Republics, was no longer even called after Russia. It is true that a 'Russian Soviet Federative Socialist Republic' (RSFSR) was created within the Soviet Union – indeed it was the largest and most populous republic – but unlike the others it was not established on any ethno-territorial principle. It was simply the territory left over after all the other nationalities had received their republics. It included many non-Russians, some of whom were awarded 'autonomous' territories of their own within the RSFSR, and it did not include all Russians, many of whom lived in Ukraine, in Belorussia, in Kazakhstan (after that was finally established in 1936) and elsewhere. It was certainly not a Russian homeland: virtually all Russians, if asked, would have identified their country as the Soviet Union, not the Russian Republic (Kaiser 1994: Chapter 3).

Within the ethno-territorial republics, national minorities were allowed to set up their own smaller sub-units, wherever they lived in compact groups, right down to village soviet level. Thus, in the Ukrainian Soviet Socialist Republic, there were designated lower-level territories for Poles, Germans,

Jews, Greeks and Armenians and others – but not for Russians. If Russians had been given equivalent rights, then whole large cities, like Khar'kov and Donetsk, would have had to be handed over to them. The Russians were simply too numerous and historically too dominant for their own good (Martin 2001: 35–48).

Even more telling, although the Ukrainians, Georgians, Kazakhs, etc. all had their own Communist parties, there was no Russian Communist Party. Since the Communist Party was the focus of power and the bearer of the messianic vision which animated the new state, that lack was a peculiarly sensitive one. Russia had no effective autonomous political existence within the Soviet Union. The Russian-American scholar Yuri Slezkine has likened the situation to that of a communal apartment in which the various non-Russians – Ukrainians, Georgians, Kazakhs, etc. – each had their own room, with a door to shut against the world. The Russians lived in the kitchen, bathroom, corridor and hall: they ran the place and got in everyone else's way, but they had no room of their own (Slezkine 1994).

For Russians, the effects of these policies were deepened by the fact that the revolution had eliminated so much of their cultural and institutional memory. All the institutions of the old regime had been destroyed, including the police, local government, the financial and legal systems. Many Russian social and cultural institutions had either been destroyed with them or had been transformed beyond recognition: the mass media, the education system, the professions. The Orthodox Church, perhaps the Russian people's most distinctive cultural marker, had been disestablished, expropriated and deprived of its central institutions in 1918, while during the 1920s and 1930s nearly all monasteries and most parishes were closed. Monks and priests were exiled, arrested, not infrequently simply murdered. One crucial institution, the village commune, which survived and even flourished during the 1920s, was supplanted by a party-dominated caricature during the establishment of collective farms in the 1930s.

In spite of all the damage inflicted on Russian institutions and symbols, however, there was still something Russian about the Soviet Union, even in its first decade. First of all, socialism. Many Russian intellectuals had always believed that capitalism was alien to Russia, a foreign import imposed by the Tsarist regime. They argued that Russians were more attuned to collective production and burden-sharing rather than private property and individual economic enterprise. In particular, they held that in Russia the land belonged to no individual, but was a common resource, available to anyone who needed it and was prepared to cultivate it. The 1917 Revolution in the countryside suggested that peasants shared that viewpoint. Vera Tolz has called socialism 'the first nationalist ideology which ... could help Russia define a comfortable place and role in the world for itself' (Tolz 2001: 98).

Second, universalist messianism. It was no longer Orthodox Christianity which Russia's new rulers wished to disseminate, but socialism. As Lev Kopelev, staunch Communist of the 1920s and 1930s, commented: 'The party became our militant church, bringing all humanity eternal salvation, eternal peace and the bliss of an earthly paradise' (Kopelev 1978: 271). Aleksandr Blok (1999) actually combined the two forms of messianism in his 1918 poem *The Twelve*, which ends with the figure of Jesus Christ leading a detachment of Red Army soldiers on their mission:

> Thus they advance with state-bearing step,
> Behind them a hungry cur,
> Whilst at their head with bloody banner,
> Invisible in the snowstorm,
> Impervious to the bullets,
> At a gentle pace above the storm,
> In the pearly scattering of snow,
> With a wreath of white roses,
> Before them all walks Jesus Christ.

The Bolsheviks believed that Russian egalitarianism could and should be spread around the world, freeing the workers from exploitation in capitalist countries, and emancipating whole peoples from imperialist domination in the colonies. They saw themselves as ushering in a new era of history whose culmination would be the construction of an international proletarian state. This expectation was shared by many Communists *outside* the USSR as well. Eric Hobsbawm (2002: 137), British Marxist of the 1930s, recalls in his memoirs: 'Ours was a movement for *all* humanity and not for any particular section of it. It represented the ideal of transcending selfishness, individual and collective.' So Soviet Russian Marxists did not just *imagine* they were leading a worldwide movement: they really were. Their conviction was embodied in the Communist International, or Comintern.

As it happened, too, the idea of the 'single Soviet people' was more appealing to the Russians than to any other nationality, since they were the most numerous, and their language was the official language and that of inter-ethnic communication. They – together with Ukrainians and Belorussians – were the most geographically mobile ethnos, migrating into all parts of the Soviet Union in various capacities. From the 1920s through to the 1950s, despite *korenizatsiia*, they were often desperately needed as skilled workers, technical specialists and administrators, especially where new industry or mining was being developed. They concentrated mainly in the towns; by 1939, for example, they constituted 35.7 per cent of the urban population of Azerbaijan, in Uzbekistan 35 per cent and in Kazakhstan a huge 58.4 per cent. They usually expected the Russian language, not the local one, to be used in dealing with them (Kaiser 1994: 113–24; Kozlov 1998: 14–47). They often behaved in practice, then, as if the 'single Soviet people' were already a reality, and its native language were Russian.

Gradually, the Soviet state began to sanction and then to adopt these attitudes. During the 1930s and thereafter, a more explicitly Russian content was grafted on to Soviet state symbolism. As early as 1930 Stalin reminded the poet Demian Bednyi that one could not write off all Russians. 'In the past there existed two Russias, revolutionary Russia and anti-revolutionary Russia', while today's Russian working class, which had emerged from the former, was the most advanced in the world. In a later speech he added: 'In the past we had no fatherland and could not have one. But now that we have overthrown capitalism, now that power is with us, the people, now we have a fatherland, and we shall defend its independence' (Vdovin *et al.* 1998: 125–9). By the mid-1930s things had gone much further: it was not only revolutionary Russia or its working class which Stalin was rehabilitating, but the tsars who had created and defended the Russian Empire, and had thus made the Soviet Union possible. In the schools Russian victories were once again celebrated, while Ivan the Terrible, Peter the Great and Alexander I were extolled as great leaders. As before 1917 the history of the non-Russian peoples was presented in school textbooks as part of the history of the Russian people, which had the mission of integrating them into a new and higher supra-national community (Tolz 2001: 183–6).

The Soviet Army was also turning into something more like the old Russian imperial army. Exemptions from service for certain non-Russians were abolished, and territorial reserve units were phased out from 1935. These had been locally based units whose members did a few days' training every month, and attended a summer camp each year. In regions of mixed nationality the smaller formations had generally been ethnically homogeneous, with training and command in the appropriate language. These ethnic formations were abolished from 1938. Russian was made the language of command, and in July 1940 army tuition in Russian was provided for those recruits who did not speak it (Reese 1996: 26–7, 32–3, 39–40).

In the 1930s the Soviet leaders also tried to do something to make up for the absence of a social and cultural memory. They set about creating a specifically Soviet culture, not as a denial of the aristocratic and bourgeois cultures which had preceded it, but on the contrary as their culmination in a new mass culture. A Union of Soviet Writers was established to supersede the feuding literary 'groupuscules' of the 1920s and to propagate a single literary mainstream, largely traditional and realist in form, but also specifically 'socialist realist', depicting Soviet society in the light of its great future, its 'revolutionary development'. Several distinguished European writers were invited to the first congress – André Malraux, Louis Aragon, Theodor Plievier, Ernst Toller – to substantiate the claim that contemporary Russian literature was building on the best of European culture (Robin 1986).

Russian was projected as the senior literary culture among the Soviet peoples, patron and protector of the others, which were due to develop themselves following the Russian example. The Pushkin celebrations of 1937 (the 100th anniversary of the poet's death) exemplified this aspiration. His poem 'Exegi monumentum' was much quoted, for it contained the lines:

Stories of me will spread all over Great Rus, and my name will be
uttered in every one of its tongues, by the proud descendant of the Slavs
and by the Finn, by the now still savage Tunguz, and by the Kalmyk,
son of the steppes.

The implication was that Pushkin would be translated into all the Soviet
languages, and also that non-Russians would learn Russian, and thus
become full Soviet citizens, by reading him (Slater 1999; Petrone 2000:
126–31). He was also projected as the precursor of a truly international
culture in which Russia would take the lead: 'Pushkin long ago outstripped
the borders of his country. All progressive, cultured humanity bows before
his genius. Pushkin is deeply national. For that very reason he became an
international poet' (Slater 1999: 414–15).

In the other arts, a similar process went forward: warring factions were
closed down, a single consolidated association was created to resurrect traditional skills and train young practitioners in them, taking Russian as the
mainstream Soviet culture and then projecting it as the zenith of world
culture. In architecture one can still see the results today just by walking
around the centre of any ex-Soviet city, where the main buildings exhibit an
enlarged neo-classical style, with neo-baroque decorations, usually either the
hammer and sickle, friezes of soldiers or workers, or ethnic motifs from the
non-Russian republics (Croft Brumfield 1993: 485–92).

Because of inadequate resources, poorly qualified teachers, and pupils
often distracted by other matters, there was always a tendency for students,
schoolchildren and the general public to oversimplify what was put before
them, to ignore the subtleties and residual internationalist reservations of
the party line and to interpret it in terms of simple-minded Russian military
and statist patriotism. This tendency was naturally especially strong during
the Second World War. It represented not just a revival of pre-1917 patriotism, which, as we have seen, had been diffuse and uncertain except among
an educated elite, but a genuinely new popular Russian national feeling,
strongly felt for the first time by all social strata (Brandenberger 2002:
Chapters 6, 10, 14).

We should note, though, that this rehabilitation of Russia was entirely
imperial, not ethnic. It was, if you like, *neo-rossiiskii*, not *russkii*. Stalin
despised ethnic Russia and during the 1930s he had never ceased pursuing
policies aimed at the destruction of its two most important aspects: the
Orthodox Church and the village commune. Parishes were being closed,
church buildings sequestrated, priests were arrested and often were
murdered. Peasant households were being herded into collective farms and
the most productive farmers exiled to Siberia and Kazakhstan, where they
were unable to continue their traditional way of life. Russian literature, art
and music which did not conform to the new state-imposed canon was
suppressed or at best subject to unpredictable persecution. Nor was
korenizatsiia terminated.

During the Second World War, there was a change in this policy: concessions *were* made to ethnic Russia. Peasant households were granted greater freedom to decide what crops to grow and to trade them on the open market. The Orthodox Church was rescued on the brink of extinction and permitted to recreate its patriarchate (which had lapsed in 1925) and to reopen many of its closed parishes. Some Russian writers banned throughout the 1930s were again allowed to publish their work. But these concessions were purely instrumental: they were calculated to help the Soviet Union win the war against Nazi Germany. To this end, too, most of the internationalist features of Soviet culture were abandoned or severely downgraded, giving way to unyielding nationalism. The war was presented as being fought not between workers and capitalists, but between Russians and Germans: that was the way nearly all Soviet citizens saw it. The Communist International was abolished and the slogan 'Workers of the world unite!' was replaced by 'Death to the German occupiers!' (Kopelev 1978: 221; Hosking 2002).

The new nationalist propaganda was not, however, accompanied by any special concern for the Russians as a people, or indeed for any other Soviet ethnos. Red Army soldiers captured by the enemy were confined in POW camps where the Germans made little attempt to keep them alive. The Soviet government, when approached by the International Red Cross about possible help for them, refused to cooperate, indicating that it considered them traitors (Kromiadi 1953: 194; Konasov and Tereshchuk 1996). When Russians or other Soviet citizens who had lived on occupied territory returned to the Soviet Union, they had to undergo a humiliating political investigation before they could be allowed to return to their normal life. It was carried out in filtration centres which differed little from hard-regime labour camps, and it sometimes ended with their arrest or exile (Naumov 1996). These practices suggested that the regime distrusted all its peoples, Russians as much as the others.

The Russians' claim to be, as it were, a nation above nations, peacefully and benignly integrating other ethnic groups into a harmonious multi-national state, was starkly refuted by the brutal deportation of hundreds of thousands of Estonians, Latvians, Lithuanians, Belorussians, Ukrainians and Moldavians, when those republics were annexed in 1939–40, and even more by the deportation of whole ethnies from the north Caucasus in 1944–5. Of course these deportations were implemented not by Russians alone, but the peoples affected made no such subtle distinctions: they regarded the attempted genocide against them as the work of Russians, Communists and the Soviet state, and in consequence they loathed all three, an attitude which persisted till the very end of the Soviet Union, and helped to bring it about (Bugai 1990; Gross 2002).

From the 1950s to the 1970s national identity was becoming more confidently and consistently articulated in the non-Russian ethno-territorial republics. The long-term effects of *korenizatsiia* plus urbanisation and mass education had brought into the cities of many republics a confident and quite well-educated class of young people of local nationality, well equipped to move into the top jobs, to compete for elite housing and other privileges and to assert their own view of the world in the competing symbolic discourses of Soviet politics. In the republican academies and universities, research into national history, culture, folklore and traditions became more popular and sometimes resulted in publications which were condemned by ideological watchdogs for 'bourgeois nationalism'. By the 1970s linguistic assimilation had begun to slow: the use of Russian as a second language continued to grow, but attachment to the local national language for everyday purposes remained strong in most republics. In all of them except Ukraine and Belorussia more than 90 per cent of the titular nation regarded their own language as native. Non-Russian republican elites were assisting this sense of national distinctiveness by competing to claim a larger share of all-Union economic resources for their own territory. There was evidence too that the burgeoning underground economy was being run by local people under the protection of those elites. Nepotism and corruption figured prominently among the charges levelled at republican leaders purged during the 1960s and early 1970s in Ukraine, Georgia, Kazakhstan, Latvia and Azerbaidzhan (Rakowska-Harmstone 1974).

This local national assertiveness did not necessarily mean that Russians were hated. In most republics this was not the case, and Russians on the whole continued to behave without racial prejudice towards other Soviet ethnic groups. The Baltic republics, western Ukraine and the north Caucasus constituted an exception, as we have seen above. There Russians were hated by most of the population as 'occupiers'. In Latvia and Estonia the feeling was intensified by the fear that Russians (or Slavs) were gradually swamping them: already by 1970 there were fewer Letts than Russians in the Latvian capital, Riga, and by 1979 Estonians formed only half the population of their capital city, Tallinn. The situation was even worse in other Estonian towns, and by 1989 Russians formed 59 per cent of the republic's urban population (Misiunas and Taagepera 1993: 214–18; Kozlov 1998). In the north Caucasus the legacy of bitterness left by the deportations had been exacerbated by conflict over places of settlement since the return of the deported nationalities after 1957 (Bugai and Mikhailov 2000).

Even where they were regarded without open hostility, however, Russians could no longer take for granted that their superior culture and education gave them an automatic advantage in the competition for administrative and professional jobs, and with them the superior housing and other privileges reserved for the elite. This deterioration in Russians' life-chances did not lead before the late 1980s to appreciable emigration from the non-Russian republics. On the other hand, net immigration from the European parts of the USSR to Central Asia and the Caucasus was ceasing by the late 1960s, and because of the slower growth rate of the Russians (and Slavs generally), their proportion of the population in those regions was declining (Table 8.1).

Table 8.1   Russians in Union Republics, 1959–89 (in 000s, with percentage of total republican population)

	1959		1970		1979		1989	
	Total	Urban	Total	Urban	Total	Urban	Total	Urban
Georgia	403	327	397	328	372	n/a	341	264
	10.1%	19.1%	8.5%	14.6%	7.4%		6.3%	8.7%
Armenia	56	40	66	52	70	n/a	52	44
	3.2%	4.5%	2.9%	3.8%	2.3%		1.6%	1.5%
Azerbaijan	501	439	510	470	475	n/a	392	372
	13.6%	25%	10%	18.3%	7.5%		5.6%	9.8%
Kazakhstan	3974	2343	5522	3818	5991	n/a	6228	4823
	42.7%	59%	42.4%	59.3%	40.8%		37.7%	50.1%
Turkmeniia	263	248	313	300	349	n/a	334	326
	17.3%	34.9%	14.5%	29%	12.5%		9.5%	20.3%
Uzbekistan	1091	913	1474	1312	1666	n/a	1653	1567
	13.4%	33.5%	12.5%	30.6%	10.8%		8.3%	19.3%
Tajikistan	263	228	344	323	395	n/a	388	365
	13.3%	35.3%	11.9%	30%	10.4%		9.6%	21.9%
Kirgiziia	624	360	856	564	912	n/a	917	641
	30.2%	51.7%	29.2%	51.4%	25.7%		21.4%	39.1%

Note: Percentage of total republican population shown.

Source: Kozlov (1998: 21–3)

The prospect of the 'single Soviet people' was receding, not getting nearer (Erofeeva 2001).

By the 1970s evidence was also beginning to emerge that in some respects the Soviet Union was having a damaging effect on Russians as a people. The population of the three Slavic peoples was experiencing a natural growth slower than that of any other republics. This was partly because of continued out-migration to other republics, but mainly because their birth rate was lower than anywhere else except Latvia and Estonia. That low birth rate was in its turn partly explained by a high divorce rate and also by the immigration of Slavs into towns, and especially into very large towns. From the 1940s to the 1960s Russian villages, notably in the non-Black Earth regions, saw many of their inhabitants depart, particularly the young, the men and the better qualified. The authoritarian collective farm system offered the enterprising and skilled few opportunities for enrichment or self-development, while the introduction of facilities now considered as essentials, like electricity and tele-phones, was proceeding very slowly. The Russian countryside had become the preserve of women, the unskilled and old people, no longer the guarantor of high population growth, as it had been throughout the nineteenth century and up to 1930 or so (Denisova 1996).

Quite a few villages had become totally depopulated. In 1984 Viktor Petrovich Beliaev, after a lifelong career in Moscow, visited the village in Kostroma oblast which he had left fifty years earlier as a thriving community:

> There were eight houses still standing. They were quite robust and were not boarded up, as the owners usually do on taking their departure. They had simply been abandoned. The doors were not locked, and some of them stood wide open. On the porch of the house nearest to the river stood a samovar ... The village streets were covered in grass, and in the garden plots nettles and burdocks were growing profusely. The field which the collective farmers had cleared and sown with oats in 1928 was now overgrown with trees and bushes. The magnificent meadows, where four villages had mown hay for the whole year, had now become swampy and choked with sedge.
>
> (Beliaev 1998)[1]

Meanwhile, in the towns, communal apartments and the high employment rate of women discouraged childbirth. Few married couples had the space, the service facilities or the time left over from work and commuting to devote to bringing up a family (Seniavskii 1995: 166–81). Meanwhile in the Caucasus and (especially) Central Asia, where more people stayed in the villages, the birth rate remained high (Perevedentsev 1972: 8; 1989). The long-term result was foreseeable: the Russians would soon fall below half the Soviet population, and long before that they would lose their predominance in the Soviet Army.

The increased influx of Central Asian and Caucasian troops into the army aggravated the problem of *dedovshchina*, which was already serious enough without it. *Dedovshchina* was the practice according to which second and third year conscripts would co-opt new recruits as personal servants, to clean their weapons and uniforms and keep the barracks tidy. To humiliate them, the *stariki*, or senior soldiers, would give their 'fags' obscene nicknames, beat them and even rape them. Because many of the Central Asian and Caucasian, as well as the Baltic, recruits could not speak Russian, the treatment meted out to them was especially brutal. In this way the Soviet Army, which had once been held up as a model of inter-ethnic harmony, was turning into the opposite, a nursery of ethnic hatred (Odom 1998: 286–9).

The result was that some Russians began to question whether the USSR was really so good for Russia as a nation, and whether Russians might not do better to cultivate their own national health rather than promote internationalism. The first thinker to articulate this line unambiguously was Aleksandr Solzhenitsyn (2001: 60–94). In his 'Letter to the Soviet Leaders' of 1973 (not of course published in the Soviet media), he accused his addressees of undermining Russia for the sake of international revolution. Through over-centralised political control, misplaced gigantism in the military–industrial complex and insistence on unproductive collective agriculture, they had enfeebled the economy, disfigured Russia's cities, distorted the education system, suppressed the national culture, driven men to alcoholism and imposed on women a demeaning and exhausting way of life which reduced their fertility. He accused the Communist leaders of being mainly responsible for the loss of 66 million lives in the civil upheavals of the twentieth century. Anticipating a coming war with China, he warned them that they would soon need the convinced patriotism of the Russian people, and for its sake would have to ditch their ideology and the concomitant international burdens, which were incompatible with patriotism. 'By giving up the Ideology, your party would merely be renouncing impractical dreams of world domination, which we do not need, and would be fulfilling national obligations: to save us from war with China and from technological disaster' (Solzhenitsyn 2001: 91).

No other writer articulated as unambiguously as Solzhenitsyn the incompatibility of Russian national life and Communist Party domination, but some officially published literary journals began to express alarm at decline of the Russian way of life. As so often in Russia, this alarm was most clearly expressed in fiction. From the mid-1960s to the mid-1980s, novels published by so-called 'village prose' writers were at the centre of literary discussion. Writers such as Vasilii Belov, Sergei Zalygin, Fedor Abramov, Boris Mozhaev and Valentin Rasputin depicted the Russian village as they had known it in their own lifetimes, from the flourishing and diverse communities of the 1920s right through to the devastated and demoralised villages of the 1980s. Their work was not the heralding of a great future, but a lament for the past. They showed village people in the grip of an alien bureaucracy and an encroaching urban civilisation, losing their community traditions and even their agricultural skills. The principal characters in their novels derived their inspiration not from any vision of the future, but from ordeals and hard work shared together in the past. Especially striking for some readers was the relatively candid description of the disruption caused by collectivisation and dekulakisation in the early 1930s, a much franker account than Soviet historians were allowing themselves at the time (Parthé 1992; Brudny 1998; Hosking 2001).

Village prose was widely read, because it reflected what might be called the 'master narrative' in the biography of many Russian townsfolk. Millions of them had been born and brought up in the village, but had left it with relief to secure an education or a career in the city. As a result, the village was dying, and many of them looked back at their own lives with unease and even guilt. As Sergei Zalygin commented:

> I feel that the roots of my nation are indeed in the village, in the ploughed field, in daily bread. Furthermore, it seems that our genera-tion [he was born in 1913] will have been the last to see with its own eyes the 1000-year old [peasant] way of life, in which each of us grew up. If we do not tell about it and about its radical alteration in a short period of time, who will?
>
> (Brudny 1998: 77)

The evils disclosed by the 'village prose' writers did not provoke anything like a national liberation movement. Russians were still accustomed to regard the Soviet Union as their homeland, and even those who bitterly criticised the oppressive Communist regime did not intend to break it up. When by the late 1980s it became possible to vent their grievances openly and to mobilise politically, they agitated over issues such as freedom of speech, the dangers of nuclear power and the degradation of the environ-ment. They initially assumed that the solutions they envisaged would apply to the Soviet Union as a whole. For political reasons, though, Russian liberals and anti-Communists soon found themselves in alliance with non-Russian national liberation movements: after all, they shared a common enemy, the oppressive, over-centralised Soviet state and Communist Party. But the non-Russians started out from the opposite assumption: that seces-sion from the Soviet Union was a prerequisite for dealing with any problems (Beissinger 2002).

Quite rapidly Russian politicians began to adopt a similar anti-centralist, ethnically based approach. Prior to 1990 there is little evidence that Boris Yeltsin regarded the status of the Russian Republic as a serious issue, but he took it up successfully in the soviet elections in March that year and by June the RSFSR Supreme Soviet had declared sovereignty. The Russian public appeared to support them: by September an opinion poll showed that 48 per cent of the RSFSR population thought their republic should have the right to revoke decisions of the Soviet government on their own territory, while only 22 per cent disagreed (ibid.: 409–12).

Different Russians had different reasons for their opinion, however. For liberals, thwarting oppressive rule and carrying out reform remained the main motive. Paradoxically, some of their opponents now also wanted to strengthen Russia, mainly in order to have a secure base from which to attack the current Soviet leader, Gorbachev, whose policies they thought were in danger of destroying the Soviet Union. It was one of the village prose writers, Valentin Rasputin, who in May 1989 first raised the possibility that Russia might secede from the Soviet Union. He did so, not as a serious proposal, but as a rhetorical gesture, to emphasise that Russians now felt exploited and discriminated against by non-Russians, especially in the Caucasus and Baltic.[2] However, the logic of his witticism was compelling, and it led in 1990, for the first time, to the formation of a Russian Communist Party as a distinct entity within the all-Union party. Its ideologues warned that the imperialists were intriguing to tear the Soviet Union apart, separating Russia from its natural partners, and in particular that the US pro-Israeli lobby aimed to detach the Muslim peoples from the USSR and establish a '"green empire", whose northern border has already been drawn along the Urals and the river Volga' (Prokhanov, quoted in Dunlop 1993: 174).

In that way the scene was set for the putsch of August 1991, when for three days a so-called Emergency Committee seized power in Moscow. Their action precipitated a showdown, not, as might have been expected, between Communists and anti-Communists, but between the Soviet Union and Russia. The Emergency Committee accused 'extremist forces' of having 'adopted a course towards the liquidation of the Soviet Union, the collapse of the state and the seizure of power at any price'. Yeltsin, on the other hand, having recently become the legitimately elected Russian head of state, called on the population to 'unswervingly follow the constitutional Laws and Decrees of the President of the RSFSR' (Dunlop 1993: 214).

Russia won, at least in appearance. Only, of course, at the same time, Russians found that they had lost a major proportion of what they had always considered their homeland. The other Union Republics declared their independence, some of them with great rejoicing as the culmination of their national liberation, others with more reluctance. The Russians were left with their residual territory, and with a great many of their co-nationals living 'abroad', having 'emigrated' without moving a single step. The Russians were the victims of their own greatest triumph.

Strangely, their political behaviour at this stage was rather similar to that of the English within the United Kingdom. Consider the following judgement from a recent work on British national identity: 'The problems which the English faced when their partners became unhappy with the arrangement arose not from the fact that they had forgotten how to be English, but that they had forgotten how to articulate their national identity politically' (Weight 2002: 10). Russians had the same problem, and, when they were suddenly compelled to articulate their national identity politically, they were unable to avoid doing so in such a way that they destroyed the country they had always considered their homeland, the Soviet Union (Zhirinovsky 1996).

All in all, the Russians offer one of the most extreme examples of a people whose national identity has been vested almost entirely in their state rather than in the customs and traditions we normally associate with ethnicity. In part, this has been a result of their geo-political situation on the vast north Eurasian plains, where a strong state was needed to guarantee any form of stable existence and where the intermingling of peoples made peaceful inter-ethnic relations a practical necessity. For that reason, the term 'ethnos' is actually rather difficult to apply to them. One might almost say that their 'dominance' has been purchased at the cost of their 'ethnicity'.

Acknowledgements

The research for this chapter was undertaken while I was the holder of a Leverhulme Personal Research Chair. I am most grateful to the Leverhulme Trust for their support.

Notes

© Geoffrey Hosking

1   Rossiiskaia biblioteka-fond zarubezh'ia, archive fund R-385, V.P. Beliaev, *Svidetel'stvuiu o vremeni*, Moscow, 1998, list 3.
2   *Pervyi s"ezd narodnykh deputatov SSSR: stenograficheskii otchet*, Moscow: Politizdat, 1989, vol. 2, 458–9.

References

Beissinger, M. (2002) *Nationalist Mobilization and the Collapse of the Soviet State*, Cambridge: Cambridge University Press.
Blok, A. (1962) 'Intelligentsiia i revoliutsiia', in A. Blok, *Sobranie sochinenii*, Moscow/Leningrad: Gosudarstvennoe izdatel'stvo khudozhestvennoi literatury 6(9).
—— (1999) *Polnoe sobranie sochinenii i pisem*, vol. 5, Moscow: Nauka.
Brandenberger, D. (2002) *National Bolshevism: Stalinist Mass Culture and the Forma-tion of Modern Russian National Identity, 1931–1956*, Cambridge, MA: Harvard University Press.
Brudny, Y.M. (1998) *Reinventing Russia: Russian Nationalism and the Soviet State, 1953–1991*, Cambridge, MA: Harvard University Press.
Bugai, N.F. (1990) *Tak eto bylo: natsional'nye repressii v SSSR*, Moscow: Nauka.
Bugai, N.F. and Mikhailov, V.A. (eds) (2000) *Reabilitatsiia narodov Rossii*, Moscow: INSAN.
Croft Brumfield, W. (1993) *A History of Russian Architecture*, Cambridge: Cambridge University Press.
Denisova, L.N. (1996) *Ischezaiushchaia derevnia Rossii: nechernozem'e v 1960–80ye gody*, Moscow: Institut Rossiiskoi Istorii RAN.

Dixon, S. (1996) 'Russia and the Russians', in Graham Smith (ed.) *The Nationalities Question in the Post-Soviet States*, 2nd edn, London: Longman.

Dunlop, J. (1993) *The Rise of Russia and the Fall of the Soviet Union*, Princeton, NJ: Princeton University Press.

Emmons, T. (ed.) (1988) *Time of Troubles: The Diary of Iurii Vladimirovich Got'e*, Princeton, NJ: Princeton University Press.

Erofeeva, I. (2001) 'Slavianskoe naselenie Vostochnogo Kazakhstana v xviii–xx vekakh: migratsionnoe dvizhenie, stadii sotsiokul'turnoi evoliutsii, problemy reemigratsii', in *Etnicheskii natsionalizm i gosudarstvennoe stroitel'stvo*, Moscow: IV RAN – Natalis, pp. 358–60.

Fennell, J. (ed.) (1964) *Pushkin*, Harmondsworth: Penguin.

Gross, J.T. (2002) *Revolution from Abroad: The Soviet Conquest of Poland's Western Ukraine and Western Belorussia*, 2nd edn, Princeton, NJ: Princeton University Press.

Hobsbawm, E. (2002) *Interesting Times: A Twentieth-Century Life*, London: Allen Lane.

Hosking, G. (1980) *Beyond Socialist Realism: Soviet Fiction since Ivan Denisovich*, London: Granada.

—— (1997) *Russia: People and Empire, 1552–1917*, London: HarperCollins.

—— (2001) *Russia and the Russians*, Cambridge, MA: Harvard University Press.

—— (2002) 'The Second World War and Russian national consciousness', *Past and Present*, 175: 162–87.

Kaiser, R.J. (1994) *The Geography of Nationalism in Russia and the USSR*, Princeton, NJ: Princeton University Press.

Kappeler, A. (1992) *Russland als Vielvölkerreich: Entstehung, Geschichte, Zerfall*, Munich: Verlag C.H. Beck.

Konasov, V.B. and Tereshchuk, A.V. (1996) 'K istorii sovetskikh i nemetskikh voennoplennykh (1941–3)', *Novaia i noveishaia istoriia*, 5: 54–72.

Kopelev, L. (1978) *I sotvoril sebe kumira*, Ann Arbor, MI: Ardis.

Kozlov, V.I. (1998) 'Russkie v novom zarubezh'e (statistiko-geograficheskii obzor)', in *Russkie v sovremennom mire*, Moscow: Institut etnologii i antropologii, 17: 19.

Kromiadi, K. (1953) 'Sovetskie voennoplennye v Germanii v 1941g', *Novyi zhurnal*, 32: 194.

Martin, T. (2001) *The Affirmative Action Empire: Nations and Nationalism in the Soviet Union, 1923–1939*, Ithaca, NY: Cornell University Press.

Misiunas, R.J. and Taagepera, R. (1993) *The Baltic States: Years of Dependence, 1940–1990*, London: Hurst.

Naumov, V.P. (1996) 'Sud'ba voennoplennykh i deportirovannykh grazhdan SSSR: materialy kommissii o reabilitatsii zhertv politicheskikh repressii', *Novaia i noveishaia istoriia*, 2: 91–112.

Odom, W.E. (1998) *The Collapse of the Soviet Military*, New Haven, CT: Yale University Press.

Parthé, K. (1992) *Russian Village Prose: The Radiant Past*, Princeton, NJ: Princeton University Press.

Perevedentsev, V.I. (1972) *Naselenie SSSR: vchera, segodnia, zavtra*, Moscow: Mysl' 9.

—— (1989) *Kakie my? Skol'ko nas?* Moscow: Mysl'.

Pervyi s"ezd narodnykh deputatov SSSR: stenograficheskii otchet (1989) vol. 2, pp. 458–9, Moscow: Politizdat.

Petrone, K. (2000) *Life Has Become More Joyous, Comrades: Celebrations in the Time of Stalin*, Bloomington: Indiana University Press.

Rakowska-Harmstone, T. (1974) 'The dialectics of nationalism in the USSR', *Problems of Communism*, 23(3): 1–22.

Reese, R.R. (1996) *Stalin's Reluctant Soldiers: A Social History of the Red Army, 1924–1941*, Lawrence, KS: University of Kansas Press.

Robin, R. ([1986] 1992) *Socialist Realism: An Impossible Aesthetic* (trans. C. Porter from *Le Réalisme socialiste: une esthétique impossible*), Stanford, CA: Stanford University Press.

Rogger, H. (1986) *Jewish Policies and Right-Wing Politics in Imperial Russia*, Berkeley, CA: University of California Press.

Seniavskii, A.S. (1995) *Rossiiskii gorod v 1960–80ye gody*, Moscow: Institut Rossiiskoi Istorii RAN.

Slater, W. (1999) 'The patriots' Pushkin', *Slavic Review*, 58: 407–27.

Slezkine, Y. (1994) 'The USSR as communal apartment, or how a socialist state promoted ethnic particularism', *Slavic Review*, 53(2): 414–52.

Solov'ev, S.M. (1960) *Istoriia Rossii s drevneishikh vremen*, book 2, Moscow: Izdatel'stvo Sotsio-ekonomicheskoi Literatury.

Solzhenitsyn, A. (2001) *Sobranie sochinenii*, vol. 7, Moscow: Terra – knizhnyi klub.

Tishkov, V. (1997) *Ethnicity, Nationalism and Conflict in and after the Soviet Union: The Mind Aflame*, London: Sage.

Tolz, V. (2001) *Russia: Inventing the Nation*, London: Arnold.

Vdovin, A.I., Zorin, V.Iu. and Nikonov, A.V. (1998) *Russkii narod v natsional'noi politike: xx vek*, Moscow: Russkii Mir.

Vitte, S.Iu. (1960) *Vospominaniia*, vol. 3, Moscow: Izdatel'stvo Sotsio-Ekonomicheskoi Literatury.

Weight, R. (2002) *Patriots: National Identity in Britain, 1940–2000*, London: Macmillan.

Zhirinovsky, V. (1996) *My Struggle: The Explosive Views of Russia's Most Controversial Political Figure*, New York: Barricade Books.

Part III
Dominant ethnicity resurgent

9 Citizenship, immigration and ethnic hegemony in Japan

Keiko Yamanaka

Introduction

The rapid economic reconstruction of Western Europe in the 1950s and 1960s is to a significant extent attributable to the massive deployment of foreign labour in heavy manufacturing industries. Governments in this region commonly adopted policies permitting guest workers to reunite with their families in the host society. As a result, by the 1980s these societies had witnessed permanent settlement of large numbers of immigrants and the resultant growth of diverse ethnic communities within their territories. In an effort to incorporate these non-citizen populations, including refugees and asylum seekers, into their legal and political structures, the governments have gradually expanded the social, economic and political rights available to their non-citizen, permanent residents. Consequently, by the 1990s citizenship has ceased to be a factor determining eligibility for most public services, economic activities and political participation at local levels. In post-national Western Europe, therefore, rights of immigrants have been increasingly determined by residence rather than citizenship (Soysal 1994).[1]

In a similar vein, since the 1960s the large numbers of foreigners working in the manufacturing and construction industries in Asia's newly industrialised countries/economies, such as Singapore, Malaysia and Hong Kong, have contributed greatly to their rapid economic development (e.g. *ASEAN Economic Bulletin* 1995). By the 1990s Japan, Korea and Taiwan had imported foreign labour in order to boost their increasingly labour-short industries. With more than five million migrant workers, East and Southeast Asia thus became one of the world's most active sites of international migration (Yamanaka 1999). In sharp contrast to Western Europe, however, Asian host governments have commonly adopted policies that rotate a pool of temporary workers with little concern for their labour, human and citizenship rights (Battistella 2002). Migration scholars have explained that many Asian governments still engage in the process of post-colonial nation-state building as a result of which they tend to construct and maintain sharp boundaries between citizens and non-citizens (Soysal 1994: 150; Castles and Davidson 2000). Some Asian states emphasise 'Asian values' in order to uphold collective values while dismissing individual and human rights as 'Western values' (Bauer and Bell 1999).

Japan occupies a unique position between post-national Europe and post-colonial Asia regarding its immigration policy and citizenship rights for migrant workers. The country stands out, on the one hand, as the only Asian coloniser in the pre-World War II period and 'the only longstanding Asian democracy' in the post-World War II period (Castles and Davidson 2000: 196). Having achieved rapid economic reconstruction and development, post-war Japan resembles Western Europe in its high technological and living standards, large middle-class population and solid nation-state foundation. On the other hand, unlike its European counterparts, Japan has adopted a policy to receive only skilled foreigners, while unofficially admitting more than half a million *de facto* guest workers (as discussed below). Because they lack citizenship, most of these newcomers are denied rights to family reunification and access to public services. In its exclusive policy on immigration and citizenship, Japan resembles its Asian post-colonial neighbours. The contradiction between Japan's advanced capitalism and its obsolete immigration policies requires explanation.

In this chapter, I focus on ethno-historical forces as a possible explanation for Japan's efforts to maintain sharp boundaries between citizens and non-citizens despite the fact that its economy benefits greatly from foreign workers. In addition to these newcomers, like all nation-states, Japan contains within its population a number of long-term and indigenous ethnic minorities with distinct histories and cultures. This is a result of nation-building efforts since the 1860s that forced ethnic minorities – Koreans, Chinese, Ainu, Okinawans, *Burakumin* and others – to assimilate into the national culture and polity dominated by the majority Japanese population who comprise the country's long-established *ethnie*, to use Anthony Smith's term. According to him, an *ethnie* is defined as 'a named unit of population with myths of common ancestry, shared memories and culture, an association with a homeland and sentiments of "social solidarity"' (Smith 1999: 191).[2]

By tracing the history of nation building, ethnic hegemony and what I term 'disposable citizenship' during the two distinct periods before and after World War II, I investigate how the ethnic nationalism that defines Japan as an ethnically homogeneous nation has contributed to the country's political and economic development in times of war and peace. The analysis demonstrates a close association between definitions of who belongs to the *ethnie* and who belongs to the nation and territory. These definitions are alterable, however, as national goals and boundaries shift with the rapid changes in international politics and economy. In the last section of the chapter, therefore, I discuss recent challenges to the Japanese myth of ethnic homogeneity in the age of global capitalism and migration, based on my ten years of research on a large influx of 'Third World' immigrant workers in Hamamatsu City, Shizuoka Prefecture.

Inclusive citizenship in a multi-ethnic empire: 1868–1945

'Modern Japan was characterized by (multiethnic) imperialism, not (monoethnic) nationalism' (Lie 2001: 112). By the turn of the twentieth century, as a result of victory in two successive wars Japan had achieved two external colonies – Taiwan in 1895 and Korea in 1910 – outside of its traditional territory composed of its four major islands plus the Ryukyu (now Okinawa Islands). From this period until the end of World War II, Japan was a multiethnic empire and home to diverse ethnic minorities who altogether accounted for 30 per cent of the then total 100 million people in the territory ruled by Japan (Oguma 1995: 4). How to manage and control this unprecedented ethnic diversity was therefore a topic intensely debated by intellectuals and political leaders throughout the imperial period (Oguma 1995, 1998). From the 1868 *Meiji* Restoration until the territorial expansion of 1910, the country had already been undergoing rapid social, economic and political changes, transforming itself from an agrarian feudal society into a modern industrial nation. During these four decades, national leaders made concerted efforts to bring together the then loosely connected population to participate in the national project of constructing a new modern nation and economy (Gellner 1983). Europe and the United States had provided them with advanced technologies and models of judicial and political institutions. These were adopted by Japanese in a way that enabled them to fit into their own traditional cultural milieu and indigenous knowledge system. Under constant threat from Western colonialism, throughout this period the national leaders also made every attempt to raise educational standards, promote industrialisation, facilitate transportation and communication, strengthen military power and uplift patriotic ideology.

In the early stage of forging the new nation, the *Meiji* government engaged in what Smith (1999: 194) calls a process of 'vernacular mobilisation' in order to unite the population under a single national identity. The new state required grassroots support for its nation-building efforts. Thus began the political process of inventing spiritual leadership, often by returning to the roots of the ethnic community. In its first step, the *Meiji* state revived the ancient emperor system, replacing the feudal *Shogunate* system by designating the emperor as the divine ruler and the rest as his subjects.[3] The *Meiji* Constitution (promulgated in 1899) invested sovereignty in the emperor whose power was based on ancient myths about the origins of the nation and the unbroken line of emperors (Brownlee 1997: 7). In the second step, the government institutionalised belief in the myths of such ancestors and their pristine past through education, religion and other means of persuasion. *Shinto* (literally the way of deities) was regarded as the national religion because of its close association with the imperial household. Over many years, *Shinto* priests and scholars created a series of 'ancient' rituals, ceremonies and pageants engaged in by the emperor himself (Fujitani 1996). Historians studied the myths, legends and folklore in search of 'truths' of the imperial tradition (Brownlee 1997). Schoolchildren learned them in textbooks that began with the genesis of Japan by many deities in the ancient period. Those who voiced doubts or criticisms of these myths were regarded by the state as subversive traitors.

Such myths, legends and folklore originated long before any kind of nation was founded. In the 710s, at the dawn of the *Nara* Period (710–93), they were compiled into two volumes as the nation's first histories, *Kojiki* (Record of Ancient Matters, 712) and *Nihon Shoki* (Chronicles of Japan, 720). The two books, written in Chinese characters, tell stories of nation-building by a deity couple, *Izanagi* and *Izanami*, and their numerous descendants (Matsumae 1974; Tooyama 2001). Especially important among them was the Sun Goddess *Amaterasu*, who sent her Heavenly Grandchild down from the Plain of High Heaven to the Central Land of Reed Plains (Japan). It was believed that some generations after the descent of the Heavenly Grandchild, the first human emperor, *Jinmu* (divine warrior), conquered many clans and groups that had resisted his reign. He then unified the nation and declared his ascension to the imperial throne in Kashihara, near Nara, in 660 BC (Brownlee 1997: 2–7). In this foundation myth, the divine emperor and his descendants had been benevolent rulers of their subjects, including those they had conquered. Under the universal and fatherly love of the emperors, all people, regardless of their origins, were treated impartially as being the emperors' children. As such, they were able to assimilate easily into Japanese society and culture. The mythical Japan thus founded comprised not only Japanese – the dominant majority – but also large numbers of people of diverse and mixed ancestry, therefore constituting a multi-ethnic and cosmopolitan nation (Oguma 1995).

Until 1945, historians commonly adopted a view, based on these ancient myths, that Japanese were people of hybrid or mixed ethnicity whose ancestors had migrated from various parts of East and South-east Asia in the pre-historic period. Since the 1910s this view accommodated conveniently to the fact that Japan was a multi-ethnic empire comprising diverse ethnic groups with distinct histories and cultures. The fictitious blood-ties among the emperor's subjects provided a link to establish brotherhood between Japanese and non-Japanese groups (Oguma 1995). In this 'imagined' family state, the emperor was the household head, the majority Japanese were the first son, and colonial nationals were their 'younger' brothers. Furthermore, the alleged superiority of Japanese culture provided the state with the justification to force its assimilation policies upon non-Japanese so that they would improve their 'inferior' cultures. At the outset of the rapid industrialisation and territorial expansion in the 1910s and 1920s, the ideology of a family state thus contributed significantly to the development of the concept of a Greater East Asian Co-Prosperity Sphere – a racialised 'imagined community' (Anderson 1983) dominated by Japan – in the Far East on the basis of 'shared' ancestry, myths and culture (Armstrong 1989; Weiner 1994). The ideology of social homogeneity also helped the state and the national majority to ignore the reality of the Japanese Empire in which the 100 million population was deeply divided according to ethnicity, class, region, history and gender.

A contradiction between the state goal and the real life of different peoples was apparent in ethnic and class relations. Despite the official rhetoric of equality among different groups, throughout the imperial period the state adopted a policy of 'separate but equal', granting colonial subjects fewer rights than Japanese. Bureaucrats in an administrative office recorded on the household registration card ethnic Japanese as *Naichijin* (inner territory people) and others as *Gaichijin* (outer territory people). Citizenship rights were weighted accordingly. Although Koreans were Japanese nationals, the Governor-General of Korea controlled migration of Koreans to and from the inner territory (Japan), whereas citizens of Japanese origin were not under such control (Yamawaki 2000: 39). In the Korean Peninsula, Koreans did not have suffrage rights, whereas those in the inner territory did and even had the right to be elected representatives.[4] In the 1920s and 1930s, however, most Koreans in Japan were unskilled labourers who had migrated in search of economic opportunities not available in their homeland now under foreign rule. By 1925, 150,000 Korean men and women worked in jobs shunned by Japanese in such labour-intensive and often dangerous industries as mining, construction, arms and other manufacturing. This number had risen dramatically to 800,000 by 1937, the year Japan declared war on China. Poor and uneducated, the migrant workers in tattered clothes, living in filthy tenements, were an easy scapegoat for the fears and anxieties widespread among members of the Japanese working class (Weiner 1994)[5] At the height of the Pacific War (1942–5), more than 2 million Korean Japanese nationals became an important source of conscripted, and later forced, labour working under extremely harsh and brutal conditions (ibid.).

Exclusive citizenship in a mono-ethnic nation, 1945–89

> In prewar Japan, everyone said that Yamato Japanese people are hybrid people (*zasshu minzoku*), and mixed people (*kongo minzoku*) ... But, rather strangely, in the postwar period, beginning with progressive intellectuals, people began to say that Japan is monoethnic. There is no basis for this.
>
> (Kamishima, cited by Lie 2001: 137)

This statement by the political scientist Jiro Kamishima, who lived in both pre- and post-war Japan, points to the complete reversal in intellectual discourse and public views about the ethnic composition of the Japanese population from pre- to post-war periods. This can be partly explained by the fact that Japan had lost colonies as a result of defeat in World War II and the subsequent denationalisation of former colonial residents in the country. The discursive shift from multi-ethnicism to mono-ethnicism was also closely related to ethnic and cultural nationalism that arose between the late 1940s and 1950s as part of national efforts to rebuild the nation as a peaceful, democratic country with a prosperous economy. By the late 1960s, when Japan was acclaimed as the country with the highest rate of economic growth, Japanese nationality provided its citizens with a source of ethnic pride. In the 1970s and 1980s, a new economic and cultural nationalism emerged in which citizens in all walks of life – intellectuals, politicians, businessmen and ordinary folk – were engaged in '*Nihonjinron*' (discussions of the Japanese) in search of a new identity suitable to their now affluent 'First World' country.

Japan's surrender in 1945 liberated its Korean colonial subjects, the majority of whom soon repatriated to their homeland. One-quarter of them (600,000), however, chose to remain in Japan for political, economic and familial reasons. With the looming threat of war in the Korean Peninsula, their repatriation efforts were postponed further (Lie 2001: 197). For seven years, between 1945 and 1952, the Japanese government regarded its former nationals of colonial origin (*Gaichijin*) as foreigners, excluding them from political participation and requiring them to register as foreign residents (Onuma 1993; Tanaka 1995). In 1951, Japan signed the San Francisco Peace Treaty with the United States with the result that the country was restored to full independence and re-entered the international community. In April of the following year, when the Treaty took effect, the Ministry of Justice issued a communication by which the 600,000 Koreans were formally deprived of Japanese citizenship.[6] In 1950, when the 1899 Nationality Law was revised, Japan had retained the principle of *jus sanguinis* (law of blood) through paternal lineage as defining Japanese citizenship. As a result, descendants of non-Japanese nationals, including Koreans, are to this day defined by law as foreigners no matter how long or over how many generations they have lived in Japan (Miyajima 1997: 126). In 1965, the Japan–Korea Peace Treaty imposed South Korean nationality on most ethnic Koreans in Japan, and granted permanent resident status to Koreans of the first and second generations of residence in Japan.[7] By 1990, the Korean population had increased to 700,000, constituting Japan's largest foreign population. From 1945 until the early 1980s, the loss of Japanese citizenship had denied Koreans most of the benefits of public services to which Japanese citizens are entitled, including national health insurance and workers' pensions – this despite their obligation to pay taxes on their earnings (Miyajima 1997: 127).

In 1952, at the outset of Japan's post-war economic reconstruction, the denationalisation of 600,000 Koreans had reinforced the post-war Japanese myth of ethnic homogeneity in the country of then 100 million (Onuma 1993; Oguma 1995). The *Showa* Constitution (promulgated in 1946) renounced war while, in Article 1, defining the emperor to be 'the symbol of the State and of the unity of the people, deriving his position from the will of the people with whom resides sovereign power'. In reconstructing the nation and economy in the post-war period, therefore, the emperor symbolised peace, unity and eternity of the Japanese people and culture. In the late 1950s, when the country's post-war 'economic miracle' was to take off, the notion of 'one nation, one people' served as a new dominant ethnic ideology to reunite the nation and the labour force in pursuit of goals to reconstruct the economy. The fact that Japan is a nation of islands geographically separated from the rest of the Far East together with its two centuries of diplomatic isolation (1633 to 1868) added to the consolidation of its myth of ethnic homogeneity. The emphasis on its collective oneness was also closely linked to political objectives of the time – the development of post-war democracy and the welfare state, based on the assertion that 'everyone is equal because everyone is Japanese'. Being Japanese has thus meant that one is a Japanese national (citizen), who is born to a Japanese family (father), speaks the same language (Japanese), receives the same (standardised) education, has the same (Japanese) face, and therefore behaves in the same way as everyone else ('us'), as opposed to non-Japanese ('them').[8]

In reality, such a sweeping ideology of nationalism, based on the shared experience and identity of the majority group, had long been belied by the presence of diverse ethnic minority communities (notably Okinawans, Ainu, and *Burakumin*, in addition to Koreans) (Weiner 1997).[9] It also overlooked the labour market exploitation of female and older workers, the underdevelopment of peripheral regions, and the victimisation wrought by environmental pollution at the hands of large corporations (see Upham 1987; Brinton 1994). Emergence of monoethnicity as a major post-war national ideology also allowed the Japanese to conveniently sever the peaceful present from a past badly damaged by military aggression and brutal colonialism (Lie 2001). As a result of the history taught in the post-war educational curriculum, post-war generations – comprising two-thirds of the nation's population – are today unaware of Japan's multiethnic history and its contemporary legacy. They have therefore accepted the idea of 'monoethnic Japan' uncritically. In their minds, Japanese nationality (citizenship) is synonymous with Japanese ethnicity (ibid.).

The unprecedented economic growth following the 1960s led to a turning point in Japanese post-war nationalism in the 1970s and 1980s. From the *Meiji* modernisation to post-war reconstruction, the goal of rapid economic development had been to 'catch up' with the West, perceived by many Japanese to be the model for advanced technology (Nakamura 1993: 570). Achievement of the 'economic miracle' in the late 1960s became a source of national pride. Some argued that Japanese technology had now surpassed Western technology. At the same time, increased international contact through trade, travel and the mass media made the Japanese conscious of their image in the eyes of the others, especially of the West. They thus began to forge the new image of selfhood and history in the international context.[10] Beginning with a book, *The Japanese and the Jews* by Isaiah BenDasan (1970) (*nom de plume* of Shichihei Yamamoto), a series of printed and broadcast materials led people to engage in *Nihonjinron* discussion, examining Japanese origins, identity, customs, behaviour and ways of thinking, which were in sharp contrast to those of any other society. Most of these media productions were non-scientific and aimed at the lay public, but *Nihonjinron*'s surging popularity suggested its strong cultural appeal to all categories of Japanese. According to Yoshino (1998: 16), the *Nihonjinron* is characterised by its holistic 'culturalistic' approach that is compatible with 'racialistic' thinking, in which a particular culture belongs to a particular 'race'. Such a cultural, racial (ethnic) and national discourse is deeply embedded in the historical notion of Japan as a family nation in which blood-ties, beliefs and ethnicity were conflated to generate a strong sense of oneness (ibid.: 19).

In parallel with this ethno-cultural, inward-looking construction of nationhood, increased international contact also gave rise to respect for individual rights, tolerance of cultural difference, and universal human rights. At the state level, this change was inseparable from the rapid economic success that had elevated Japan to become one of the most influential nations in world affairs. One result of this global recognition was the fact that Japan became signatory to many international conventions on human rights proposed by the United Nations and other international organisations (Takafuji 1991; Gurowitz 1999).[11] These conventions are based on the principle of equality for all nationalities and races, and between genders (Takafuji 1991). Once it has signed an international convention, a government is obliged to make every effort, including legislation, to eradicate inequalities built into institutional arrangements in the country. Among the international conventions ratified by Japan during the post-war era, the International Convention on the Status of Refugees and Protocol (ratified in 1981) has proven to be most important in eliminating existing discrimination embedded in laws and administration against non-citizen residents (Takafuji 1991; Tanaka 1995). As a result of its ratification, the Japanese government was obliged to revise domestic laws by which foreign, mostly Korean, residents had been treated unequally, especially in the areas of social security and welfare. Consequently, Japanese nationality was no longer required for eligibility to obtain the benefits of social services, including health insurance, worker pensions and public housing (Miyajima 1997).[12] Subsequently, the 1985 ratification of the International Convention on Eliminating All Forms of Discrimination against Women led the government in 1984 to revise the Nationality Act, so that women became equal to men in determining the nationality of their children.[13]

Challenge to ethnic hegemony in the age of global migration: from 1990 onwards

The arrival of the age of global migration in the late 1980s opened a new chapter in Japan's ethno-national history. Its growing labour needs increasingly challenged the myth of a monoethnic population. As migrant workers arrived, not only from East, South-east and South Asia but also from South America, the reality of a 'multiethnic Japan' could no longer be denied (Lie 2001). The 1990 Revised Immigration Law made it officially illegal to hire unskilled foreigners, while it opened new channels through which migrants could legally enter, work and live in Japan. A result is a sudden influx of more than 200,000 Brazilians of Japanese ancestry and their families who have arrived in many industrial cities throughout Japan and rapidly developed their ethnic communities replete with Brazilian culture and enterprises (Yamanaka 2000a). This has resulted in increasing everyday contacts between these 'foreigners' and ordinary Japanese. Consequently in these locales, as citizens and municipal governments struggle to cope with problems of face-to-face interactions with the new local residents, there has emerged a dialectical social process in which Japanese of all levels are engaged in daily negotiation to construct the emerging new national identity. In this process, they are increasingly confronted with the notion of universal equality among all residents regardless of nationality and ethnicity. As a result, 'ethnic' citizenship, rigidly defined on the basis of national membership, is challenged to expand its boundary in order to include these newcomers who have heretofore been denied rights because they lack citizenship.

Between the late 1960s and early 1970s, Japan's rapid and prolonged economic boom required unprecedented amounts of labour, which caused severe labour shortages. Although foreign labour was requested by employers as a way to alleviate the labour shortages, the government advocated other solutions.[14] These included: increasing productivity by introduction of automation, exporting production to low-wage countries (especially in Asia), mobilising unutilised labour (e.g., women and elderly), allowing inflation to increase, and permitting the transfer of income from capital to labour (Bartram 2000: 19). Consequently, as a result of having virtually avoided importation of labour for four decades, Japan became an anomaly among highly industrialised countries with similar problems of labour supply during the post-war economic boom. Most of the others had chosen to rely heavily on foreign labour as a solution (Bartram 2000: 15). By the mid-1980s, however, all signs pointed to the fact that Japan was attracting global immigrant workers (Yamanaka 1993). From the late 1980s to early 1990s, no less than 200,000 unskilled foreigners (mostly from neighbouring Asian countries) entered the country's labour force illegally by over-staying their short-term visas issued to tourists, students, business personnel, company trainees and entertainers (Morita and Sassen 1994).

Faced with the dilemma of how to ameliorate the shortage of labour, on the one hand, and maintain social and class homogeneity on the other, the Ministry of Justice came up with a solution. In June 1990, it implemented the Revised Immigration Law without changing its central provision that had restricted imported labour to skilled occupations. The revision entailed the introduction of the following two measures designed to increase the supply of inexpensive labour while stemming the tide of unwanted foreigners (Cornelius 1994; Weiner and Hanami 1998). First, the Revised Immigration Law made employers of illegal workers subject to criminal penalties: two years' imprisonment or a maximum fine of two million yen ($20,000). Second, it established a new 'long-term resident' (*teiju*) visa category, exclusively for non-citizens with Japanese ancestry (*Nikkeijin*) up to the third generation. This new category allowed *Nikkeijin*, regardless of nationality, to stay for up to three years in Japan with no restriction on their socio-economic activities (Yamanaka 1996). Their spouses and children were also permitted to stay, usually up to one year. Visas of both the *Nikkeijin* and their families in this category could be easily renewed, as a result of which many of the immigrants remained beyond the initially designated periods. The change in the law had an immediate effect on migration flows into Japan. In 1990, the year the law was implemented, there was an influx, over the next five years, of more than 200,000 *Nikkeijin* immigrant workers, mostly from Brazil where the largest overseas Japanese population lived. The same law, however, closed the door to other unskilled workers, most of whom were Asians without Japanese ancestry (e.g., Yamanaka 2000b). Many Japanese employers, threatened by criminal penalties, discharged unauthorised workers and replaced them with *Nikkeijin* and company trainees, the other legal category of migrant workers.

A case study of changing ethnic hegemony from Hamamatsu

The section will comprise a case study I conducted from 1998 to 2003 in Hamamatsu City, where most Japanese have faced day-to-day interaction with mostly Japanese Brazilian immigrants, following their sudden and large influx since 1990.[15] It provides data from which to analyse dynamic but contradictory social processes in the changing ethnic hegemony of Japanese as they realise that authorised foreigners are also 'local citizens' (Tegtmeyer Pak 2000) who deserve and can demand legal rights equal to those of Japanese citizens.

Hamamatsu, a city of half a million located 257 kilometres south-west of Tokyo, is one of the many cities that since the late 1980s have received an influx of migrant workers, both authorised and unauthorised. As home to the headquarters of such large manufacturing corporations as Suzuki, Yamaha and Honda, the city has attracted skilled foreigners as well as thousands of unskilled workers including both authorised Japanese Brazilians and unauthorised Asians throughout the 1990s. By 2001, the city was home to 12,000 Brazilians and 8,000 other registered foreign nationals who together accounted for 3.5 per cent of the city's total population. Ethnographic and sociological analyses of Brazilian immigration in Hamamatsu and other cities have commonly reported systematic 'differential exclusion' (Castles 1997: 115–17) of Brazilian immigrant workers at the hands of Japanese industries, employers, brokers, workers and bureaucracy (Yamanaka 1996, 2000a; Roth 2002; Tsuda 2003). According to these studies, upon arrival in Japan, the majority of working-age Brazilian men and women have been employed on assembly lines and shop floors in factories producing and assembling automobile parts, electric appliances and other manufactured goods. They have usually signed short-term contracts with labour brokers (*assen* or *haken gyosha*), who in turn dispatched them to the factories where they worked as temporary labourers separated from the formal labour force (Roth 2002). The formal labour force comprises Japanese (male) employees who can look forward to permanent employment. As this suggests, most Brazilian workers, despite their authorised status, lack job security, labour union membership, unemployment insurance, old-age pension and the wide variety of fringe benefits to which Japanese permanent employees are entitled. Because the majority of them lack Japanese citizenship, they are also ineligible for the National Health Insurance Plan. In the housing market, Brazilians routinely encounter discrimination by landlords. As a result, job brokers often sublet apartments to their foreign employees during the period of their employment contracts. The sublet system severely restricts foreigners' choice of residence, and consequently limits their occupational mobility. In children's education, Portuguese-speaking Brazilian children enrolled in Japanese public schools often find it difficult to understand Japanese instructions. Consequently, many of them soon drop out of school to work in factories or they roam the streets, remaining unschooled.

The contradictory ethnic and class selection criteria employed by the government in seeking to attract inexpensive Brazilian labour to Japan underlie the discriminatory treatment these workers experience (Yamanaka 1996). By law, Japanese ancestry has privileged ethnic Brazilians over other foreign workers by offering them long-term residence visas irrespective of occupation. The majority of them, however, work as temporary manual workers in factories. According to Castles (1984: 12), guest worker systems embody institutional discrimination designed to recruit and control such temporary migrant workers. For local industries, the advantage of hiring migrant workers from the Third World rests on their vulnerability as a result of their dire economic need, non-citizen status, linguistic handicaps, and unfamiliarity with local labour customs. Foreign workers provide a cheap alternative labour pool that carries out essential manual jobs shunned by Japanese. Their work requires physical strength and on-the-job experience but no complex technical or communication skills. It exposes them to danger and stress while providing no prospect of promotion and none of the fringe benefits their Japanese co-workers enjoy. In times of recession, they are the first to be laid off, while Japanese co-workers' jobs and wages remain secure. Brazilian workers of Japanese ancestry are no exception to this kind of systematic labour discrimination.

My research in Hamamatsu suggests that responses to the emergence of this new but marginalised ethnic community on the part of both the municipal government and the public have been complex and often contradictory.

On the one hand, the systematic exclusion of Brazilians as described above has reinforced the cold reception they receive from Hamamatsu citizens. Discrimination commonly occurs in such public spaces as stores and restaurants that serve immigrant customers. Having experienced difficulty in communicating with foreign customers, the majority of whom are Portuguese-speaking Brazilians, some merchants become reluctant to serve them. The mass media have paid a great deal of attention to police reports of increasing conflicts, violence and crimes attributed to foreigners (Herbert 1992). These reports have further reinforced the public perception that foreigners are not only cultural strangers but also troublemakers, even criminals.

Such social and political processes of constructing 'foreignness', as opposed to perceived 'Japaneseness', in Hamamatsu culminated in a lawsuit charging discrimination brought in August 1998 by Brazilian television journalist Ana Bortz, the non-*Nikkeijin* wife of a Japanese Brazilian newspaper reporter, against a local merchant.[16] Two months earlier, Bortz had entered a downtown jewellery store whereupon the owner, Takahisa Suzuki, asked her nationality. When Bortz revealed her Brazilian nationality, Suzuki pointed to a home-made sign in Japanese, 'No foreigners allowed in this store', and demanded that she leave. When Bortz refused, protesting that exclusion of foreigners from the store is a violation of their human rights, the proprietor called the police who arrived soon but left without taking any action. Bortz then left as well, but subsequently sued the owner for discrimination on the basis of race and nationality. In the absence of any applicable Japanese law, she cited the authority of the International Convention on Eliminating All Forms of Racial Discrimination, which Japan had ratified in 1995.

Fourteen months later, in October 1999, a District Court judge astounded the nation when he ruled that (1) in view of Japan's ratification of the International Convention, its provisions serve as the standard by which racial discrimination must be determined in Japan; and (2) because its provisions provide the grounds upon which Japanese Civil Law takes effect, the victim is entitled to compensation.[17] The defendant filed no appeal and full compensation was awarded. My research on the social impact that this unprecedented court ruling had on citizens' perceptions of foreigners suggests that many of them thought the defendant Suzuki did the 'right' thing in order to protect his business from a foreigner – a potential criminal (Yamanaka 2003a). They also expressed vague fears generated by the fact that a foreigner (Bortz) had dared to challenge Japanese authority and hegemony in a Japanese city. In reply to a question of how strained relationships between Japanese and Brazilians could be improved, the majority of my informants cited communication – not law and litigation – as the best method for ending discrimination.

In their view, both Japanese and foreigners should try hard to understand cultural differences and to establish common rules for dealing with them. They believed that the use of law and litigation to enforce racial equality would result in the mere appearance of racial harmony and would therefore be counterproductive.[18] The long-term impact of the court ruling on public perceptions and attitudes towards ethnic minorities is yet to be seen in Hamamatsu. It is evident at this point, however, that the issue of racial equality and human rights that was emphasised in the court ruling remains a remote concept to the majority of citizens who have never doubted their entitlement to ethnic (national) hegemony in the Japanese territory, thus accepting discrimination against foreigners.

On the other hand, some Hamamatsu citizens, having witnessed the legal and social barriers faced by foreign workers and residents, have responded with empathy for their plight and have been moved to action. Small but dedicated groups of such citizens have formed grassroots organisations to meet the needs of foreigners whose lack of citizenship has denied them public services, legal rights and political participation. Their voluntary activities include not only providing the foreigners with information and services but also carrying out cultural and educational projects jointly with immigrant groups and organisations (Yamanaka 2003b). Citizen volunteers also negotiate with the local administration for immigrant rights, and they campaign to raise multicultural awareness among the general public. (Yamanaka 2003c)

Underlying this unprecedented surge of community activities in Hamamatsu is a broad and growing emphasis on self-governance at the grassroots throughout Japan. Arising from the ashes of the 1995 Kobe earthquake, this new civil society movement stresses voluntarism, public interest, non-profit, and non-governmental organisations (Tajiri 2001: 19). In contrast to traditional activism serving the interests of specific neighbourhoods, and the 1960s' radical citizens movement for social justice and equality, recent community activism has undertaken to address broad societal concerns such as ageing, disability, health, environment, migration, human rights, etc. Ordinary citizens, often middle-class women, volunteer their efforts in networking, providing services and advocating the rights of those who are disadvantaged because of existing legal, institutional and cultural barriers. Under increasing budgetary constraints coupled with rapidly ageing populations, local governments have been inclined to delegate policy projects to non-governmental and non-profit-making organisations (Sakuma 2001: 147–8). In this age of economic liberalism and power decentralisation, the partnership between local governments and non-governmental organisations has been consistent with the interests of the national government as well.

My research demonstrates that Hamamatsu citizens' grassroots activities comprise a basis for the small-scale but tangible form of transnationalisation now occurring in this non-metropolitan city where, before 1990, most citizens rarely had contact with non-citizens (Yamanaka 2003b). Citizens and immigrants have begun to interact with one another at work and in community activities, as a result of which the two parties, in the absence of shared national citizenship, are developing a sense of shared 'global citizenship' (Soysal 1994; Lister 1997). That is, by carrying out responsibilities and projects together, they are in the process of achieving a collective identity and a shared societal history that crosses national boundaries. They have thus triggered 'grassroots transnationalisation', a form of social transformation in which everyday practices and relations of ordinary people generate 'multiple and counter-hegemonic powers' for promoting equality and multiculturalism (Mahler 1998: 64). At the national level, my research also points to the growing and glaring contradictions between governmental immigration policy and practice in Japan. One such contradiction is the significant gap between the national government and local governments in their policies relating to the incorporation of immigrants into the political, social and legal structure of the state (Tsuda and Cornelius forthcoming; Kondo 2003). Local governments, such as that of Hamamatsu, are becoming responsive to their immigrants' needs and interests, and have moved towards incorporating them into the local polity.[19] The government of Japan, by contrast, remains indifferent to such policies because it denies that Japan is a country of immigration and has therefore adopted an immigration law that merely regulates border control while ignoring the plight of immigrants. As a result, local administrations and concerned citizens are left to struggle for practical solutions to the mounting problems associated with immigrant health, housing, education, culture and human rights within their own jurisdictions in the context of severe budgetary constraints and limited resources at the grassroots. Without governmental efforts to build a consensus at the national level, local autonomy is prevented from being achieved, while voluntarism is inadequate to address them. Solutions to these problems require fundamental changes in national policies defining identity and citizenship.

Conclusion

This comparative analysis of Japanese citizenship in the process of nation-state building during the pre-war and post-war periods highlights the critical importance of the 'ethnic' component in defining who belongs to the state. It also reveals the great discretion exercised by the state in constructing the boundaries between citizen and non-citizen at each historical turning point. For more than a century, the core ideology of a family state (one nation and one people) has shaped and reshaped Japanese national identity according to national goals and strategies in order to attain those goals in the rapidly changing world of politics, economy and demography. In times of war and patriotism, the 'imperial' Japanese state broadened the boundary of nationality in order to mobilise colonial subjects into its labour force and military.

In times of peace and prosperity, the 'democratic' state constricted the boundary to exclude former colonial nationals from political and social participation. In this period of global capitalism, the 'neo-liberal' state has redefined Japanese ethnicity to include foreign nationals of Japanese descent in the shrinking labour force, but has stopped far short of including them within the political and ethnic community.

This repeated pattern of redrawing the boundary of citizenship throughout Japanese modern history clearly suggests that the state has negotiated and manipulated the boundary of who belongs to the nation-state. It also indicates that the dominant ethnic Japanese have accepted uncritically the changing definition of ethnicity and nationality. The fluid and 'disposable' nature of citizenship, then, suggests the possibility of an expanded 'civic' component in the redefinition of Japanese citizenship, in response to the growing emphasis on universal human rights in the increasingly deterritorialised world.[20] Such change may occur in Japan in the near future, but only if the state and the majority Japanese accept the fact that Japan is and has been multiethnic, and that it has in the long run benefited greatly from its ethnic diversity. The case study of Hamamatsu described above indicates that the paths to building a multiethnic community are not smooth but rocky with much social and political tension embedded in the process of breaking the old myths and creating the new. In this process, international law and grassroots activism have proven to be two powerful new forces in broadening the ideological scope and legal frameworks of citizenship towards including civic and participatory defini tions. More research will be necessary to predict how and to what extent these two forces – one from 'above' and the other from 'below' – can bring significant change to the century-old ethnic nationalism that has defined who is, and who is not, Japanese.

Notes

1 Soysal (1994) has analysed the incorporation of guest workers and their dependants who have become permanent residents into the state's political structure since the 1970s in six Western European countries (Sweden, Netherlands, Germany, France, Switzerland and Britain). Guest worker populations from non-EU member countries, such as Turkey and those in North Africa, however, still face many forms of exclusion in the political, social and economic institutions in receiving countries, while refugees are largely excluded from most political institutions (Piper 1998).

2 The name 'Yamato' is frequently used to designate the majority Japanese (e.g. Lie 2001: 3). According to Bestor (2001: 1140), it is used by archaeologists and historians to distinguish Japanese artistic genres from their Chinese counterparts. In contemporary usage, it is strongly associated with the imperial and military system. Today, most Japanese call themselves *Nihonjin* or *Nipponjin* (Japanese people) deriving from *Nihon* or *Nippon* (Japan), meaning 'origin from the sun'.

3 Throughout Japanese history until the *Meiji* Restoration, emperors were dominated by a succession of court families and military (*samurai*) rulers, although state authority was in theory concentrated in the hands of the emperor (Lock 1993: 105).

4 The 1925 Universal Manhood Suffrage Act enfranchised men over the age of 25, including Koreans living in Japan. In the national and local elections between 1929 and 1936, 46 out of 153 Korean candidates were elected to public office (Weiner 1994: 149).

5 For example, in the aftermath of the Great Kanto Earthquake of 1923, approximately 6,000 Koreans were massacred by the Japanese military, police and populace (Yamawaki 2000: 45).

6 The San Francisco Peace Treaty had formally ended the seven-year occupation of Japan by the United States. In April 1952, when the Treaty took effect, the Japanese government exercised its sovereignty by legally defining former colonial citizens as foreigners, thereby completing their exclusion from membership in the nation-state (Onuma 1993: 264).

7 Both the Japanese government and leading Korean organisations regarded all Koreans in Japan as foreigners or sojourners despite the fact that their lives had already taken deep root in the country (Lie 2001: 108).

8 Kelly (1993: 192) argues the importance of analysing how government policies and people's choices have contributed to the incorporating and differentiating effects of institutions and ideologies in post-war Japan. As a result, this period has been characterised less by 'homogenisation' than by the 'standardisation' of diversity, enforced by governmental policies and reinforced by the choices people have made.

9 It should be emphasised that Japan has never been ethnically homogeneous. Between the fourth and eighth centuries, Chinese and Koreans frequently migrated and settled in the country, bringing with them foreign technology and culture. They were called *Kikajin* (naturalised people). Under rules of military regimes from the late twelfth to mid-nineteenth centuries, those who engaged in certain stigmatised occupations (e.g., leather workers, undertakers, executioners, scavengers, beggars and itinerants) were collectively treated as a distinct 'untouchable', even subhuman, population, that today comprises the two to three million *Burakumin* in Japan (Price 1967: 13). During the nation-building of the nineteenth and twentieth centuries, territorial expansion incorporated two other ethnically distinct populations, today numbering 1.6 million Okinawans in Japan's far south, and the variously reported 25,000 to 300,000 Ainus indigenous to the far north (Lie 2001: 94).

10 Yoshino (1998: 13–14) calls this kind of nationalism 'secondary nationalism'. In contrast to 'primary nationalism', which is concerned with the creation of a nation's original identity, secondary nationalism emerges to preserve and enhance national identity in an already well-established nation.

11 In 1979 Japan ratified both the International Covenant on Civil and Political Rights and the International Covenant on Economic, Social and Cultural Rights. This was followed by the 1981 ratification of the International Convention on the Status of Refugees and Protocol, and the 1985 ratification of the International Convention on Eliminating All Forms of Discrimination against Women. Ten years later, in 1994, Japan also signed the International Convention on Rights of Children, and in the following year the International Convention on Eliminating All Forms of Racial Discrimination.

12 In August 1999, in response to years of protest by Koreans and their Japanese supporters, the Revised Alien Registration law abolished the notorious practice of fingerprinting all foreigners (Gurowitz 1999: 431).

13 This has had a significant impact on the Korean population because it opened a legal window through which children born of marriage between Japanese and Koreans could be Japanese citizens. By 1985 an estimated 70 per cent of marriages by second- and third-generation Koreans were to ethnic Japanese (Kang and Kim, cited by Lie 2001: 109).

14 In the late 1960s, when these allegedly labour-saving measures proved to be inadequate to alleviate labour shortages, Japan resorted to some attempts to recruit foreign workers from neighbouring Asian countries (Lie 2001: 10). But by 1975, OPEC's oil embargo had triggered a serious economic recession, and demands for labour quickly fell from high to minimal. The recession lasted for ten years, creating a surplus of labour until the mid-1980s (Bartram 2000: 26).

15 It is part of my broader sociological study of the Japanese Brazilian community in Hamamatsu and its vicinity, which began in 1993. To understand the 'return' migration experiences of Japanese Brazilians, between 1994 and 1995, I interviewed migrants in the Hamamatsu area and in São Paulo, Londrina and Porto Alegre, Brazil (Yamanaka 2000a). For four months in fall 1998, and several shorter periods thereafter, I lived in Hamamatsu (where I had spent much of my youth) in order to carry out this research on social interaction between local citizens and immigrants.

16 Because of a relatively high rate of interracial marriage in Brazil, the Japanese Brazilian population in Japan includes a substantial number of non-*Nikkeijin* Brazilian spouses of *Nikkeijin* Brazilians and their *mestiços* children.

17 This court ruling was front-page news in the *New York Times* of 15 November 1999 under the headline ' "Japanese only" policy takes body blow in court' (French 1999).

18 For example, in an interview with *Newsweek* magazine (2003: 51), Hisao Yasui, Director of the International Affairs Office of the Hamamatsu Municipal Government, said, '[Racial discrimination in Japan] is not a kind of problem that the Western way of judging good or bad can solve. Taking up negative examples would only result in stirring Japanese nationalism.'

19 For example, in 2000, Hamamatsu City established the Foreign Citizens Assembly. There, selected members of the city's foreign communities discuss problems faced by foreign residents and present proposals to the city government. The effect of the Assembly on the city's policy-making is questionable, however, as many problems of concern to the Assembly, such as children's education and access to inexpensive health care, remain largely unsolved (Yamanaka 2003b, 2003c).

20 See Kashiwazaki (2000: 461–6) for further discussion of policy implications of the changing politics of citizenship in Japan.

References

Anderson, B. (1983) *Imagined Communities: Reflections on the Origin and Spread of Nationalism*, London: Verso.

Armstrong, B. (1989) 'Racialisation and nationalist ideology: the Japanese case', *International Sociology* 4(3): 329–43.

ASEAN Economic Bulletin (1995) 'Labour migration in Asia' (special issue), 12: 2.

Bartram, D. (2000) 'Japan and labor migration: theoretical and methodological implications of negative cases', *International Migration Review*, 34(1): 5–32

Battistella, G. (2002) 'International migration in Asia vis-à-vis Europe: an introduction', *Asian and Pacific Migration Journal* 11(4): 405–14.

Bauer, J.R. and Bell, D.A. (eds) (1999) *The East Asian Challenge for Human Rights*, Cambridge: Cambridge University Press.

BenDasan, I. ([1970] 1972) *The Japanese and the Jews* (trans. R.L. Gage from *Nihonjin to Yudayajin*, Tokyo: Yamamoto Shoten), New York: Weatherhill.

Bestor, T.C. (2001) 'Japan', in M. Ember and C.R. Ember (eds) *Countries and Cultures*, vol. 2, New York: Macmillan Reference USA.

Brinton, M. (1994) *Women and Economic Miracle: Gender and Work in Post-war Japan*, Berkeley, CA: University of California Press.

Brownlee, J.S. (1997) *Japanese Historians and the National Myths, 1600–1945: The Age of the Gods and Emperor Jinmu*, Vancouver: UBC Press.

Castles, S. (1984) *Here for Good: Western Europe's New Ethnic Minorities*, London: Pluto Press.

—— (1997) 'Multicultural citizenship: the Australian experience', in V. Bader (ed.) *Citizenship and Exclusion*, New York: St Martin's Press.

Castles, S. and Davidson, A. (2000) *Citizenship and Migration: Globalization and the Politics of Belonging*, New York: Routledge.

Cornelius, W.A. (1994) 'Japan: the illusion of immigration control', in W.A. Cornelius, L. Martin and J.F. Hollifield (eds) *Controlling Immigration: A Global Perspective*, Stanford, CA: Stanford University Press.

French, H.W. (1999) '"Japanese only" policy takes body blow in court', *New York Times*, International Edition, 15 November: A1, A14.

Fujitani, T. (1996) *Splendid Monarchy: Power and Pageantry in Modern Japan*, Berkeley, CA: University of California Press.

Gellner, E. (1983) *Nations and Nationalism*, Ithaca, NY: Cornell University Press.

Gurowitz, A. (1999) 'Mobilizing international norms: domestic actors, immigrants, and the Japanese state', *Journal of Asian Studies* 51(3): 413–45.

Herbert, W. (1992) 'Conjuring up a crime wave: the "rapid growth in the crime rate among foreign migrant workers in Japan" critically examined', *Japan Forum* 4 April: 109–19.

Kashiwazaki, C. (2000) 'Citizenship in Japan: legal practice and contemporary development', in T.A. Aleinikoff and D. Klusmeyer (eds) *From Migrants to Citizens: Membership in a Changing World*, Washington, DC: Carnegie Endowment for International Peace.

Kelly, W. (1993) 'Finding a place in metropolitan Japan: ideologies, institutions, and everyday life', in A. Gordon (ed.) *Postwar Japan as History*, Berkeley, CA: University of California Press.

Kondo, A. (2003) 'The development of immigration policy in Japan', *Asian and Pacific Migration Journal*, 11(4): 415–36.

Lie, J. (2001) *Multiethnic Japan*, Cambridge, MA: Harvard University Press.

Lister, R. (1997) *Citizenship: Feminist Perspectives*, New York: New York University Press.

Lock, M. (1993) 'Japanese', in P. Hockings (ed.) *Encyclopedia of World Cultures*, vol. V: *East and Southeast Asia*, Boston: G.K. Hall & Co.

Mahler, S. (1998) 'Theoretical and empirical contributions toward a research agenda for transnationalism', in L.E. Guarnizo and M.P. Smith (eds) *Transnationalism from Below*, New Brunswick, NJ: Transaction Publishers.

Matsumae, T. (1974) *Nihon no Kamigami, Chuko Shinso 372*, Tokyo: Chuokoron Shinsha.

Miyajima, T. (1997) 'Immigration and the redefinition of "citizenship" in Japan: "one people – one nation"', in T.K. Oommen (ed.) *Citizenship and National Identity: From Colonialism to Globalism*, New Delhi: Sage.

Morita, K. and Sassen, S. (1994) 'The new illegal immigration in Japan 1980–1992', *International Migration Review*, 28(1): 153–63.

Nakamura, E. (1993) *Showashi II 1945–89*, Tokyo: Toyo Keizai Shinposha.

Newsweek, Japanese edition (2003) 'Gaikokujin Okotowari', 26 February: 48–53.

Oguma, E. (1995) *Tanitsu Minzoku Sinwa no Kigen: Nihonjin no Jigazo no Keishin*, Tokyo: Shinyosha.

—— (1998) *Nihonjin no Kyokai: Okinawa, Ainu, Taiwan, Chosen Syokuminchi Shihai kara Fukki Undo made*, Tokyo: Sinyosha.

Onuma, Y. (1993) *Tanitsu Minzoku Shakai no Shinwa wo Koete: Zainichi Kankoku, Chosenjin to Shuntsunykoku Taisei*, Tokyo: Toshindo.

Piper, N. (1998) *Racism, Nationalism and Citizenship: Ethnic Minorities in Britain and Germany*, Aldershot: Ashgate.

Price, J. (1967) 'A history of the outcaste: untouchability in Japan', in G. De Voss and H. Wagatsuma (eds) *Japan's Invisible Race: Caste in Culture and Personality*, Berkeley, CA: University of California Press.

Roth, J.H. (2002) *Brokered Homeland: Japanese Brazilian Migrants in Japan*, Ithaca, NY: Cornell University Press.

Sakuma, T. (2001) 'Global jidai no borantia katsudo wo kangaeru', in Editorial Committee (eds) *Borantia Hakusho*, Tokyo: Nihon Seinen Hoshi Kyokai.

Smith, A.D. (1999) *Myths and Memories of the Nation*, Oxford: Oxford University Press.

Soysal, Y.N. (1994) *Limits of Citizenship: Migrants and Postnational Membership in Europe*, Chicago: University of Chicago Press.

Tajiri, K. (2001) 'Kininaru "borantia" to "NPO" no kannkei', in Editorial Committee (eds) *Borantia Hakusho*, Tokyo: Nihon Seinen Hoshi Kyokai.

Takafuji, A. (1991) 'Gaikokujin rodosha to wagakuni no shakai hoshosei', in Shakai Hosho Kenkyujo (ed.) *Gaikokujin Rodosha to Shakai Hosho*, Tokyo: University of Tokyo Press.

Tanaka, H. (1995) *Zainichi Gaikokujin: Ho no Kabe, Kokoro no Mizo, Shiban, Iwanami Shinsho 171*, Tokyo: Iwanami Shoten.

Tegtmeyer Pak, K. (2000) 'Foreigners are local citizens, too: local governments respond to international migration in Japan', in M. Douglass and G. Roberts (eds) *Japan and Global Migration: Foreign Workers and the Advent of a Multicultural Society*, London: Routledge.

Tooyama, M. (2001) *Tenno Tanjo, Chuko Shinso 1568*, Tokyo: Chuokoron Shinsha.

Tsuda, T. (2003) *Strangers in the Ethnic Homeland: Japanese Brazilian Return Migration in Transnational Perspective*, New York: Columbia University Press.

Tsuda, T. and Cornelius, W. (forthcoming) 'Immigration to Japan: myths and realities', in W.A. Cornelius, T. Tsuda, J. Hollifield and P. Martin (eds) *Controlling Immigration: A Global Perspective*, 2nd edn, Stanford, CA: Stanford University Press.

Upham, F. (1987) *Law and Social Change in Postwar Japan*, Cambridge, MA: Harvard University Press.

Weiner, M. (1994) *Race and Migration in Imperial Japan*, London: Routledge.

—— (1997) *Japan's Minorities: The Illusion of Homogeneity*, London: Routledge.

Weiner, M. and Hanami, T. (eds) (1998) *Temporary Workers or Future Citizens? Japanese and US Migration Policies*, New York: New York University Press.

Yamanaka, K. (1993) 'New immigration policy and unskilled foreign workers in Japan', *Pacific Affairs*, 66(1): 72–90.

—— (1996) 'Return migration of Japanese-Brazilians to Japan: the Nikkeijin as ethnic minority and political construct', *Diaspora*, 5(1): 65–97.

—— (1999) 'Illegal immigration in Asia: regional patterns and a case study of Nepalese workers in Japan', in D.W. Haines and K.E. Rosenblum (eds) *Illegal Immigration in America: A Reference Handbook*, Westport, CT: Greenwood Press.

—— (2000a) '"I will go home, but when?" Labor migration and circular diaspora formation by Japanese Brazilians in Japan', in M. Douglass and G. Roberts (eds) *Japan and Global Migration: Foreign Workers and the Advent of a Multicultural Society*, London: Routledge.

—— (2000b) 'Nepalese labour migration to Japan: from global warriors to global workers', *Ethnic and Racial Studies*, 23(1): 62–93.

—— (2003a) 'A breakthrough for ethnic minority rights in Japan: Ana Bortz's courageous challenge', in M. Morokvasic-Muller, U. Erel and K. Shinozaki (eds) *Gender and Migration: Crossing Borders and Shifting Boundaries*, vol. 1 International Women's University Series, Opladen: Verlag Leske & Budrich.

—— (2003b) 'Feminized migration, community activism and grassroots transnationalization in Japan', *Asian and Pacific Migration Journal*, 12(1–2): 155–87.

—— (2003c) 'Migration, differential access to health services and civil society's responses in Japan', paper presented at the Workshop on Migration and Health in Asia, Singapore-Bintan, 22–4 September (organised by the Asian Meta Centre for Population and Sustainable Development Analysis, Singapore).

Yamawaki, K. (2000) 'Foreign workers in Japan: a historical perspective', in M. Douglass and G. Roberts (eds) *Japan and Global Migration: Foreign Workers and the Advent of a Multicultural Society*, London: Routledge.

Yoshino, K. (1998) 'Culturalism, racism, and internationalism in the discourse on Japanese identity', in D.C. Gladney (ed.) *Making Majorities: Constituting the Nation in Japan, Korea, China, Malaysia, Fiji, Turkey and the United States*, Stanford, CA: Stanford University Press.

10 Towards a theory of ethnocratic regimes

Learning from the Judaization of Israel/Palestine

Oren Yiftachel and As'ad Ghanem

Introduction

The rapidly changing international political landscape has exposed the poverty of tools and concepts currently used for regime analyses, with the academic discourse unduly constrained by a binary democracy–non-democracy framework (for example, Axtmann 1996; Linz and Stepan 1996; Dahl 1995). This has caused many scholars to overlook the existence, and recent consolidation, of a regime type we term here 'ethnocracy', which is neither democratic nor authoritarian. It is a regime designed for, and by, a dominant ethnic majority, which has appropriated the state apparatus to advance its control over a contested territory and power apparatus. In this chapter we aim to define a model of 'open' ethnocratic regimes, examine its impact on ethnic relations, and illustrate its dynamics by briefly analysing the case of Israel. Our analysis centres on the mechanisms of the regime, which explain both its persistent patterns of ethnic dominance and its instability.

Our approach is multidisciplinary, focusing mainly on the fields of political geography and political science. The approach is also critical, exploring and questioning the causes and consequences of processes and institutions, often accepted as 'natural' under the current geopolitical order. Theoretically, the critical approach casts doubt on the common use of ethnicity as an unproblematic social category in many of the social sciences, usually attached to minorities.

We aim to show that ethnicity is often constructed as a tool of oppression by ethno-national majorities, particularly in cases of territorial conflicts. It is never a mere 'identity' or set of social and cultural markers sailing neutrally through history, but generally a product of specific power relations, human geographies and material conditions (see Gellner 1996 as opposed to Smith 1996). In cases of territorial conflict, ethnicity often becomes an essentializing and stratifying mechanism, drawing on the ability of the state and dominant majority to shape and mobilize identities. Empirically, our critical approach also aims to question the common representation of Israel as a democratic state (Barak 1998; Dowty 1998; Gavison 1999; Smooha 2002). We show below that the examination of the Judaization of Israel/Palestine, and the associated minority marginalization and oppression, make Israel a prototype ethnocratic state.

Ethnocratic regimes – structure

We define ethnocracy as a particular regime type, frequently found on the world political map, but rarely studied by social scientists. This regime facilitates the expansion, ethnicization and control of a contested territory and state by a dominant ethnic group. In this chapter we focus on ethnocracies which exercise selective openness. They possess a range of partial democratic features, most notably political competition, free media and significant civil rights, although these fail to be universal or comprehensive, and are typically stretched to the extent they do interfere with the ethnicization project.

As elaborated elsewhere (Mann 1999; Yiftachel 1999), expanding ethnic regimes emerge from the time–space fusion of three main historical-political forces: (a) settler-colonialism, which may be external (into another state or continent) or internal (within a state) (Lustick 1993; McGarry 1998); (b) ethnonationalism, which draws on the international legitimacy of national self-determination to buttress the political and territorial expansionist goals of the dominant ethno-nation (Connor 1994; Mann 1999); and (c) a conspicuous 'ethnic logic' of capital, which tends to stratify ethnic groups through uneven processes of capital mobility, immigration and economic globalization (Sassen 1998; Soysal 2000).

Ethnocracies are driven, first and foremost, by a concerted collective project of exerting ethnonational control over a territory perceived as the nation's (exclusive) homeland. The regime is thus propelled by a sense of collective entitlement among the majority group to control 'its' state, and 'its' homeland, as part and parcel of what is conceived as a universal 'natural' right for self-determination. But given the perennial existence of multi-ethnic and multi-national territories, the imposition of ethnic control over a mixed territory (and at times beyond) is likely to cause bitter and protracted conflicts generated by rival claims for the same territory made by other groups, typically those controlling the areas in different historical periods (Hakli 2001; Murphy 2002).

The manipulation of ethnic political geographies is hence one of the central pillars of all ethnocratic regimes; that is, the ethnicization of political space. The legal, political, cultural and demographic 'bases' of the regime, as elaborated below, all facilitate this collective goal (Paasi 1999; Murphy 2002). But the geographical process in which ethnocratic regimes are enmeshed also expose their long-term weakness: as shown by the recent work of social and political scientists such as Brubaker (1996), Gurr (2000), Mann (2000), McGarry (1998) and Hechter (2000), the process of state-led ethnic territorial expansion dispossesses and marginalizes minorities to such an extent that their resistance often generates serious threats to the regime, most commonly on a regional or transnational scale. The remaking of ethnic geography is also closely related to another key component of most ethnocratic regimes – the harnessing of religion to advance the ethnic project.

These settings mean that ethnocratic regimes reflect, and at the same time reproduce, patterns of ethnic stratification and discrimination. The parallel workings of these structural forces have shaped several key regime characteristics – all enhancing the process of ethnicizing a contested territory:

- Ethnicity, and not citizenship, forms the main basis for resource and power allocation; only partial rights and capabilities are extended to minorities; there is a constant ethnocratic–civil tension.
- The dominant ethnic nation appropriates the state apparatus and shapes the political system, public institutions, geography, economy and culture, so as to expand and deepen its control over state and territory.
- Political boundaries are vague, often privileging co-ethnics of the dominant group in the diaspora over minority citizens; there is no clearly identified 'demos'.
- Rigid forms of inter-generational ethnic segregation and socio-economic stratification are maintained, despite countervailing legal and market forces.
- Religion is often ethnically exclusive, and used to strengthen group boundaries and stratification.
- Politics is ethnicized, as the ethnic logic of power distribution polarizes the body politic and party system.
- State ethnocratic policies generate, over time, growing resistance from marginalized minorities, causing structurally destabilizing dynamics.

Significantly, in ethnocratic regimes the notion of the 'demos' is crucially ruptured. That is, the community of equal resident-citizens (the 'demos') does not feature high in the country's policies, agenda, imagination, symbols or resource distribution, and is therefore not nurtured or facilitated. But the 'demos' forms the necessary basis for the establishment of democracy ('demos-cracy'), and as a foundation for the most stable and legitimate form of governance known to human society. Needless to say, the concept of the 'demos' is open to many interpretations, as evidenced by the variety of federal, multi-cultural or unitary state structures (Dahl 1995; Kymlicka 2001). Yet, the consistent diminution of the demos by ethnocratic regimes highlights their qualitative and structural difference from the norms and practices of democratic state building.

The Israeli regime: Judaizing the homeland

Following half a century of Jewish colonization of (mainly Arab) Palestine, tacitly supported by the British rulers, Israel gained its independence in 1948. This followed a failed UN partition attempt, rejected by the Arabs, and a Palestinian–Jewish war, in which Arab states attacked the Zionist community, and during which some 700,000 Palestinians fled or were driven out of their homeland.

Both ethno-national groups claim to have historical rights over the country. The Palestinian-Arabs claim continuous residence as indigenous people, and a natural right for self-determination in a national homeland. The Jewish-Zionist justification rests on the existence of ancient Israelite kingdoms on the land before the Jews were exiled, and on sacred Jewish texts, which promise the land to the Israelite 'chosen people'. The Zionist movement claims that Jews maintained in their diasporas a continuous bond with the 'promised land' and that, following the eruption of genocidal European anti-Semitism, the Land of Israel (Palestine) became the rightful and natural site in which to build a safe, independent, Jewish state (Kimmerling 2001).

During the 1947–49 war Israel seized control over 78 per cent of Mandatory Palestine, about 40 per cent larger than the territory allocated to it by the UN plan. In 1949, only 160,000 Palestinian-Arabs remained in Israel and received state citizenship. In the next five decades, Israel absorbed some 2.7 million Jewish refugees and immigrants, and prevented the return of the Palestinian refugees. In 2002, Palestinian-Arabs constituted 17 per cent of Israel's citizens, while Palestinians in the entire Israel/Palestine area between the Jordan River and the Sea (conquered by Israel in 1967 and still under its control), accounted for 47 per cent. Palestinians are expected to form a majority in this area by 2010 (CBS 2002).

Following independence, Israel began a concerted and radical strategy of *Judaization*. The expulsion and flight of Palestinian refugees created large 'gaps' in the geography of the land, which the authorities were quick to fill with Jewish settlements. This strategy also entailed the destruction of over 400 Palestinian-Arab towns, villages and hamlets (Falah 2003). During the first decade of independence, Israel built 350 Jewish settlements, and during the following four decades added a similar amount. As a result, over 950 Jewish settlements, towns and cities exist today in Israel/Palestine, while the number of Arab localities has remained virtually unchanged since 1948, despite a five-fold increase in population (see Figure 10.1). The duality of the Israeli state can thus be traced to its early days: it created a state with several democratic features and formalities, but at the same time established legal, institutional and cultural spheres which advanced an undemocratic project of Judaizing (and hence de-Arabizing) the country. This duality became obvious again following the seizure of further Palestinian territories in 1967, but it existed before, and still exists today, in 'Israel Proper' (within the 'Green Line' – the state's recognized sovereign borders), where laws, policies and institutions facilitate the Judaization project. Most conspicuous among these was the highly restrictive military government imposed on the Arab citizens until 1966, and a set of land laws and policies to be discussed below.

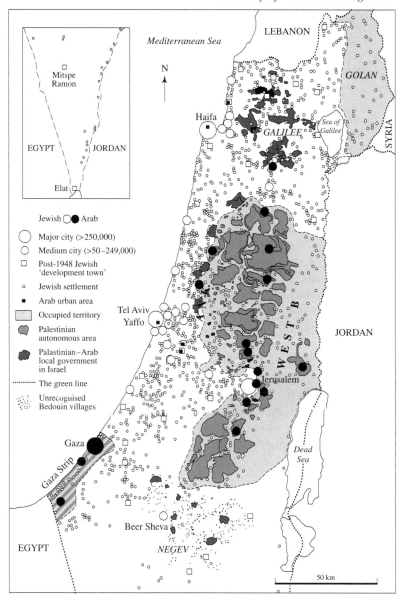

Figure 10.1 Ethnic geography in Israel/Palestine, 2000

In this context, it is analytically and morally important to distinguish between the pre-1948 period, when Jews arrived in Palestine mainly as refugees fleeing genocidal European anti-Semitism, in a population movement Yiftachel has conceptualized as a 'colonialism of survival' (1997), and later periods, which see the Israeli state engaging in internal (post-1948) and external (post-1967) colonialism, encroaching into the territories and rights of Palestinians (Ghanem 1998; Kimmerling 2001; Yiftachel 2002).

Within this setting, several key democratic principles are routinely violated, including the equality of citizens under the law, the universality of elections, or the preservation of basic rights such as freedom of speech, political organization and religious faith – all due to the ethnocratic nature of the regime. Consequently, Israel never had a constitution, and basic human rights and capabilities are thus not protected by special legislation; there is no separation between state and church; while there are some twenty pieces of legislation which discriminate against Arab citizens (Kretzmer 1990; Adalah 1998, 2003).

This political design is premised on a hegemonic perception, cultivated since the rise of Zionism, namely that 'the land' (*Haaretz*) belongs to the Jews, and only them. A rigid form of territorial ethnonationalism developed from the beginning of Zionist settlement, in order to quickly 'indigenize' immigrant Jews, and to conceal, trivialize or marginalize the existence of a Palestinian people on the same land. The frontier became a central icon, and its settlement was considered one of the highest achievements of any Zionist 'returning' to the revered homeland. A popular (and typical) youth-movement song, frequently sung in schools and public gatherings and known to nearly every Jew in Israel during its formative years, illustrates the powerful construction of these icons and myths.

We shall build our land, the homeland (Nivne Artzenu Eretz Moledet)

We shall build our country, our homeland
Because it is ours, ours, this land
We shall build our country, our homeland
It is the command of our blood, the command of generations
We shall build our country despite our destroyers
We shall build our country with the power of our will
The end to malignant slavery
The fire of Freedom is burning
The glorious shine of hope
Will stir our blood
Thirsty for freedom, for independence
We shall march bravely towards the liberation of our people.
                    (A. Levinson, translated by Oren Yiftachel)

Such sentiments were translated into a pervasive programme of Jewish-Zionist territorial socialization and indoctrination, expressed in school curricula, literature, political speeches, popular music, and other spheres of public discourse (Bar-Gal 1993; Ram 1995). The vision promoted was that of a 'pure' ethnic state, following the East European examples from which the founding elites had arrived. Frontier settlement thus continued as a cornerstone of Zionist nation-building, even well after the establishment of a sovereign state, forming a central part of the sacred values, the heroes, the mythology and the internal system of legitimacy and gratification of the settler society (Kimmerling 1983; Shafir and Peled 2002).

Jewish frontierism has gained new energies following the 1967 War, after which Jewish control was extended to the entire historic Palestine/Eretz Yisrael and beyond. The scope of this chapter does not permit full discussion of the significant impact of the semi-official inclusion of the Occupied Territories into the realm of the Israeli regime, and the changes which have occurred since the 1993 Oslo Agreement (Kimmerling 2001). Let us just note that the mutual recognition between the Jewish and Palestinian national movements and the establishment of the Palestinian Authority (PA) have so far failed to halt the Judaization process. To date, the PA has gained only tenuous control over small parts of the Occupied Territories. Further, since the eruption of the 'second Intifada' (Palestinian uprising) in October 2000, and the spectre of intensifying state violence and anti-Jewish terror, the Judaization project has gained new prominence in Israeli-Jewish society, followed by corresponding military, settlement and development policies.

The making of 'ethnocracy'

The Judaization strategy and its counter-forces, especially Palestinian resistance, became the main 'axis' around which both Zionist and Palestinian societies developed in Israel/Palestine. The main spheres in which the ethnocratic regime has developed include Israel's Jews-only *immigration* policies (and the prevention of the return of Palestinian refugees); the state's *legal system* and constitutional foundations, which enshrine its Jewishness; its *development* strategies which heavily favoured Jews over Arabs, but at the same time also create ethno-class gaps between the dominant Western Jews (Ashkenazim) and other immigrant groups, most notably 'Eastern' Jews ('Mizrahim'); the central role assigned to the *armed forces* in shaping state policies; these forces exclude the vast majority of Arabs, while exacerbating socio-economic stratification in Israeli society; and the firm imposition of the *Jewish and Hebrew culture* (mainly in its Ashkenazi guise) as the dominant medium of communication, norms and social customs. These aspects of Israeli society are discussed by a vast literature (Rouhana 1997; Kimmerling 2001; Shafir and Peled 2002; Yonah and Shenhav 2002).

The last major ethnocratic sphere concerns spatial policies, governing land, settlement, boundary and planning policies. Here there are several mechanisms, which work powerfully and systematically to transfer the ownership, control and use of space from Palestinian-Arabs to Jewish hands and at the same time stratify Jewish and Palestinian societies (Kedar 2001; Yonah and Saporta 2000). One striking example in the area of land ownership: prior to 1948, Jews owned only 7 per cent of the land, but have increased control to over 96 per cent at present (land belonging to the state, the Jewish National Fund and Jewish individuals).

The Judaization of space has been achieved through a range of legal and planning means, most conspicuously the confiscation of refugee property, the state appropriation of all land without formal title, and the imposition of Jewish municipal control over 97 per cent of the state (Kedar 2001; Yacobi and Yiftachel 2003). Another striking example of this process has been the institutional prevention of Arab citizens from purchasing land in nearly all of Israel's Jewish non-urban municipalities, which cover 84 per cent of the state (Yiftachel 1999). In addition, the spatial Judaization process has been unidirectional, as, under Israeli basic law, state land cannot be sold, and has included the Occupied Territories where 54 per cent of the land has been either transferred to state ownership or to exclusive Jewish use (Benvenisti 2001; Kedar 2001).

The control of land enabled the establishment of 700 Jewish settlements in Israel/Palestine since 1948, while at the time no new Arab settlements were allowed, except for towns built to concentrate Bedouin tribes. Since 2000, with the intensification of hostilities, Israel has accelerated its settlement programme, which had previously declined for more than a decade, by building dozens of new settlements on both sides of the Green Line, and by seizing large tracts of Palestinian lands for new roads and for a massive security fence planned in the West Bank.

The foundations of the Israeli ethnocracy are buttressed by the declaration of the state as 'Jewish', and not 'Israeli' as would be required under the internationally accepted (territorial) application of the right for self-determination within the nation-state order. The difference between 'Jewish' and 'Israeli' is not mere semantics, but a profound obstacle to the imposition of democratic rule, which should be premised on the empowerment of a sovereign 'demos'. To illustrate: the state prohibits any candidate to compete in elections who advocates a change to the Jewish character of the state. This clearly impinges on the basic right of non-Jewish groups to campaign by democratic means for their political goals.

Another striking facet of this distorted setting is the hierarchy of Palestinian-Arab rights under the Israeli regime, which are stratified legally and institutionally between Druze, Bedouin, Palestinian-Arab citizens, Jerusalem Palestinian residents, and 'subjects' of the Palestinian Authority, split between Gaza and the West Bank. This stratified citizenship is a vivid illustration of the workings of the ethnocratic regime, which uses ethnicity and geography to manipulate identities and unevenly distribute resources (Yiftachel 2001).

The ethnocratic nature of the regime is also conspicuous in the selective imposition of boundaries and borders (Kemp 1998; Newman 2001). For example, the Green Line (Israel's pre-1967 border) functions only as a barrier to the movement of Palestinian-Arabs, but not for Jews, who can freely cross it and settle in the Occupied Territories. Another illustration is the myopia towards the Occupied Territories during Israeli elections, which are described by nearly all commentators as free, 'universal' and democratic.

Yet, Jews residing in the Territories have determined the election of right-wing governments four times during the 1980s and 1990s, while the Palestinians, who were subjects of the Israeli regime, remained disenfranchised. This process, coupled with the stratification of Arab citizenship, is akin to a 'creeping apartheid', increasingly institutionalized and accepted by the Israeli regime and society (Yiftachel 2001). Hence, the Israeli regime has no clearly identifiable 'demos', but rather a complex and layered set of stratified groups.

As noted, the nature of the Israeli ethnocracy has not only discriminated against Palestinians, but also against 'Eastern' Jews (Mizrahim), hailing from the Middle East. The control policies towards the Mizrahim have been less visible, expressed mainly by the imposition of informal economic, cultural and geographical barriers to their mobility within Ashkenazi-dominated society. These are intimately linked to the de-Arabization process, which has worked to delegitimize Arab culture, politics and capital. Given their Arab cultural background, this has structurally marginalized most Mizrahi Jews (Shohat 1997; Peled 2001; Shenhav 2000).

But the comparison between Palestinians and Mizrahim should be qualified: we do not claim that the two groups are of equal status, but rather that the ethnocratic 'western' structure of the Judaizing state *vis-à-vis* Palestinian-Arabs has affected the Mizrahim adversely in a range of cultural, economic and geographic matters. But the oppression of the Palestinians has of course been far more profound, while Mizrahi Jews (and not the Palestinians) have had the option of integrating into the Israeli mainstream and its growing middle classes.

Against this process, it is illuminating to note that the Ashkenazim became a numerical minority in Israel already during the early 1950s, but the working of the ethnocratic settling regime, and the fusion of their identity with a general form of 'Israeliness', 'modernity' and 'development', enabled them to maintain long-term dominance (Swirski 1989; Shohat 2001). This has been aided by the influx of nearly a million immigrants from the former Soviet Union during the 1990s. Despite forming initially a distinct cultural community, they are likely to merge with the Ashkenazi group over the next few decades, thereby maintaining its societal dominance.

The processes described above, however, must not be viewed as static or unidimensional. First, they should be viewed as dialectical and dynamic. That is, ethnocratic forces tend to intensify in the face of resistance, especially when faced with violence and terror. Hence, the activities of the Israeli regime must be understood *vis-à-vis* the ongoing violent Zionist–Palestinian conflict, and the changing relations between Israel's Arab citizens and the state.

Indeed, Israeli ethnic oppression has met with increasing minority resistance. This has been expressed by periodical waves of protest against state policies and political polarization. Protest reached two notable peaks: the first Land Day in 1976, in which six Arab citizens were killed when protesting the confiscation of their lands; and in October 2000, when thirteen Arabs (and one Jew) were killed during mass demonstrations, protesting Israel's ongoing oppression of the Palestinians, on both sides of the Green Line. Political polarization has thus been deepening between the two ethnic groups, with an increasing proportion of Arab votes going to non-Zionist Arab parties, reaching 70 per cent in 1999, and an all time high of 18 per cent in the 2003 elections. In the special Prime Ministerial elections of 2001, 82 per cent of Arab citizens boycotted the vote in protest over their treatment by the Jewish state, signalling again the intensifying process of polarization.

In sum, the Israeli regime, ruling over Israel/Palestine, demonstrates the deep logic of ethnicization behind state structure and policies. It adopts a structure of an 'open' formal democracy, but at another level has set into motion an ethnic transformation of the state from a mainly Arab country into a thoroughly Judaized space and power structure. The new state structurally discriminates against most of its Palestinian-Arab citizens and residents, and actively facilitates the ongoing Judaization of institutions, politics, culture and territory. Drawing on the Israeli example, and keeping in mind the prevalence of similar ethnocratic process in a wide range of other states, such as Serbia, Estonia, Latvia, Sri Lanka, pre-1974 Cyprus, pre-1999 Northern Ireland, and Malaysia, we can now return to our theoretical discussion.

Ethnocracy and regime components

Ethnocracy and democracy

Our discussion of ethnocratic regimes aims to formulate a critique of their frequent representation as democratic. On the one hand, such regimes claim to be full (and often even liberal) democracies, while on the other they routinely oppress and marginalize peripheral minorities, and constantly change the state structure in the majority's favour. The oppression of minorities is often exacerbated by the legitimacy granted to the state as 'democratic' in the international arena. The common representation of these regimes as democratic has been labelled by some scholars as 'conceptual stretching' (Collier and Levitski 1997; Zakaria 1997)

This critique emerges from two main positions. First, we employ a Gramscian-informed perspective that seeks to discover the underlying logic of power relations within a system of hegemonic cultures (for elaboration, see Gramsci 1971; Laclau 1994; Said 1994; Hall 1997). This perspective is suspicious of official rhetoric and declarations, constantly searching for the deeper political and historical forces, and for hegemonic norms, often unseen or silent, which navigate these forces. Second, the critique emerges after privileging a look at society 'from the periphery into the core', hence 'peeling off' much of the self-legitimizing democratic narrative held by society's mainstream. This angle often reveals the impregnable, stratifying, and non-democratic nature of the ethnocratic regime.

Importantly, we do not use the term 'democracy' uncritically. We recognize that it is a contested concept, hotly debated, rarely settled and widely abused, particularly in multi-ethnic states (Mann 1999). It is an institutional response to generations of civil struggles for political and economic inclusion, gradually incorporating and empowering the poor, women and minorities into the once elitist polity (Held 1990a; Tilly 1996).

This is not the place to delve deeply into democratic theory. Suffice it to say that several key principles have emerged as foundations for achieving the main tenets of democracy – *equality* and *liberty*. These include equal citizenship, protection of individuals and minorities against the tyranny of states, majorities or churches, and a range of civil, political and economic rights (Held 1990b). A stable constitution, periodic and universal elections and free media generally ensure these (Dahl 1995). In multi-ethnic or multinational polities, as illustrated by the seminal works of Lijphart (1984), Kymlicka (1995) and most recently Rawls (1999), a certain parity, recognition and proportionality between the ethnic collectivities are prerequisites for democratic legitimacy and stability. While no state ever implements these principles fully, and thus none is a pure democracy, ethnocratic regimes are conspicuous in breaching the spirit, purpose and major tenets of the democracy ideal.

To further fathom the workings of 'open' ethnocracies, we differentiate analytically between regime features and structure. As noted in Figure 10.2, some ethnocracies possess 'visible' democratic features, such as periodic elections, free media, relatively open gender relations, and an autonomous judiciary which protects, and even (some) human rights legislation. But these tend to work on a surface level, while the deeper structure of such regimes is undemocratic, mainly because it facilitates and promotes the seizure of territory and power by one ethnos. It thus undermines key democratic principles, such as civil and legal equality within agreed state boundaries (the 'demos'), protection of minorities, maintenance of equality and proportionality among main social groups, separation between religion and state law, and the enjoyment of substantive rights and capabilities by all long-term state residents.

The analytical differentiation between 'features' and 'structure' highlights the selective and mainly hollow use of the term 'democracy' by the dominant ethnic group. But the use of a democratic discourse, hollow as it is, has the effect of legitimizing the regime, especially in the eyes of the majority group, as is so vividly evident in the Israeli case. The distinction between 'features' and 'structure' is of course not rigid or stable, with a constant flow of mutual influences. For example, elections can bring political change at the levels of features, but this may lead to structural change through the accumulation of small reforms in legislation, resource allocation and representation. However, during the intense process of state-building, the ethnocratic logic of the regime structure generally dictates the terms of much of what transpires in the more visible arenas of political features.

Ethnocracy Regime: Structure and Features
A Conceptional Framework

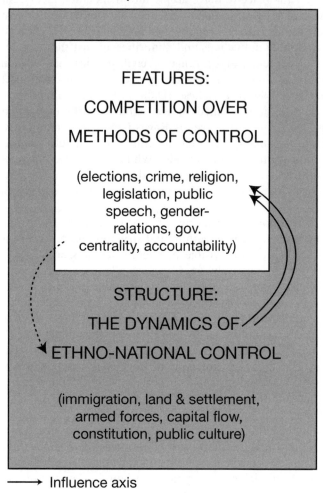

FEATURES:

COMPETITION OVER

METHODS OF CONTROL

(elections, crime, religion,
legislation, public
speech, gender-
relations, gov.
centrality, accountability)

STRUCTURE:

THE DYNAMICS OF

ETHNO-NATIONAL CONTROL

(immigration, land & settlement,
armed forces, capital flow,
constitution, public culture)

⟶ Influence axis

Figure 10.2 Ethnocracy regime: structures and features

Ethnocracies thus operate simultaneously in several levels and arenas, and create a situation where political struggles are often waged around the state's features, while little is said and relatively few battles are fought over the deeper hegemony which makes it 'natural' and 'taken-for-granted' that the state is controlled by one ethnic group. As powerfully argued by Antonio Gramsci (and synthesized by Sassoon 1987: 232), a 'moment' of hegemony is marked by 'the unquestioned dominance of a certain way of life ... when a single concept of reality informs society's tastes, morality, customs, religious and political principles' (ibid.: 232).

The hegemonic order reflects and thus reproduces the interests of the dominant 'ethnie', by representing the 'order of things' in a distorted manner as legitimate, democratic and moral, and by concealing its oppressive or more questionable aspects. This public perception is maintained by preventing, deflecting or ridiculing voices that challenge the regime structure, thereby containing public debate within the 'shallower' bounds of regime features.

Given the analytical distinction between features and structure, and drawing on the case of Israel described above, as well as comparable ethnocratic states analysed elsewhere (Yiftachel 2002), we have identified several structural 'bases', which constitute the foundation of ethnocratic regimes. These are key components of the dominant hegemony, which are generally protected by the boundaries of public discourse and political discussion. Let us emphasize again that we see the structural bases of the regime as *dynamic*, never reaching a state of sustainable stability. These bases evolve over time, but face many challenges and modifications in an effort to maintain their 'natural' status. As part of the ethnocratic regime, they are never sustainable in the long term. The main regime bases thus include:

- *Immigration and citizenship*: rights of entry and membership into the political community define the all-important boundaries of political (and by implication social) power. In ethnocracies, immigration and citizenship are chiefly determined by affiliation with the dominant ethnic-nation.
- *Land and settlement*: land and territory are absolutely central for ethnonational politics. As such, the ownership, use and development of land, as well as planning and settlement policies, are shaped by the state's project of extending ethno-national control over its (multi-ethnic) territory.
- *Armed forces*: violent force is critical in assisting the state to maintain (oppressive) ethno-national control over contested regions and resisting groups. To that end, the armed forces (the military, the police), which bear the name of the entire state, are predominantly affiliated with the leading ethnic nation.

- *Capital flow*: the flow of capital and development patterns are deeply influenced by an 'ethnic logic', privileging the dominant ethno-classes; notably, these market mechanisms are often represented as 'free' or 'neutral' and hence beyond challenge.
- *The legal system*: legalism often depoliticizes and legitimizes patterns of ethnic control. Such controls are often premised on redundant, absurd, non-existent or only partially functional constitutions. This is often presented as 'the law of the land', and subsequently placed outside the realm of legitimately contestable issues.
- *State culture*: the ethnocratic public culture is formulated around a set of symbols, representations, traditions and practices, which tend to reinforce the narratives of the dominant ethno-national group while silencing, degrading or ridiculing contesting cultures or perspectives.

These regime bases, each separately and in varying combinations, powerfully mould ethnic relations in contested territories, but are rarely subject to day-to-day or electoral deliberation. Genuine debate on these 'taken-for-granted' issues is generally absent from public discourse, especially among the dominant majority. When these issues are questioned by resisting groups (say, in the parliament, or through the media), they are usually ignored, silenced or ridiculed. But the dominance of the various 'truths' behind these regime 'bases' is of course not absolute, and may be exposed and resisted as political entrepreneurs exploit the tensions and contradictions in the system, particularly between the declared 'democracy' and its substantive discriminatory manifestations. When such topics enter the public arena and become subject to genuine public debate, cracks are likely to appear in the ethnocratic structure.

Ethnocracy and minorities

A hallmark of the ethnocratic system is its ability to maintain the dominance of the leading ethnic group while excluding indigenous or national minorities. This is premised on the exclusion, marginalization or assimilation of minority groups. But not all minorities are treated equally. Some are constructed as 'internal', whereas others are marked as 'external'. In the essentializing discourse of ethnocratic societies, a critical difference exists between those considered part of the 'historical' or even 'genetic' nation and others whose presence is portrayed as mere historical coincidence, or as a 'danger' to the security and integrity of the dominant ethnos. These discourses strip 'external' minorities from means of inclusion into the meaningful sites of 'the nation' (Penrose 2000).

Ethnocracies are driven, first and foremost, by a sense of collective entitlement among the majority group to control 'its' state, and 'its' homeland, as part and parcel of what is conceived as a universal right for self-determination. Thus, belonging to the dominant 'ethnie' is the key to mobility and resources among peripheral groups, and so forms the strategy adopted by most immigrant minorities, who thereby distance themselves from indigenous or other 'external' minorities. As such, ethnocratic societies continuously maintain an 'ethnic project', which, similarly to the 'racial project' identified by Omi and Winant (1993) for American society, attempts to build an informal public image of separate and unequal groups. This image is diffused into most societal arenas (such as public culture, politics, universities, the economy), causing long-term reproduction of ethnic inequalities.

The dominant ethnic group generally forms the state's elites and upper strata, and tends to play a dual game *vis-à-vis* peripheral minorities. On the one hand, it articulates a discourse of belonging which incorporates immigrant and peripheral groups not associated with any 'external' or 'rival' nation, 'inviting' them to assimilate into the moral community of the dominant ethno-nation. But on the other hand, it uses this very discourse of inclusion and belonging to conceal the uneven effects of its strategies, which often marginalize the immigrants and 'deviant' groups, economically, culturally and geographically. It would be a mistake, however, to treat this as a conspiracy; it is rather an expression of broad social interest, generally unarticulated, privileging social circles that are closest to the ethno-national core. This 'natural' process tends to broadly reproduce, though it never precisely replicates, patterns of social stratification.

The strategy towards indigenous and/or national minorities, or fragments of rival nations, is generally more openly oppressive. They are represented and treated, at best, as 'external' to the ethno-national project, or, at worst, as a subversive threat. As illustrated by the Israeli example, the tenets of self-determination are used only selectively, pertaining to ethnicity and not to an inclusive geographical unit, as required by the basic principles of democratic statehood. Many of the expansionist projects typical of ethnocracies – namely, ethnic settlement, land seizure, cultural dominance, military expansion or uni-ethnic economic development – encroach into the sphere of local minorities. This is often 'wrapped' in a discourse of modernity, progress and democracy, but the very material reality is unmistakable, entailing minority dispossession and exclusion.

However, the self-representation of most ethnocracies as democratic creates profound structural tensions, because it requires the state to go beyond lip service and empower external minorities with some (though less than equal) formal political powers. It is the 'cracks' and 'crevices' between the claims for democracy, the denial of political equality, and the associated material encroachment into minority spaces and resources which harbour the tensions and conflicts typical of ethnocratic regimes.

Looking ahead

This chapter presents a framework for ethnocratic theory. It shows that, in certain geographical and political circumstances, various forces combine to create ethnocratic regimes. It focuses on 'open' ethnocracies, where the state represents itself as democratic while simultaneously facilitating the seizure of a contested territory and power by a dominant ethnic nation. It outlines the characteristics of such regimes, shows their distinctiveness from the 'normal' nation-state model, and analyses their ability to maintain ethnic dominance. The chapter also discusses the relation of ethnocratic regimes with minorities, democracy and political instability, and explores the tensions and contradictions which generate their decline and transformation.

Our framework here is both broad and preliminary. It needs to be tested, challenged and expanded, in order to gain depth, validity and robustness. This can advance in various directions, the most obvious are: (a) comparative research which would test, calibrate and modify the assertions made above; (b) in-depth case studies, which would study the more detailed and subtle forms of ethnocratic expansion and hegemony, as well as the forms of resistance and challenge to the system; and (c) theoretical explorations and modifications, especially *vis-à-vis* new structural forces influencing the nation-state, such as the increasingly globalizing world economy and/or the growing force and influence of the discourse of human rights and multi-culturalism. Efforts in these directions have been initiated by the authors in this volume, but further research is needed to enrich our understanding of ethnocratic states, and their volatile ethnic relations.

References

Adalah (1998) *Legal Violations of Arab Rights in Israel*, Shefa'amre: Adalah.
—— (2003) *Law and Politics in the Or Commission*, Shefa'amre: Adalah.
Axtmann, R. (1996) *Liberal Democracy into the Twenty-First Century: Globalization, Integration, and the Nation-State*, Manchester: Manchester University Press.
Barak, A. (1998) 'The role of supreme court in a democracy', *Israel Studies*, 3(2): 8–16.
Bar-Gal, Y. (1993) *Moledet (Homeland) and Geography in a Hundred Years of Zionist Education*, Tel Aviv: Am Oved, Hebrew.
Benvenisti, M. (2001) *Sacred Landscapes*, Los Angeles: University of California Press.
Brubaker, R. (1996) *Nationalism Reframed: Nationhood and the National Question in the New Europe*, London: Cambridge University Press.
CBS (Central Bureau of Statistics) (2002) *Statistical Data on Israel*, Jerusalem: Government Printers.
Collier, D. and Levitski, S. (1997) 'Democracy with adjectives: conceptual innovation in comparative research', *World Politics*, 49 (April): 430–51.
Connor, W. (1994) *Ethnonationalism: The Quest for Understanding*, Princeton, NJ: Princeton University Press.
Dahl, R. (1995) *Democracy and its Critics*, New Haven, CT: Yale University Press.
Dowty, A. (1998) *The Jewish State: One Hundred Years Later*, Los Angeles: University of California Press.

Falah, G. (2003) 'Dynamic patterns of shrinking Arab lands in Palestine', *Political Geography*, 22: 179–209.

Gavison, R. (1999) 'Jewish and democratic? A rejoinder to the "ethnic democracy" debate', *Israel Studies*, 4(1): 44–72.

Gellner, E. (1996) 'Do nations have navels?', *Nations and Nationalism*, 2(3): 366–71.

Ghanem, A. (1997) 'The limits of parliamentary politics: the Arab minority in Israel and the 1992 and 1996 elections', *Israeli Affairs*, 4(2): 72–93.

—— (1998) 'State and minority in Israel: the case of ethnic state and the predicament of its minority', *Ethnic and Racial Studies*, 21(3): 428–47.

—— (2000) *The Palestinian-Arab Minority in Israel, 1948–2000*, Albany, NY: SUNY Press.

Gramsci, A. (1971) *Selections from Prison Notebooks*, New York: International Publishers.

Gurr, T. (2000) *Peoples Versus States: Minorities at Risk in the New Century*, Washington, DC: US Institute of Peace.

Gurr, T. and Harff, B. (1994) *Ethnic Conflict in World Politics*, Boulder, CO: Westview Press.

Hakli, J. (2001) 'In the territory of knowledge: state-centred discourses and the construction of society', *Progress in Human Geography*, 25(3): 403–22.

Hall, S. (1997) 'Introduction: who needs identity?', in S. Hall and P. du Gay *Questions of Cultural Identity*, London: Sage, pp. 1–18.

Hechter, M. (2000) *Containing Nationalism*, Oxford: Oxford University Press.

Held, D. (1990a) *Models of Democracy*, London: Polity Press.

—— (1990b) 'The decline of the nation state', in S. Hall and M. Jacques (eds) *New Times: The Changing Face of Politics in the 1990s*, London: Lawrence and Wishart, pp. 191–204.

Kedar, A. (2001) 'The legal transformation of ethnic geography: Israeli law and the Palestinian landholder 1948 1967', *NYU Journal of International Law and Politics*, 33(4): 997–1044.

Kemp, A. (1998) 'From politics of location to politics of significance: the construction of political territory in Israel's first years', *Journal of Area Studies*, 12(1): 74–101.

Kimmerling, B. (1983) *Zionism and Territory*, Berkeley, CA: Institute of International Studies, University of California.

—— (2001) *The Invention and Decline of Israeliness: State, Society, and the Military*, Berkeley, CA: University of California Press.

Kretzmer, D. (1990) *The Legal Status of the Arabs in Israel*, Boulder, CO: Westview Press.

Kymlicka, W. (1995) *Multicultural Citizenship: A Liberal Theory of Minority Rights*, Oxford: Clarendon Press.

—— (2001) *Politics in the Vernacular: Nationalism, Multiculturalism and Citizenship*, Oxford: Oxford University Press.

Laclau, E. (ed.) (1994) *The Making of Political Identities*, London: Verso.

Lijphart, A. (1984) *Democracies*, New Haven, CT: Yale University Press.

Linz, J., and Stepan, A. (1996) *Problems of Democratic Transition and Consolidation*, Baltimore, MD: Johns Hopkins University Press.

Lustick, I. (1993) *Unsettled States, Disputed Lands*, Ithaca, NY: Cornell University Press.

—— (2002) 'Nationalism and religion in the Middle East', *Hagar: International Social Science Review*, 3(2): 176–203.

McGarry, J. (1998) 'Demographic engineering: the state-directed movement of ethnic groups as a technique of conflict regulation', *Ethnic and Racial Studies*, 21(4): 613–38.

Mann, M. (1999) 'The dark side of democracy: the modern tradition of ethnic and political cleansing', *New Left Review*, 253 (June): 18–45.

—— (2000) 'Democracy and ethnic war', *Hagar: International Social Science Review*, 1(2): 115–34.

Murphy, A. (2002) 'The territorial underpinnings of national identity', *Geopolitics*, 7(2): 193–214.

Newman, D. (2001) 'From national to post-national territorial identities in Israel–Palestine', *Geoforum*, 53: 235–46.

Omi, M. and Winant, H. (1993) *Racial Formation in the United States: From the 1960s to the 1990s*, New York: Routledge.

Paasi, A. (1999) 'Boundaries as a social process: territoriality in the world of flows', *Geopolitics*, 3: 69–88.

Peled, Y. (ed.) (2001) *Shas: The Challenge of Israeliness*, Tel Aviv: Yediot Ahronot (in Hebrew).

Penrose, J. (2000) 'The limitation of nationalist democracy: the treatment of marginal groups as a measure of state legitimacy', *Hagar: International Social Science Review*, 1(2): 33–62.

Ram, U. (1995) 'Zionist historiography and the invention of modern Jewish nationhood: the case of Ben Zion Dinur', *History and Memory*, 7: 91–124.

Rawls, J. (1999) *The Law of Peoples*, Cambridge, MA: Harvard University Press.

Rouhana, N. (1997) *Palestinian Citizens in an Ethnic Jewish State: Identities and Conflict*, New Haven, CT: Yale University Press.

Said, E. (1994) *The Politics of Dispossession: The Struggle for Palestinian Self-Determination*, London: Chatto and Windus.

Sassen, S. (1998) *Globalisation and its Discontents*, New York: Wiley and Sons.

Sassoon, A.S. (1987) *Gramsci's Politics*, Minneapolis: University of Minnesota Press.

Shafir, G. and Peled, Y. (2002) *Being an Israeli: The Politics of Citizenship*, Cambridge: Cambridge University Press.

Shenhav, Y. (2000) 'What do Palestinians and Jews-from-Arab lands have in Common? Nationalism, ethnicity and the compensation question', *Hagar: International Social Science Review*, 1(1): 70–116.

Shohat, E. (1997) 'The narrative of the nation and the discourse of modernization: the case of the Mizrahim', *Critique*, Spring: 3–19.

—— (2001) *Forbidden Reminiscence: Towards Multi-Cultural Thought*, Tel Aviv: Bimat Kedem (in Hebrew).

Smith, A.D. (1995) *Nations and Nationalism in a Global Era*, Cambridge: Polity.

—— (1996) 'Nations and their pasts', *Nations and Nationalism*, 2(3): 358–65.

Smooha, S. (2002) 'Types of democracy and modes of conflict management in ethnically divided societies', *Nations and Nationalism*, 8(4): 423–31.

Soysal, Y. (2000) 'Citizenship and identity: living in diasporas in post-war Europe?', *Ethnic and Racial Studies*, 23(1): 1–15.

Swirski, S. (1989) *Israel: The Oriental Majority*, London: Zed Books.

Tilly, C. (1996) *Citizenship, Identity and Social History*, London: Cambridge University Press.

Yacobi, H. and Yiftachel, O. (2003) 'Urban ethnocracy: ethnicization and the production of space in an Israeli "mixed" city', *Environment and Planning D: Society and Space*, 21(3): 322–43.

Yiftachel, O. (1997) 'Israeli society and Jewish–Palestinian reconciliation: "ethnocracy" and its territorial contradictions', *Middle East Journal*, 51(4): 505–19.

—— (1999) 'Ethnocracy: the politics of Judaizing Israel/Palestine', *Constellations*, 6(3): 364–90.

—— (2001) 'From "peace" to creeping apartheid: the emerging political geography of Israel/Palestine', *Arena*, 16(3): 13–24.

—— (2002) 'Territory as the kernel of nationalism', *Geopolitics*, 7(3) (special issue on 'When/Where the Nation?'): 215–48.

Yiftachel, O. and Kedar, S. (2000) 'Landed power: the emergence of an ethnocratic land regime in Israel', *Teorya Uvikkoret* (*Theory and Critique*), 19(1): 67–100.

Yonah, Y. and Saporta, Y. (2000) 'Land and housing policy in Israel: the discourse of citizenship and its limits', *Teorya Uvikkoret* (*Theory and Critique*), 18: 129–52.

Yonah, Y. and Shenhav, Y. (2002) 'The multicultural condition' (Hebrew), *Teorya Uvikkoret* (*Theory and Critique*), 17: 163–87.

Zakaria, F. (1997) 'The rise of illiberal democracy', *Foreign Affairs*, 76(6): 22–43.

11 'Majority ethnic' claims and authoritarian nationalism

The case of Hindutva

Chetan Bhatt

[T]here is no need to unmask what are so patently selective readings of an ethnic past. Yet selection can take place only within strict limits, limits set by the pre-existing myths, symbols, customs and memories of vertical *ethnies*.

(Smith 1989: 356)

The jeering, hooting young men who battered down the Babri Masjid are the same ones whose pictures appeared in the papers in the days that followed the nuclear tests. They were on the streets, celebrating India's nuclear bomb and simultaneously 'condemning Western Culture' by emptying crates of Coke and Pepsi into public drains. I'm a little baffled by their logic: Coke is Western Culture, but the nuclear bomb is an old Indian tradition? Yes, I've heard – the bomb is in the Vedas. It might be, but if you look hard enough, you'll find Coke in the Vedas too. That's the great thing about all religious texts. You can find anything you want in them – as long as you know what you're looking for.

(Roy 1998)

Introduction: civic bifurcation and Indian nationalism

The violent eruption of Hindu nationalist mass movements, organisations and a political party of governance in India since the 1980s was most brutally illustrated during the pogroms in Gujarat during 2002 against Indian citizens, mainly Muslims. During the pogroms, state authorities and sections of the police force acted in collusion with Hindutva organisations against minority groups. Some 2,000 adults and children were killed and an estimated 150,000 people displaced during the violence. Even if the atrocities which accompanied previous Hindutva mobilisations can still be conceived as 'communal violence', the Gujarat events pointed to a far bleaker situation of an organised, systematic pogrom. Gujarat's Christians, targets of Hindutva violence since the late 1990s, are now subject to a systematic, state-sponsored enumerative surveillance. In 1998, the Hindu nationalist BJP (Bharatiya Janata Party) announced its coming to power, as head of an unstable coalition government, by ordering the testing of nuclear devices and long-range nuclear weapon delivery systems. A political party which had come to power by invoking the sacred landscape of Bharatmata was inducting weapons of mass destruction on her sacrosanct soil.

The move to the centre of Indian polity and civil society of previously marginal bodies such as the Rashtriya Swayamsevak Sangh (RSS, the foundational organisation of contemporary Hindu nationalism), the BJP, the Vishwa Hindu Parishad (VHP) and their numerous offshoots has sometimes been represented as the politicised expression of the 'dominant majority' Hindu population. This is seen as India's own 'majority' fundamentalism, an empirical illustration of intensified expression and conflict based on nationalism, ethnicity or religion in various regions of the world since the early 1980s. This can lead to an academic rendition of 'Hindu' nationalism as the most recent expressive mode of a 'dominant *ethnie*' comprised of the Hindus of India, counterposed to the minority 'ethnicities' of Muslim, Sikh and Christian populations.

There are formidable complexities, historical and contemporary, in explaining Hindu nationalism in terms of extant and readily describable majorities and minorities, ethnicity, ethnic religions and the like. The political languages of majority and minority, and an ethnic-territorial conception of religious identity, are also ones which have provided potent sources of legitimation for Hindu nationalists themselves, though the idea of an all-embracing Hindu identity is alien to 'traditional' Hinduism. The complexities are further compounded in attempts to conceive of Indian histories, social formations, civil societies, polity, national, federal and district state formations and Indian nationalism in the languages of 'ethnicity', 'majority' or 'minority'. The formation of the Indian nation-state, and much of the content of pre- and post-Independence Indian politics, were partially the result of institutionally embedded, deeply politicised logics set in motion from the 1870s, and based on modernist enumerative reasoning, statistically defined population blocs, group calculus, and an arithmetic (zero-sum) conception of political and civil power dependent on ascribed and hermetic group identities. Partition was one horrifying consequence, based as it was on population demographics and the demand for a separate state for Muslims in order to protect their interests against 'Hindu majority' domination. Post-Independence Indian political culture (and administration) have also been subject to communitarian reasoning, often characterised by a ready slippage from impermanent, contingent and varying political majorities as necessary features of the democratic, civic-nationalist project, to permanent, reductively (and sometimes legally) defined majorities and minorities, groups and communities, electorates and representation, discrimination and reservation, secession and national belonging.

Since its inception in the late nineteenth century, Hindu nationalism has contained an ideology of majoritarian dominance and Hindu supremacy. From the early decades of the twentieth century, this took the form of a crude demand that the nation-state, nationalism and national culture reflect the culture and aspirations of what was conceived as an overwhelmingly 'majority Hindu' population, and that minorities must demonstrate unconditional and unceasing obeisance to an exclusive 'Hindu nation-state' (*Hindurashtra*). Following Independence, Indian nationalism, especially its Gandhian 'multicultural' and Nehruvian secularist version, was construed as an illegitimate and inauthentic imposition upon an already constituted 'Hindu majority' conceived as the natural inheritor of the land. Secularism is seen to favour Muslim and Christian minorities of India. Hindus, in this discourse, are rendered as the perpetually suffering victims of a 'western pseudo-secular' nationalism that is claimed to be based, against all reason and empirical evidence, on the 'appeasement' of minorities and systematic historic discrimination against the 'majority Hindus'.

Since the first decade of the twentieth century, advocates of Hindu nationalism have also unceasingly claimed to be the sole representatives of the 'majority Hindu' population of India and the legitimate guardians of its evidently calculable 'interests'. However, historically Hindu nationalism has never been able to represent the aspirations of what is claimed to be a 'Hindu majority' constituency, nor has it yet managed to achieve an unfettered electoral legitimation by that putative constituency. Hence, Hindu nationalism has often been characterised as a '*communal*' movement, one which cannot name itself as such (Datta 1999), in which previously marginal organisations and a minority Hindu nationalist electoral constituency have made illicit majoritarian claims based on appeals to 'dominant' religion and culture. Hindu nationalism is thus seen not as a competing nationalism that has the capacity to replace or usurp Indian nationalism, but is instead a 'communal' movement representing a severely narrow and limited political interest, though being no less dangerous for that. From this 'anti-communal' perspective, Indian nationalism has a distinct genealogy and content which are now being threatened by anti-secular, anti-democratic, extra-legal Hindu 'communal' forces.

However, this position has been questioned from a variety of directions (Jaffrelot 1996; Sarkar 1996; Hansen 1999; Zavos 2000). What is now conceived in post-Nehruvian terms as the secular, democratic, federal, republican and essentially civic Indian nationalism has often had a relatively close, if uneven and discontinuous, historical relationship to some strands of incipient Hindu nationalism. The argument here has to be approached carefully, and a crude equivalence of Indian and Hindu nationalism is not implied (indeed, there is great evidence to the contrary). This is also not a *post hoc* legitimation of claims (for example, of Mohammed Ali Jinnah during the 1930s) that the Indian freedom movement was, and post-Independence India would be, Hindu-dominated and hence a separate nation-state for Muslims was necessary in order to protect their interests. Nor is the argument simply that Indian nationalism was Hindu-influenced in 'ethos' and cultural symbolism. The latter is usually represented by Gandhianism, though even here one has to take care: virtually all of

Gandhi's campaigns were directed to secular matters and not to distinctly Hindu concerns, though the key exceptions – his 'fast unto death' at the prospect from 1932 of separate electorates for 'untouchables', his characterisation of dalits as 'descendants of Vishnu', and his unyielding belief in *varnashramadharma* – are highly significant because of the hegemonic Hindu upper-caste ideology they represented.

Indian nationalism is usually characterised as 'anti-communal' over much of the pre-Independence era (but see Bhatt 2001; Tejani 2002), and committed to legal and civil protection of minorities under a composite, multireligious national ideal during the Nehruvian period. However, it was unable to sufficiently register, either before or after Independence, the nature and depth of what institutional secularism and a cultural politics of secularism might mean for a complex multicaste, polyethnic, multireligious, multilingual society, governed by a federal but centrist state, comprised of many populations immediately amenable to the enchantment of religion, and structured by institutional and civil discrimination against 'lower' castes and dalits. Similarly, Indian nationalism has been unable to sufficiently inure itself against encroachments informed by Hindu majoritarian claims. Postcolonial Congress hegemony and state and political administration and governance at national, federal, district and local levels were informed by logics of group thinking and enumeration that were themselves susceptible to Hindu socio-political mobilisation and inculcation of sectarian religious interests into the apparatus of ostensibly neutral political governance and administration. Indira Gandhi's explicit appeal to Hindu nationalist senti ments following her authoritarian 'emergency' period, the anti-Sikh pogroms of the mid-1980s (following Indira Gandhi's assassination, and which implicated Congress politicians, activists and forces of law and order), as well as the increasing dominance of Hindu religious symbols and iconography in state-run and independent media and political campaigns are examples of the interpenetration of Hindu religious symbolism into Indian politics since the early 1980s. These processes worked to the favour of, and were readily exploited by, Hindu nationalist organisations during the 1990s.

Dominant ethnicity?

If there were important, even if uneven, associations between varieties of Hindu majoritarian thinking and Indian nationalism, can either be characterised as the manifestation of a 'dominant ethnicity'? This chapter argues against the conceptual application of the idea of 'dominant ethnicity' to Hindu nationalism or, indeed, to Hinduism. Similarly, India provides neither a nation-state nor a nationalism that is based on (a dominant) ethnicity, nor can one feasibly conceive of the organisation and multiplicity of its various civil societies, caste hierarchies, regional vernaculars, religious traditions (Hindu or otherwise), local anthropologies and national and federal institutions as determined under an unproblematic 'ethnic' description, let alone

one that can be extended from 'dominant ethnicity' to ethnic nationalism. It is not disputed here that *both* Indian and Hindu nationalism are conceivable in terms of upper-caste hegemony, power, domination, ideology and systematic institutional discrimination against 'scheduled castes and tribes' and 'other backward' classes. Nor is it disputed that 'secular' forms of Indian nationalism have been historically dominated by upper caste groups and enunciated through political ideologies of nationalism that are reflective of upper-caste belonging (for example, a core aspect of Gandhi's Indian nationalism was the interpellation of dalits as 'harijans', and illustrated a caste Hindu claim *over* a population structurally outside of and discriminated against by Hinduism.) However, it would be difficult to meaningfully apply a framework of 'ethnicity' to describe dominant caste configurations in India. The term 'ethnicity' is normatively used in Indian sociology and anthropology, as elsewhere, to describe minority groups, in the Indian case usually *adivasi* (tribal) and smaller linguistic communities. Inverting this paradigm to interrogate and expose a set of dominant ideologies based on caste that are masked under a universal nationalism may be necessary. But it would be difficult to characterise socially, economically and politically dominant groups under *ethnic* descriptions, nor would it be accurate to conceive of caste elites under *ethnic* taxonomies.

Parallel arguments apply to what is now conceived as a 'world religion' called Hinduism, an idea partially sustained as a result of Durkheimian functionalist paradigms in religious studies. A 'syndicated' or unanimist conception of Hinduism is itself a recent, political claim, but is not empirically or historically justifiable (Thapar 1985, 1989). Similarly, the idea that Hindu nationalism represents a resurgence of 'dominant *ethnic*' expression, and cognately that a 'dominant ethnicity' either has or should have some substantive relationship to Indian nationalism, is not only an intellectually unwarranted reification, but an ethically problematic one, not least because it is at the core of the political claims made by Hindu nationalists in their attempts to violently subvert the rule of law and replace the republican, secular and democratic constitution of India with that representing an exclusive, anti-minority, caste-based Hindu nation-state (*Hindurashtra*).

The broader set of issues here concern the disciplinary reification of slippery concepts like ethnicity and nationalism, the confluence of description, explanation and legitimation that can emerge from typological schemes, and the destabilising of emic-etic boundaries to the advantage of those who seek to naturalise ethnicity, ethnic belonging, culture, homeland, tradition and authenticity. Hindu nationalist claims are frequently mobilised using the same kinds of taxonomic framework as are employed in some academic characterisations of ethnicity (typically related to shared myths, histories, culture, kinship and homeland): what, then, is the ethical consequence of the intellectual reification of euhemerism? An adjacent question, especially pertinent to colonial and post-colonial nationalisms, is what can an allegedly 'shared' history of myth, symbol, culture and homeland mean if the content, limits and boundaries of the latter were definitively brought into relief, historicised, rendered as systems of belief and hierarchy, indeed often fashioned, during the ventures of eighteenth- and nineteenth-century comparative philology, mythology, and 'ethnology'? One need not concur with a flattening, hermetic conception of 'Orientalist' scholarship to also recognise the 'paradox' of an allegedly authentic Hindu nationalism in its dense and thorough embedding in colonial scholarship. This raises deeper questions about the invention of ethnicity during the colonial era and its post-colonial consequences (Ranger 1999).

This also leaves open a more difficult set of historical questions, both about the over-integrated, homogenising conception of an ethnicised and territorial Hinduism as a world religion, and the troubled relationship from the nineteenth century onwards of that Hinduism to incipient secular or religious nationalisms. The conception of Hinduism as a relatively coherent, unified (even if occasionally rendered *sui generis*) conglomeration of cognate traditions, rituals, cosmologies and practices is itself recent, arising from the eighteenth century (von Stietencron 1989, 1995; Inden 1990; but see Lorenzen 1999). This is usually related to a relatively recent reductive condensation of Hinduism to an authoritative, if diffuse, Vedic and Indo-Aryan origin, emanationistic and monistic pantheism (usually Upanishadic), 'post-Vedic dualism' (*advaita Vedanta*) and associated idealist cosmologies, three main devotional sects (Vaishnavite, Shaivite, Shakta) and some conception of caste-based hierarchical ordering. This also represents a reduction of diverse geographical and linguistic caste Hindu traditions to those related to northern India, Sanskrit and Hindi, while eliding the traditions and cosmologies of *shudras* and *dalits*. The rendition of Hinduism as *sanatana dharma* (the eternal or 'perennial religion'), which has also emerged at the core of Hindu nationalist claims that *sanatana dharma* is the primordial religion of humanity, arising from the first ever civilisation, and first discovered by Hinduism, can be traced to complex nineteenth-century currents, including disputes between what are now rendered as 'modernist' and 'traditionalist' sectarian tendencies (such as the Arya Samaj and its various adversaries, including the Sanatan Dharm Sabha). The characterisations of Hinduism as 'tolerant', 'non-violent', 'liberal', 'inclusive', 'metaphysical', 'spiritual' or 'other-worldly' are each relatively recent products (Halbfass 1988; von Stietencron 1995; Pinch 1996; Sarkar 1996). Each of these areas is also susceptible to a peculiar euhemerism and instinctive use of supramundane metaphors such that, in a remarkable recuperation of Hegel, 'Hinduism' is displaced beyond and outside histories and societies, process and transformation.

The unremitting historicity and incompleteness of this process (by no means restricted to Hinduism) are paradoxically at the core of the early twentieth-century Hindu nationalist compulsion to conclusively define and proscribe what being a Hindu means (Savarkar [1923] 1989; Golwalkar [1939] 1944), not least because of the absence of an unambiguously autochthonous origin for the term 'Hindu' itself (and the lack, from the colossal Hindu pantheon, of a single deity that represents *Hindurashtra*). It is additionally significant that a key focus of the activities of Hindu nationalists since the late nineteenth century has concerned numerous Indian groups and communities that are syncretic, hybrid, and which cannot be classified unambiguously by any particular religious or ethnic taxonomy. In other words, one strand in the emergence of Hindu nationalism has been the existence of genuinely authentic Indian traditions in which ethnic boundaries are simply not commensurable, and which therefore pose the threat of impurity and danger.[1] Equally of significance is the observation that the iconographies of contemporary Hindu nationalism have, by and large, been those refashioned from northern Indian Vaishnava repertoires, historically associated with a range of devotional traditions and movements (*bhakti*) which developed in the medieval period, often in opposition to structural and scriptural forms of authority derived from the Vedas; the Hindu nationalist attempt to collapse and homogenise these historically opposed traditions under a single territorial carapace is a hegemonic, upper-caste claim. It is also possible to explain the emergence and periodic resurgence of Hindu nationalism as an upper-caste response to 'lower'-caste and dalit socio-political movements and social mobility. The view of Hinduism as an ethnicity or ethnic religion is itself compromised by the relatively recent genealogy of this conception in a variety of attempts to provide a systematic and over-integrative description of caste, race, tribe, lineage, ritual, endogamous practices and perceived social order (Dumont 1980; Inden 1990; S. Bayly 1995, 1999b, 1999a; Trautmann 1997). As consequential have been earlier colonial historicisations of an hermetic Hinduism and its archaic *civilisational* period, usually one rendered as Vedic in originary belief, Aryan in 'ethnology' and definitively Sanskritic in 'culture' (Thapar 1996).

It is not being argued here that the nineteenth-century colonial period is the sole epistemic source for the depth, content, history and mythopoesis of what is known as Hinduism. But equally, the memorialisation of those traditions and their contemporary significance cannot be understood simply as extant history relatively independent from the impact of historiographical efforts during the long nineteenth century. These areas are distinct from a different set of complex historical debates about the import of regional, pre-colonial *patries* in India (C. Bayly 1998), pre-colonial conflicts between polities, kingdoms and groups, or the changing histories of caste, religious movements and their various xenologies. These areas complicate debates about ethnicity and nationalism among modern constructivist, ethnic primordialist and neo-traditionalist tendencies. The question here becomes not simply one about the masking of dominant ethnicity under universal nationalism by an extant and describable 'ethnic core', but about how particular intellectual *epistemes* of social and cultural historiography, and the histories they make available, have become dominant since the early nineteenth century, and which allow (certain) conceptions of time, space, tradition, authenticity, genos and xenos to be constituted in and as politics. One need neither deny the enduring political and affective power of ethnicity, nor accept a voluntarist or epiphenomenal conception of cultural transformation to also acknowledge the recent history of conceptions of tradition, authenticity, indigenism and their associated claims.

In the specific example of Hindutva ('Hinduness' but now synonymous with 'Hindu nationalism'), a term which originated during the 1860s and was reinforced in novel form in the early 1920s, there is little question that the phenomenon is very recent, irreducibly modern and stiffly resistant to an easy accommodation within whatever is meant by Hindu traditions, even as it now claims hegemony over all the 'traditions' of the latter. It is one characteristic of contemporary 'Hindu' nationalism that its core ideologies, impulse, forms of organisation, and socio-political mobilisation owe little of significance to what may be conceived as extant Hindu traditions. Indeed, one influential 'neo-traditional' tendency locates Hindu nationalism as a product of an inauthentic *secular* modernity, against which authentic Hindu traditions can be readily and sharply counterpoised (Nandy 1985; Badrinath 1993; Madan 1997). At which point, then, does the malleable nature of claims about the content of a putative ethnicity or nationalism become so removed from what is conceived as an historical or 'ethnic' tradition that to conceive of the former and the latter as both sharing related 'myths of a common ancestry, historical memories and a distinct culture' (Smith 1999: 127) can become a presentist reading that is at least partially at risk of acknowledging the veracity of an interested political claim? Similarly, when does the western origin, content and form discerned in an allegedly indigenous 'ethnic' claim make it 'modern' to the extent of rendering filiations to whatever is conceived as 'tradition' irrelevant and immaterial? If the appropriation of Hegel, James Mill, Friedrich Schlegel, Arthur Schopenhauer, Friedrich Max Muller, Mazzini, Herbert Spencer and Mussolini is at least as important in describing the form and content of Hindu nationalism as are appeals to 'Hindu traditions', what precisely is the *ethnie* that is being mobilised?

The origins of Hindu nationalism

Unsurprisingly, the cluster of ideas that India constituted a nation symbolised by unitary *genos*, an evident territorial boundary and upper-caste Hindu precepts rendered in archaic and civilisational terms originated amongst sections of elite, primarily intellectual urban groups living under colonial domination in the latter half of the nineteenth century, and gained force in several periods of which the 1860s, late 1880s, after 1905 (the 'first partition' of Bengal), the inter-war period and the mid-1930s were the most important (Jaffrelot 1996; Datta 1999; Zavos 2000). The importance of regional vernacular elites is of particular significance here, especially in Bengal and Bombay Presidency (now Maharashtra), though these two 'centres' by no means completed the efforts of Hindu religious-nationalist emergence (Jones 1976; Dalmia 1997). Similarly, late nineteenth- and early twentieth-century claims made for unitary, homogeneous nationalism, whether secular Indian or religious Hindu, were informed by an overfamiliar cultural epistemology of time and space: a founding archaic genius, consequent civilisational atrophy, present vitalism and a future redemption which, for Hindu nationalists, could be condensed into a geopious territorialism and an ethnic-religious nation-state. India constituted a primogeniture civilisation which had fallen into degradation (and was therefore easily colonised). Hence, the necessity of nationalist renewal informed by religious, cultural or civilisational precepts, and leading ultimately to a dominion or other self-governing independent status. The nineteenth- and early twentieth-century relationships and differences between secular and religious sensibilities in the creation of Indian nationalism require much further discussion than can be provided here (Zavos 2000; Bhatt 2001). However, for incipient Hindu nationalist strands, several key themes were especially important.

Primogeniture and monumental civilisation

The nineteenth-century derivation of a primordial nationalism for India was mainly based on the foregrounding of an archetype related to the discovery of archaic 'Vedic civilisation', through which vernacular, caste and regional elites gave shape and coherence to ideas of 'national unity'; hence the importance of both the archetype and the protean form. Here, the term 'primordial' refers to an ideologically derived grid of intelligibility from which nationalism was to be understood, rather than to the development of an essential ethnic unity among Indian populations. Indeed, the flourishing of primordialist thinking in nineteenth century colonial India can be seen as resulting from the absence of an overarching 'ethnic unity' among Indian populations, rather than as its consequence.

A key aspect to these projects was the idea of evolutionary temporality in which viewing the past in linear terms was the first stage towards imagining an over-integrated national future. Nomenclature and taxonomy, functionalism and positivism were epistemologically important, but the definitive themes were: vitalism, evolution and telos, palingenesis, survival and degeneration, 'social uplift' and 'social hygiene', spirituality, enumeration, a universalising mission, ideas of ethnology, race and, for Hindu nationalists in the first decade of the twentieth century, the threat of 'racial extinction'. Early twentieth-century narratives of 'upliftment' and 'hygiene' were inextricably linked to strong themes of religious 'upliftment' and purity, and demonstrated a convergence between imperial and early nationalist 'civilising' discourses.

A central aspect of both secular and religious nationalism was their appropriation of, opposition to, and negotiation with 'Orientalist' and colonial scholarship related to the origins, languages and religions of the inhabitants of India. The dominant 'Orientalist' influence was inevitably British and in the English language. It is important though not to underestimate the influence of German 'Romantic' writers, from Herder, Friedrich and August Wilhelm von Schlegel, to Goethe, Arthur Schopenhauer and Paul Deussen, nor to understate the exchanges between Indian writers and non-British Indologists and philologists (Halbfass 1988: 218). The ideas that India was the cradle of all civilisation (Voltaire, Herder, Friedrich Schlegel among many others) or the original homeland of humanity (Schlegel, Schelling, even Kant and Hegel), that 'Hinduism' represented humanity's primal philosophy (Herder, Schlegel), or offered redemption for contemporary humanity (Schopenhauer), even that 'humanism' itself could be conceived as resultant upon 'Hindu values' (Herder), as well as the associated ideas that privileged a transcendental cultural epistemology or a 'national soul' above any determination by the state (variously Herder, Fichte, Renan among others) were widely disseminated in Europe but were also, conversely, engaged with by vernacular elites in India (Halbfass 1988; Bhatt 1999).

Especially after the early 1870s, these processes were evident in the conscious cultivation of the 'memory', indeed affective remembrance of India's archaic Hindu past by numerous societies and writers, in the burgeoning print media, by nationalist and religious leaders, British colonial officers and administrators, and western religious societies such as the Theosophists. India's ancient civilisation was demonstrated to be as old as that of the ancient Greeks and Romans and, it was speculated and then believed by some, may have been the progenitor of the latter. Its knowledge and philosophies demonstrated the superiority of its religion and culture. Its religious texts illustrated not simply the religious and (frequently) 'racial' unity of its past, but pre-eminently its national unity, as Aryavarta (the land of the Aryans) or Bharatvarsha (the kingdom of Bharat). The Vedas, Upanishads, Puranas and the Epics illustrated that ancient Hindu civilisation possessed not simply a cultural and moral greatness, but a highly developed ethical system, polity, civil society and social formation. A key component of this intellectual discovery concerned a comparison between the vitalism, dynamism and resilience of the ancient Hindus and what was perceived as the degeneration and stagnancy of contemporary Hindu society. Conversely patriotism and nationalism were seen as the mechanisms by which Hindu society would be reinvigorated. In this nineteenth century linearist paradigm of Hindu glory, degradation and invigoration, there is by and large an absence of the view that Islam was responsible for the alleged downfall of Hinduism during the medieval period, or of the view that this linear history was driven forward by a logic of Hindu war against foreign, Muslim invaders. These two elements were written more forcefully into the imagined 'history' of Hindus around the first decade of the twentieth century and were to become dominant in V.D. Savarkar's *Hindutva – Or Who Is a Hindu?* ([1923] 1989).

Aryanism and religious nationalism

One aspect of both 'Orientalist' scholarship and primordialist nationalist thinking concerned the invention of Vedic Aryanism as the ideological basis for Indian or Hindu nationality (Thapar 1992; S. Bayly 1995, 1999b). Central to this was the discovery of Vedic Aryanism in the eighteenth and nineteenth centuries by the British and German disciplines of comparative philology, mythology and 'ethnology' and its complex diffusion in colonial India. The 'Aryan myth' in Europe was consequent upon eighteenth century discoveries of the philological affinities between archaic Latin, Greek, Sanskrit and Avestan, and between these and other languages; convergences were also noted between the mythologies and deities of ancient Greeks and Indians. Hence arose the hypothesis of a common linguistic origin. The common language group was variously named 'Indo-Germanic', 'Indo-European', 'Japhetic', 'Mediterranean', and, by Friedrich Schlegel, 'Aryan' (a corruption of the Rig Vedic *'arya'*). The idea of a common linguistic origin was rapidly supplemented by epistemologically separate hypotheses of an original people and an original geographical homeland. This unwarranted equivalence between the burgeoning projects of comparative philology, ethnology and mythology was fuelled by a considerable scholarly and dilettantish literature during the eighteenth and nineteenth centuries, speculating on the Urheimat, Ursprache, Urvolk and 'Urmythus' of the Indo-European language family (Mosse 1966; Poliakov 1971; Schwab 1984). By the late nineteenth century, the Rig Veda had been interpreted by European writers as demonstrating that a powerful warrior 'race', Aryans, had entered India and conquered 'the dark-skinned, stub-nosed' original inhabitants, the *dasyus*.

For important intellectual strands in nineteenth-century colonial India, an archaic civilisational Vedic Aryanism was also, if differently, important and became a virtual 'common sense', an unquestioned backdrop, that provided a linear paradigm for what a future nationalism was to be (Leopold 1970; Dalmia 1997; Thapar 1992; S. Bayly 1999a). Both 'race' and Aryanism in colonial India signified a wide range of meanings and forms of methodological understanding that can be seen to constitute a distinctive nineteenth-century pedagogical field with its own thematic and lexical ramifications that were irreducible to, but were in negotiation and argument with, those associated with the burgeoning racial Aryanism in France, Britain and Germany. Individuals as diverse as Vivekananda, Keshab Chandra Sen of the Brahmo Samaj, the Bengal novelist and writer Bankimchandra Chattopadhyaya, the Bombay judge, social reformer and nationalist Mahadev Govind Ranade, the social reformer Har Bilas Sarda, the 'Extremist' nationalist leader Bal Gangadhar Tilak, the fiery revolutionary nationalist Aurobindo Ghose, Congress leader Annie Besant, and the founder of the Arya Samaj, Dayananda Saraswati, employed conceptions of Aryanism within their various ideals of patriotism and loyalty to the monarch, religious reinvigoration, or reformist or revolutionary nationalism (Leopold 1970). The term Aryan was widely used, including by national leaders such as M.K. Gandhi. Just as Friedrich Max Muller had articulated the visit to England of Rammohan Roy as the 'return' of a lost Aryan cousin, for Sen, Aryanism demonstrated the patriotic unity of the British and Indians, cousins lost in antiquity who had, in the colonial period, rediscovered each other (Rothermund 1986; Trautmann 1997). Conversely, for Ranade, Ghose and Tilak, the European racial connotations of Aryan supremacy, and for the latter two the idea that Indians subjugated by the British could share a common descent, were anathema. For them as for Dayananda, Aryans were not necessarily racially constituted but were often characterised through a moral and dynamic propensity that was their genius. Nevertheless, for them, it was in India that Aryans had either originated or achieved the pinnacle of their culture and civilisation which had then bestowed on the world. There is an understated link between the universalising conception of Hinduism as providing salvation, knowledge or redemption for all humanity (Hinduism's 'worldling'), and the origin of this idea in the nineteenth-century fascination with Aryans as a world-dynamic force.

The politics of devotion

However, archaic Vedism did not address the popular and devotional aspects of Hinduism. Here, in the activities of both the Bengal novelist and writer Bankimchandra and in the political activities and writings of Bal Gangadhar Tilak, the explicit intertwining within an incipient nationalism of the Puranas, Krishna and the Motherland (by Bankim), or of Ganesh, Kali, the *Bhagavadgita* and the medieval Maratha warrior Shivaji (by Tilak) may appear to confirm the political activation of an extant ethnic or religious 'core'. However, in these ventures, the transformation of aspects of the religious pantheon into a nationalist one has to be seen to be at least as inventive as it was 'traditional'. For example, Bankim's neo-Puranic, humanised Krishna is inseparable from his attempt to critically 'unite' Comte with Kant. His powerfully affective conception of a Motherland was itself a novel rendition, based on a translation of Kant's faculties of mind into a superordinate 'faculty of love' for the nation. Similarly, Tilak's 'communal' intervention in 1894 around Ganesh Chaturti was a novel transformation of a private act of devotion into an urban, public, 'communal' demonstration for home rule. Tilak's rendition of the *Bhagavadgita* as a manual providing guidance for political action was similarly novel (Wolpert 1977).

It may still be argued that, despite the obvious political exploitation and novelty of such efforts, they were nevertheless dependent on the prior existence of symbols, memories and the like within extant Hindu traditions, in the absence of which, the efforts would have been meaningless and ineffective. However, even in the case of the Ganesh Chaturti processions, their significance is elided by simply restraining analysis to the appeal to a particular religious symbol as reflective of an extant cultural ecology, one which can be counterposed to the evident absurdity of a cultural *tabula rasa* and a resulting and random ethnic voluntarism. As various writers have shown, Tilak's interventions became organised in sharp opposition to, and were therefore symbolically made inseparable from, the Muslim Muharram festival of Poona (Cashman 1970), which had traditionally been a cross-religious affair. Indeed, the Ganesh festivals were organised as a mirror-image of Muharram (Tejani 2002: 118) such that the God became adopted by Hindus who had not previously worshipped him. Prior to this, the bathing of Ganesh idols had been a private, family-oriented activity of some (mainly upper-caste) Hindus. Indeed, there is evidence that some Hindus rejected Tilak's mobilisation of their God as contrary to their actual tradition (ibid.: 117). What might it say about any putative cultural ecology that its 'ethnic' symbol, memory or tradition was introduced into it as a result of its *prior mobilisation* for nationalist purposes? Very similar arguments apply to the symbol of the Maratha warrior Shivaji, which became prominent after its nationalist abstraction by Tilak from the history of medieval Maharashtra, and its subsequent embedding in the cultural ecology of some Hindu groups, and later the imagined martial nation of the Hindus.

Hindutva and 'history'

These factors become more acute with the invention of Hindutva, now the core symbol of Hindu nationalism. The term was used by Chandranath Basu during the 1860s to describe the quality of Hinduism and its relation to the 'history' of India (Sen 1993). It was also used by Tilak in the first decade of the twentieth century. However, the ideology of Hindutva and an exclusive *Hindurashtra* (Hindu nation) is usually traced to an *English*-language pamphlet written by Vinayak Damodar Savarkar in the early 1920s ([1923] 1989). Savarkar was an anti-colonial revolutionary, now regarded as a national hero,[2] who was involved in the first decade of the century, from London, in various propaganda and arms smuggling activities in order to fight British rule in India. He was imprisoned by the colonial authorities and deported to the Cellular Jail in the Andaman Islands during which he wrote his treatise on Hindutva and Hindu identity (Keer 1988).

The content of the document, which is primarily concerned to provide a comprehensive, majoritarian definition of Hindu identity, is puzzling for several reasons. One could read it without receiving any indication from it that British colonialism was even present, or indeed that a mass, genuinely popular anti-colonial movement was taking place at exactly the time that Savarkar was writing his tract. Similarly, there is virtually no discussion in it of anything that might be conceived as Hindu custom, belief, religious practice, ritual, metaphysics, deism, and the like. Indeed, Savarkar rejected a religious conception of Hinduism as simply a western 'ism'. Given its momentous importance for Hindu nationalism, it is striking that it makes hardly any appeal, as previous religious nationalisms had attempted, to the symbols, beliefs and practices of Hinduism. There is an important reason for this, made quite explicit in the writings of Savarkar and those who followed him: the religious traditions that comprise what is now known as Hinduism are not amenable to a unified religious description without invoking fundamental contradictions of 'theology', practice, belief, tradition, boundary, inclusion or exclusion. Savarkar himself referred to the sectarian disputes between the Arya Samaj and the Sanatan Dharm Sabha as relevant in formulating his Hindutva (the suggestion being that the foremost symbol of contemporary Hindu nationalism, itself claimed to be reflective of an archaic ethnic-religious tradition, was a result of the need to suppress political difficulties between two modern 'neo-Hindu' organisations). Hence, a fundamental method of Hindu nationalist ideology, still very important today, is to displace 'religious Hinduism' (though with some important qualifications) in favour of a nationalist ideology that attempts to prescribe unambiguous criteria of inclusion and exclusion based on blood, territory, landscape, affect and culture.

Savarkar's ideology emphasised that the Hindu was defined by his (the masculine idiom is important here) 'beingness', the essence of which was Hindutva. Hindutva comprised in Savarkar's writings an indeterminate combination of several 'shared' factors: 'race', 'territory', 'culture', 'religion', 'emotion' and 'history'. Hindutva was very closely linked by Savarkar to descent defined by paternal inheritance of 'the blood' of the putative Aryans that had entered India in antiquity. Indeed, he argued that 'blood' was the most important criterion for Hindutva. He also claimed that the Aryans had in antiquity colonised the entire geographical territory occupied in his time by the British. The argument, made during the British colonial period, that ancient Hindus were also colonists is of course highly suggestive. Similarly, Savarkar's landscape of India was one of a physically bounded, tightly enclosed natural territory (though in contemporary Hindu nationalism, this territory now extends well beyond the contemporary cartography of India, Pakistan, Bangladesh, Kashmir and Sri Lanka to also include huge areas of Afghanistan, all of Burma, Tibet and Nepal, major parts of Indonesia, Thailand, Laos and various chunks of China). This conception of nationalism in which the physical geography of India acquires a sacrosanct status was dependent on earlier ideas, such as those of Aurobindo Ghose who had argued that the nation was *literally* sacred, and nationalism was *literally* a religion which had come from God.

The third important factor for Savarkar was culture, which for him meant *sanskriti* culture, bestowed upon the world by the so-called Aryan Vedic seers. Sanskriti culture inevitably relates to upper caste, typically male groups who are authorised to pronounce and interpret religious scriptures. Culture is also central to contemporary Hindu nationalism as *sanskritik rashtriyavad* (usually mistranslated as the more benign 'cultural nationalism'). This is a hegemonic upper-caste claim over all the various amorphous traditions, Vedic and non-Vedic, together with the religious traditions (Buddhism, Jainism and Sikhism) said to be indigenous offshoots of an essential Hinduism.

Savarkar came very late to defining Hindu religion (*Hindudharma*) in his text, and this was solely to exclude syncretic groups, such as Gujarati Bohras and Khojas and 'white' adherents of Hinduism (such as Annie Besant and Margaret Noble). Savarkar said that the Bohras could claim descent 'by blood' and could also claim 'sanskritic culture' as their own; however, their religious practices were based on Islam. In hence excluding Islam (and Christianity), Savarkar advanced a definition of Hindu religion (*Hindudharma*) as a territorial, hereditary and sacred conception. Only someone who considers India as their holyland (*punyabhumi*) *and* fatherland (*pitrubhumi*) could be embraced by Hindutva, and thus claim the identity 'Hindu' (Savarkar [1923] 1989: 115–19). Islam and Christianity were, for Savarkar, foreign invader religions (though he also argued that Aryans were not autochthonous to India so the progenitors of Hinduism also came from outside India). For Muslims and Christians, their 'holy land' was 'far off, in Arabia or Palestine', and so they could not be enfolded within Hindutva unless they renounced their religions, and wholeheartedly embraced and demonstrated loyalty to an ideology of Hindu supremacism that considered them enemies. *Hindudharma* also meant for Savarkar a militaristic, masculine, virile, vitalist religion born on Indian soil. This powerful, militant religion was compromised and subverted by what he considered to be its inferior offshoots, Jainism and Buddhism, the 'weak' and 'feminine' religions that were responsible for Hinduism's historic degradation. This division between masculine and feminine world civilisations was itself dependent on nineteenth century European conceptions and is resonant today in various projects of ethnic absolutism.

The civilisational rendition of Hinduism has been increasingly important for Hindu supremacism, especially in a 'globalising' period. In contemporary Hindu nationalism, 'Hinduism' is simply the name for a primordial and universal religion of humanity, arising from the first ever revelation, but which humanity has fallen from (Golwalkar [1939] 1944). This civilisational strand is based on dismissing all so-called Semitic religions (primarily Christianity and Islam) as mere ideologies, whereas Hinduism is seen as the founding civilisation of all humanity. This 'return' to the majesty and grandeur of primordial, temporally illegible civilisation crucially allows Hindu nationalists to make 'universal' claims (similar to Islamist claims about the *din al-fitra*, the primordial religion of the Abrahamic traditions). Every other religion and political ideology is seen as an illegitimate usurpation of a global religion of humankind, which now only exists as Hinduism and its immediate offshoots. Hence, an enemy of Hindutva is an enemy of humankind. Several consequences follow from this kind of view, not least the need to explain a thousand year war suffered by a superior masculine civilisation which was incapable of defeating inferior ideologies (and, for the religious imaginary, of explaining in *karmic* terms why Hindus had been victims of this monstrous genocide). But it is worth noting that the pedigree of this view of first revelation and a primordial Indian civilisation is entirely western, clearly present in the writings of Voltaire, Herder and Friedrich Schlegel among other Enlightenment and Romantic thinkers. This idea of a primordial religion of humanity has also more recently functioned to provide Hindutva organisations in the South Asian diaspora with a 'universal mission towards all humanity'. This relates the phenomenology of minority experience in the west with the 'natural homeland' of Hindus; it is also a moot point whether minority Hindu discourse in the west has itself influenced Hindu majoritarian discourse of 'rights', 'justice' and 'discrimination' in India (see the collection by Mukta and Bhatt 2000).

The history of Hindutva was, for Savarkar, that of relentless and monumental war between Hindus and invaders (indeed, *any* contact with others inevitably meant war against them). There is no virtually no content to Hinduism in his *Hindutva* unless it is defined by war, primarily an 800-year war against Muslim invaders, followed by a subsequent war against Christians (British colonists). Savarkar's crucial transformation of previous Hindu nationalism was the significance he attached to the medieval period and the rise of the Delhi Sultanate and then the Mughal period from the late 1520s. It is therefore no accident that contemporary Hindu nationalism is viscerally opposed to, and therefore inextricably linked with, Islam. In Savarkar's work there is also an exact reproduction of an Orientalist rendition of Hinduism as essentially still, heady and self-absorbed, unless it is disturbed by outsiders. In this register, time is sheer seriality unless Hinduism is disturbed by contact with outsiders. This historical imaginary of an inexorable thousand-year war against foreigners is central today to Hindutva majoritarian claims.

The Rashtriya Swayamsevak Sangh and ordered society

Savarkar's ideology of Hindutva was appropriated by a new organisation, the Rashtriya Swayamsevak Sangh (RSS), formed in the period 1924–6. The RSS was created by Nagpur brahmins as a paramilitary men's organisation influenced, as Christophe Jaffrelot and Marzia Casolari have definitively shown, by Italian Fascist youth movements such as the Balilla and Avanguardisti fascist youth groups, and during the 1930s by National Socialism (Jaffrelot 1996; Casolari 2000). Indeed, all of the RSS's life, the dictatorial metaphor (*ek chalak anuvartitva*) of its Supreme Leader, the principal one who is to be venerated (*parampoojaniya*), has been central, as has a militaristic war aesthetic exemplified by its modern uniform, flag and daily regimented drills. The RSS can legitimately be seen as one of the largest paramilitary bodies existing in any contemporary nation.

The RSS is the base or foundation of, and created, almost all the Hindutva movements and networks that currently exist in India, including the VHP and the Jan Sangh/BJP. The RSS's second leader, Madhav Golwalkar, propounded in the late 1930s a somewhat Nazi-like view of the Hindu-Aryan nation, though not out of line with that promoted by its putative founder Hedgewar, who indeed presided over meetings in Nagpur, Maharashtra, in the 1930s to promote Mussolini's fascism in India (Casolari 2000). It is difficult to conceive of Hindutva ideology after the 1930s as distinguishable from the influence of Nazism and fascism, whether promoted by the RSS or by Savarkar's Hindu Mahasabha. It is simply not the case that National Socialist and Fascist influences were minor accretions, stray infelicities or products of their time within what was otherwise an allegedly pure or traditional Hindutva uncontaminated by so-called foreign influences. If BJP's slogan of 'One Nation, One People, One Culture' might seem like an Indian rendition of New Right cultural majoritarianism, we still have to account for the grotesque appeal of Hitlerism and Aryanism today among the RSS and its affiliates. Gujarati schoolchildren are taught today about how Hitler was a great leader who instilled the spirit of nationalism, nationhood and adventure in the common people (the Holocaust not even hinted at), or that Aryans were a fair race, the most illustrious, glorious and adventurous race in human history.

Vitalism, 'eugenicism' and national soul

Central to RSS and Savarkarite ideology is a nineteenth-century conception of *vitalism*. This is the vital impulse, at once metaphysical and physiologically constitutional, that needs to be militantly reinvigorated among Hindus. Its converse, so clearly present in RSS ideology, is a forbidding critique of actual Hindus themselves as weak, emasculated, unhealthy, indolent and effeminate. This idea of the Hindu as inherently problematic permeates the writings and speeches of RSS founders in their desire to disavow existing Hindus and 'Hindu society' in favour of remoulding the Hindu man afresh in its *shakhas* (RSS branches for callisthenics, military drills, weapons training and ideological inculcation) by taking each Hindu male-child one by one and painstakingly refashioning them until they acquire the right 'face', 'appearance', disposition and body in order to serve the Hindu nation.

The key medium for this is 'culture', the repository for and guardian of the transcendental 'soul' of the nation. These are again earlier western ideas, an interesting confluence of Herder's cultural epistemology (as in the BJP's *sanskritik rashtriyavad*) and Renan's metaphysics of nation (as 'national soul' or *chiti*) that travels from Savarkar's period and into the ideology of 'Integral Humanism' developed in the mid-1960s by Deendayal Upadhyaya, and now one of the core political ideologies of the BJP. In Upadhyaya's work, the national soul (*chiti*) is associated with a natural or cosmic order (*dharma*), and is identified as completed only in the 'rule of *Dharma*'. *Dharma*, *chiti* and *rajya* (government) are the three privileged terms. Hence, democracy is invariably subsidiary to what is conceived as the natural or cosmic order, and is dispensable if it works against it (Golwalkar *et al.* 1991). Unsurprisingly, discussion of democratic governance is highly under-developed in the writings of Hindu nationalists, 'genuine democracy' reduced simply to numerical Hindu majoritarianism, and minority protec-tion (an essential component of administrative democracy) identified with 'pseudo-secularist appeasement'.

The national soul is conceived in sanctified terms. Hence, the demand of the BJP that all citizens consider the territory of India as inherently sacred. This idea of sacred nation is due to earlier influences (including Bankimchandra, Bipinchandra Pal, Har Dayal and Aurobindo Ghose) but has been importantly transformed by contemporary Hindu nationalists, especially the Vishwa Hindu Parishad, into a view that the sacred landscape of India inherently faces a grievous insult because of the presence within it of Muslims, Christians, secularists and so forth. Simply the *existence* of minorities in a democratic nation-state is perceived as a profound wounding to the Hindu nation. Hence, there is within some Hindu nationalist organi-sations a genocidal impulse, the depth of which is only marginally captured in popular Hindutva slogans which state that the only place for Muslims in India is *kabristan* (the graveyard). Hindu nationalists have also incessantly invoked the necessity of violence against non-Hindus as a binding religious obligation upon anyone who calls him or herself a Hindu, regardless of any individual aversion to violence. The combination of a metaphysics of violence, extra-legal activities by Hindutva social movements, and unevenly accountable and partisan structures of state and district level bureaucracy and law enforcement point to a very bleak scenario, independently of the activities, wishes or fortunes of the BJP at state and national levels.

The discourses of vitalism, dynamism and national soul sit alongside an overarching RSS obsession with order, conformity, obedience, hierarchy and discipline. This fetishism of order, conformity and regimented discipline is a key characteristic of the RSS's ideal structure and method of organisation (*sangathan*). The RSS arose in opposition to the national movement's efforts to 'bridge religious communities' and build a culturally and religiously composite, 'anti-communal' nationalism. However, another reason for the RSS's formation was a deep aversion to the Indian freedom movement's discourses and strategies of disobedience, disruption, liberty, equality and freedom during the 1920s, against which the RSS wished to promote its own vision of an ordered, disciplined, hierarchical Hindu nation.

There has also been within Hindu nationalist ideology a powerful and distinctive Indian variant of what can be called, tentatively, 'eugenicism'. This is not strictly based on biological or even hereditarian ideas, but contains 'social Darwinist' resources. It has been most apparent in the remarkable influence of Herbert Spencer on Savarkar's and Golwalkar's political sociology, most explicit in the physiological and organismic conception of nation and society at the heart of Hindutva. Nationalism was conceived by Savarkar and Golwalkar as the condition and the outcome of an eternal physiological competition between nations. Importantly, an indeterminate and slippery non-biological hereditarianism involving both blood and culture is central to these views. Another strand is that familiar somatic nationalism, the literal pollution of the national body by adherents of so-called foreign ideologies of Islam, Christianity, Marxism and 'Macaulayism'.

The 'eugenicist' impulse is also central to the RSS's distinctive 'man-moulding' mission, literally its belief that it is physically and ideologically moulding Hindu men one after the other in order to create a new, superior, organised, hierarchical, disciplined society of which it is the exemplar. The RSS follower was characterised by Golwalkar as 'the living limb of the corporate personality of society', moreover one prepared to make any sacrifice for the health of the whole organism, just as a biological cell allegedly sacrifices itself for the sake of the human body. The precise origins of this kind of thinking can be traced back to late nineteenth- and turn-of-the-century claims among some Hindu nationalists that Hindus were literally facing biological extinction because of the impact of Christianity as well as Islam on India. As Pradip Datta (1999) and John Zavos (2000) have shown, Hindus were seen as a 'dying race'. That these beliefs were intimately related to the decennial censuses from the latter decades of the nineteenth century (which showed an increasing Christian population) demonstrates the importance of modernist enumeration and population calculus that is at the core of contemporary Hindu nationalist obsessions with Muslim and Christian demographics and reproductive fertility. It is also not possible to understand fully the orientation of contemporary Hindutva organisations towards the large *adivasi* (tribal) and dalit populations outside this historical lineage of social hygiene, social upliftment, statistical reasoning, and the organisation of populations into a hierarchical caste order.

The resultant 'social gardening' approach is at the core of RSS philosophy. It genuinely believes it is creating within itself, and only it is capable of creating, a new society which will permeate outwards and refashion the existing fallen society in its image. Hence, the RSS and the VHP have created an extraordinarily wide range of affiliated organisations (Jaffrelot 1996), some of which are social movements in their own right, and which are focused on women, labour, farmers and peasants, *adivasis* and dalits, teachers, students and education, welfare, youth, and the religious hierarchy. In many cases, they now represent the largest such organised corporate bodies in India. In an important sense, especially since 1989, the RSS 'exists' primarily in the welfare and service organisations it has established across a diverse range of fields (*kshetra*) in Indian civil society. The projects are concerted attempts to transform the political and civic cultures of Indian state and civil society. The RSS has from its inception sought to create novel political cultures across civil society based on manufacturing permanent emotional identifications and solidarities among Hindus, and rupturing affective identifications with non-Hindus – a literal manufacture of a Hindutva majority. One way of understanding the local relationship between the BJP and the RSS–VHP is through the violent bifurcation of local civic association along bare religious lines that the latter creates, prior to its electoral manipulation and harvesting by the former. The RSS's and VHP's projects can also increasingly be seen as parastatal bodies of ambiguous legality that mirror, as well as overlap with, the structures of the regional and district state in BJP-controlled areas.

Conclusion

The xenophobic and majoritarian nationalism which the RSS has steadily been cultivating for almost eight years has come to fruition and now poses a major threat to the different memory of Indian nationalism based on a 'composite' polycultural ideal, an uneven anti-communal conception of secularism, and the heritage of anti-colonial struggle. It is unclear whether this indicates 'secularism's last sigh', or points instead to the incomplete nature of secular modernity, and the necessity of a different visionary and heterogeneous secular renewal. Hindu nationalism has, so far, remained a minority electoral force (25.6 and 23.8 per cent of the popular vote in 1998 and 1999 respectively), restricted in support primarily to the Hindi belt, Gujarat and Maharashtra. Nevertheless, Hindutva social movements have now expanded well beyond their traditional, northern confines. The sites of symbolic conflict that Hindutva movements have adeptly manufactured continue to multiply, seemingly inexorably.

The VHP has been central to these processes. Its campaigns, such as for a Ram temple to be built at the site of the demolished Babri mosque at Ayodhya, raise key questions about political affect and its relation to nationalism. What is the nature of the aesthetic charge of manufactured symbols that allows for a motile chain of potent emotional identifications to travel from the immediately familial, domestic or concupiscent to the communitarian and 'national'? The latest major VHP campaign concerns the eleventh-century Bhojshala at Dhar, western Madhya Pradesh. The medieval history of Dhar included rulership by Raja Bhoja, Mughal dominion, subsequent capture by Mahrattas, and later evolution into a chieftainship and princely state. The Bhojshala previously contained a remarkable sculpted figurine of the goddess Saraswati, created in 1034 and now said to be in a collection in London. The figurine shows the goddess's naked torso, as is traditional in representations of Saraswati. The Bhojshala had traditionally been used both as a Hindu place of worship and a Muslim shrine, without dispute and peaceably until the VHP intervened in the 1990s. From the early 1990s, Indore, Dhar and nearby towns and villages were also the focus of violent Hindutva campaigns against Christians working among *adivasi* groups. In May 1998, the VHP's youth wing, the Bajrang Dal, stormed and attempted to destroy the Bombay apartment of M.F. Hussain, a foremost contemporary Indian artist, because he (a Muslim) had allegedly painted a Saraswati nude, though the actual 'painting' was a highly stylised sketch done in 1976 in preparation for a painting of a clothed Jindal Saraswati (Swami 1998). Saraswati has also been important for recent Aryanist claims about the Indus Valley civilisation, now rapidly becoming a founding Hindutva myth. Saraswati is an important deity for Jainism, the latter considered by Hindu nationalists as simply an offshoot of a progenitor Hinduism, and hence to be enfolded into an overarching Hindutva (despite significant Jain resistance). Naturally, the VHP's demand is that the Bhojshala be cleansed of Islamic influence and converted to a Hindu temple. The strategic condensation on to Bhojshala of so many VHP agendas is important not because of an extant cultural ecology, reservoir, narrative or tradition that is being invoked, but because of the contemporary recreation of the idea of the latter. It is precisely in this determined project of authoritarian nationalism that one can see the constitution in politics of a claim about 'dominant ethnicity'.

Notes

1   One explanation for the utter ferocity of the Gujarat pogroms in 2002 relates precisely to this point: it was the closeness of, and ambiguity of religious boundary among certain rural and urban communities in Gujarat, rather than their social distance, that had to be destroyed.
2   In February 2003, a portrait of Savarkar was unveiled by the BJP president in the Central Hall of the Indian Parliament. It hangs opposite that of Gandhi. Savarkar stood trial for conspiring to murder Gandhi, but was acquitted for lack of independent corroborative evidence, though a later Commission (under Justice Kapur in 1965) was presented with new evidence of Savarkar's alleged involvement in the conspiracy. Gandhi's assassin, Nathuram Godse, was Savarkar's 'lieutenant', a senior and prominent member of Savarkar's Hindu Mahasabha, and formerly associated with the RSS.

References

Badrinath, C. (1993) *Dharma, India and the World Order*, Edinburgh: Saint Andrews Press.
Bayly, C.A. (1998) *Origins of Nationality in South Asia*, Delhi: Oxford University Press.
Bayly, S. (1995) 'Caste and "race" in the colonial ethnography of India', in P. Robb (ed.) *The Concept of Race in South Asia*, Delhi: Oxford University Press.
—— (1999a) *Caste, Society and Politics in India from the Eighteenth Century to the Modern Age*, Cambridge: Cambridge University Press.
—— (1999b) 'Race in Britain and India', in P. van der Veer and H. Lehmann (eds) *Nation and Religion: Perspectives on Europe and Asia*, Princeton, NJ: Princeton University Press
Bhatt, C. (1999) 'Primordial being', *Radical Philosophy*, 100 (April): 28–41.
—— (2001) *Hindu Nationalism: Origins, Ideologies and Modern Myths*, Oxford: Berg.

Cashman, R. (1970) 'The political recruitment of God Ganapati', *Indian Economic and Social History Review*, VII(3): 347–73.

Casolari, M. (2000) 'Hindutva's foreign tie-up in the 1930s: archival evidence', *Economic and Political Weekly*, 22 January: 218–28.

Dalmia, V. (1997) *The Nationalization of Hindu Traditions: Bharatendu Harischandra and Nineteenth-Century Banaras*, Delhi: Oxford University Press.

Datta, P. (1999) *Carving Blocs: Communal Ideology in Early Twentieth-Century Bengal*, New Delhi: Oxford University Press.

Dumont, L. (1980) *Homo Hierarchicus: The Caste System and its Implications*, Chicago: University of Chicago Press.

Golwalkar, M.S. ([1939] 1944) *We or Our Nationhood Defined*, Nagpur: Bharat Publications.

Golwalkar, M.S., Upadhyaya, D. and Thengadi, D.B. (1991) *Integral Approach*, New Delhi: Suruchi Prakashan.

Halbfass, W. (1988) *India and Europe: An Essay in Understanding*, Albany, NY: State University of New York Press.

Hansen, T.B. (1999) *The Saffron Wave: Democracy and Hindu Nationalism in Modern India*, Princeton, NJ: Princeton University Press.

Inden, R.B. (1990) *Imagining India*, Oxford: Blackwell.

Jaffrelot, C. (1996) *The Hindu Nationalist Movement and Indian Politics*, London: Hurst.

Jones, K. (1976) *Arya Dharm: Hindu Consciousness in Nineteenth-Century Punjab*, Delhi: Manohar Press.

Keer, D. (1988) *Veer Savarkar*, London: Sangam Books.

Leopold, J. (1970) 'The Aryan theory of race in India 1870–1920: nationalist and internationalist visions', *Indian Economic and Social History Review*, VII(2): 271–97.

Lorenzen, D.N. (1999) 'Who Invented Hinduism?', *Comparative Studies in Society and History*, 41(4): 630–59.

Madan, T.N. (1997) *Modern Myths, Locked Minds, Secularism and Fundamentalism in India*, New Delhi: Oxford University Press.

Mosse, G.M. (1966) *The Crisis of German Ideology*, London: Weidenfeld & Nicolson.

Mukta, P. and Bhatt, C. (eds) (2000) 'Hindutva movements in the West', *Ethnic and Racial Studies*, 23(3) (special issue).

Nandy, A. (1985) 'An anti-secularist manifesto', *Seminar*, 314 (October): 22–5.

Pinch, W.R. (1996) *Peasants and Monks in British India*, Berkeley, CA: University of California Press.

Poliakov, L. (1971) *The Aryan Myth: A History of Racist and Nationalist Ideas in Europe*, London: Heinemann.

Ranger, T. (1999) 'The nature of ethnicity: lessons from Africa', in E. Mortimer and R. Fine (eds) *People, Nation and State*, London: I.B. Tauris.

Rothermund, D. (1986) *The German Intellectual Quest for India*, New Delhi: Manohar.

Roy, A. (1998) 'The end of imagination', *The Guardian* 1 August.

Sarkar, S. (1996) 'Indian nationalism and the politics of Hindutva', in D. Ludden (ed.) *Contesting the Nation: Religion, Community, and the Politics of Democracy in India*, Philadelphia, PA: University of Pennsylvania Press.

Savarkar, V.D. ([1923] 1989) *Hindutva – Or Who Is a Hindu?*, Bombay: Veer Savarkar Prakashan.

Schwab, R. (1984) *The Oriental Renaissance: Europe's Rediscovery of India and the East, 1680–1880*, New York: Columbia University Press.

Sen, A.P. (1993) *Hindu Revivalism in Bengal, 1872–1905*, Delhi: Oxford University Press.

Smith, A. (1989) 'The origins of nations', *Ethnic and Racial Studies*, 12(3): 340–67.

—— (1999) *Myths and Memories of Nation*, Oxford: Oxford University Press.

Swami, P. (1998) 'Predatory pursuit of power', *Frontline*, 15(11).

Tejani, S. (2002) 'A pre-history of Indian secularism: categories of nationalism and communalism in emerging definitions of India, Bombay presidency c.1893–1932', unpublished PhD thesis, Columbia University.

Thapar, R. (1985) 'Syndicated Moksha?', *Seminar*, 313 (September): 14–22.

—— (1989) 'Imagined religious communities? Ancient history and the modern search for a Hindu identity', *Modern Asian Studies*, 23(2): 209–31.

—— (1992) 'The perennial Aryans', *Seminar*, 400 (December): 20–6.

—— (1996) *Ancient Indian Social History: Some Interpretations*, London: Sangam Books.

Trautmann, T.R. (1997) *Aryans and British India*, Berkeley, CA: University of California Press.

von Stietencron, H. (1989) 'Hinduism – on the proper use of a deceptive term', in G.D. Sontheimer and H. Kulke (eds) *Hinduism Reconsidered*, Delhi: Manohar.

—— (1995) 'Religious configurations in pre-Muslim India and the modern concept of Hinduism', in V. Dalmia and H. von Stietencron (eds) *Representing Hinduism: The Construction of Religious Traditions and National Identity*, New Delhi: Sage.

Wolpert, S. (1977) *Tilak and Gokhale: Revolution and Reform in the Making of Modern India*, Berkeley, CA: University of California Press.

Zavos, J. (2000) *The Emergence of Hindu Nationalism in India*, Oxford: Oxford University Press.

12 The dynamics of ethnic minority domination in Fiji

Ralph R. Premdas

Introduction

Multi-ethnic states tend to be bedevilled by persistent problems of governance in relation to the issue of representation. Regardless of whether they are democratic or authoritarian, grievances are generated over alleged domination, repression, minority infringements, majority hegemony, ethnically skewed resource allocation and preferences, recognition, etc., all in part compounded and rendered doubly difficult to manage because of the multi-ethnic condition of the state in which these problems arise. It is rare for some sort of consociation to be struck reconciling the rival claims of the communities, given that each tends to espouse its own peculiar conception of equity and justice. More frequently, political domination by members of one ethnic community is the main mode of governance. Such ethnic domination may be by either an ethnic minority or majority. It is conceivable to have benign as well repressive governance by an ethnic minority. Such domination in both democratic and non-democratic systems, however, is undergirded by some justifying principle by the dominant group based on an appeal to ethnic origins, to being historically or divinely 'chosen', to superior economic resources and talents, to numbers, to might, etc., or several of these in combination. The mode of ethnic domination by an ethnic minority or majority may be openly articulated or unobtrusively concealed. Western European states have transformed and reinvented themselves in a new self-styled civic order bound by non-ethnic principles of equality. Here, domination by a founding ethnie is a fact of life but it is not overtly articulated, rather, it is underwritten by cultural values embedded in the social system as a subtext that anoints and legitimates political rule.

Overt claims to political pre-eminence by a founding ethnie, especially in a multi-ethnic state, tend to throw up contentious issues of legitimacy and justice even where the dominant ethnic community is demographically in the majority but especially if it is in the minority. This is not likely to go uncontested by intergenerational resident immigrant communities which may not only interrogate the historical accuracy or appropriateness of the claim but also advance their own principles for establishing legitimate government.

The idea of being the indigenous or founding ethnie of a state carries a legitimating mystique in the acquisition and maintenance of rule in multi-ethnic states with immigrant populations. But indigeneity may be a hotly contested claim, regardless of whether it is authentic or invented, often running parallel to other principles of validation so that it does not automatically confer political power to rule. In a number of cases, one of which will be examined in this study, the original population had been reduced at one time to a minority while the immigrant-descended majority justified its claim to power by insisting on equality in democratic participation. Struggle between founding ethies and other contending communities, even where the latter have been around for many centuries, has become the norm in many contemporary states. In many instances around the world today, descendants of relatively recent immigrant groups have secured power so that native founding ethnies are subordinated and ruled by 'ethnic strangers' in a thorny and potentially turbulent relationship. In a few cases, the struggle between founding ethnies and immigrant communities is persistent and chronic, overtly articulated and hotly contested, often with nativist anti-immigrant movements militantly even violently engaged in clashes with immigrant elements.

Theory: plural society

The problem of ethnic domination in multi-ethnic states has been broached by several scholars (Lustick 1979; Premdas and Hintzen 1982), but the one which best helps this inquiry refers to the so-called 'plural society' theorists such as J.S. Furnivall and M.G. Smith. J.S. Furnivall, in describing a 'plural society', postulated that in this sort of setting, domination by a minority ethnic community was almost inevitable. He succinctly set forth the fundamental features of this type of society thus:

> In Burma, as in Java, probably the first thing that strikes the visitor is the medley of peoples – European, Chinese, Indians, and native. It is, in the strictest sense, a medley, for they mix but do not combine. Each group holds to its own religion, its own culture and language, its own ideas and ways. As individuals they meet but only at the market place, in buying and selling. There is a plural society, with different sections of the community living side by side, but separately within the same unit. Even in the economic sphere there is separate division of labour along racial lines.
>
> (Furnivall 1948: 304)

Typically created by the colonial importation of alien labour, plural societies, lacking a common social will, are prone to instability, requiring a system of domination to maintain order (Rabushka and Shepsle 1972). In effect, societal integration was effected by domination by the coloniser composed of a minority ethnic community. M.G. Smith, like Furnivall, elaborated on the need for a 'central regulative organisation' to impart stability and unity to the centrifugal forces which threaten to tear the plural society apart at its ethnic seams. Argued Smith:

> Even in a plural society, institutional diversity does not include differing systems of government. The reason for this is simple: the continuity of such societies as units is incompatible with the internal diversity of governmental institutions. Given the fundamental differences of belief, value, and organization that connote pluralism, *the monopoly of power by one cultural section is the essential pre-condition for the maintenance of the total society in its current form.*
>
> (1969: 6; emphasis added)

Many critics of the plural society model such as Donald Horowitz argue that 'the theory lacks a mechanism of conflict' (1985: 137). The missing trig-gering mechanism, however, has been supplied by other plural society theorists such as Arend Lijphart, who implicated the zero-sum parliamen-tary competitive party system that has been engrafted on to a multi-ethnic state by the departing colonial power (Lijphart 1977). Ethnically driven elec-tion campaigns tend to sustain a spiral of communalised conflict in which victory and control of the state apparatus are thus seen as an instrument of ethnic pre-eminence and preference (Milne 1982; Premdas 1995).

While both Furnivall and Smith had erred in arguing that cultural pluralism inevitably required a system of domination to maintain order, consociational theorists (Lewis 1965; Lijphart 1977) have proposed a special mix of consensus non-exclusivist institutions in coalition power-sharing arrangements as a democratic alternative (Premdas 1991b: 71–93). Yet, finding such systems in the real world is difficult. The political terrain is littered with the ruins of many such experiments in power-sharing, leaving a legacy of domination in its wake. Today a new temper of democratisation is current, especially in the multi-ethnic states of the Third World, arguing for a new order of democratic governance that avoids exclusivist institutions and that promotes power-sharing. One way to assist in this commendable undertaking is to examine cases in ethnic domination for lessons. The plural society model in this opinion offers some of the best insights into the form and functioning of multi-ethnic societies that are prone to deteriorate into disorder and domination (Gurr 1994).

Fiji: domination dynamics

Fiji, a former colony, became a multi-ethnic state with a preponderantly bi-polar communal structure through colonial importation of labour in support of a plantation economy (Milne 1982; Premdas 1995). From 1874 onwards, power has oscillated several times among the main ethnic communities due to demographic changes as well as political factors. When Britain took control of the Fiji archipelago, it administered the islands as a Crown Colony until 1902, when an element of representation in a local council was first introduced but power still resided in European hands for the next six decades. The indigenous Fijians, while accepting British rule, still regarded themselves as 'paramount', a concept that would become controversial in the latter half of the twentieth century as the colony moved towards self-government (Lawson 1991; Durutalo 1986). Asian Indians, a vociferous immigrant community seeking equality of representation, would become the majority population so that conflict ensued between Indigenous Fijian 'paramount' claims and the Indian quest for one man, one vote. On the anvil of this contest, which pervaded the society and polity especially in the post-WW II period of world-wide decolonisation, political power shifted at one time to Fijian control, then to Indian, then back to Fijian, then again back to Indian and finally into Fijian hands once more. These power transitions were marked by society-wide discourses on the rightful bases of establishing legitimate authority, with symbolic collective Fijian cultural arguments pitched against individualistic democratic one man, one vote propositions posited by Indians. Power shifted around alternatingly first by inter-communal consensus, then by electoral victory, then by military coup. At no time during these transition, did economic, political, cultural and demographic pre-eminence by any community coincide and synchronise around a particular community.

For instance, when Fijians ran the government from 1970 to 1987, they enjoyed neither economic nor demographic pre-eminence in the society, but cultural priority. They were therefore a politically dominant ethnic minority. When Europeans in the early part of the twentieth century held political control, they possessed unrivalled economic power and imposed cultural ascendancy. But they lacked demographic superiority. When Indians enjoyed *de facto* pre-eminent political influence after the 1987 elections, while they were demographically in the majority and were economically dominant also, they were culturally a marginal community. Presently, with Fijians enjoying political power, while they are now in a demographic majority and possess cultural pre-eminence, they do not have control over the main economic resources of the state. Hence, political, economic, demographic and cultural pillars of pre-eminence were never simultaneously controlled by any of the communities (Table 12.1).

The shifts in the ethnic centre of governmental power were always intensely contested but were resolved both by peaceful electoral methods and military intervention. Through successive struggles conducted over half a century, the society became increasingly divided communally with no consensus on the legitimating principles in the calculus of power. From the persistence of the conflicts, refugee and diasporic communities were created, international actors entered the fray, and while the uncompromising arguments over the relative merits of collective group rights versus individual rights in a liberal democratic order remained unsettled, the threat of military intervention hovered as the final arbiter. We examine the Fiji case, looking at

Table 12.1 Phases of ethnic domination in Fiji

Date	Ethnic domination
1874–1904	European colonial control. Crown Colony
1904–1966	European control through communal representation
1966–1970	Fijian limited control. Period of limited internal self -government
1970–1987	Fijian Minority government
1987–33 days	Temporary Indian-dominated government with a Fijian Prime Minister
1987–1999	Fijian Minority government. Military intervention
2000–2001	Indian-dominated coalition government
2001–present	Fijian-dominated government. Fijian majority

these factors and forces in the issue of ethnic minority domination by Fijians from 1970 to 1999. This stretch of time consisted of two periods of Fijian rule separated temporarily by the accession to power of a new government dominated by an Indian electoral base but led by a Fijian Prime Minister.

Political domination refers to control over the decision-making (legislative) and executive arms of the government. It is rare to find cases where domination occurred simultaneously along all four axes: political, economic, cultural and demographic. We theorise that it is in part this asymmetry that has accounted for instability in these states, leading to the quest for ethnic ascendancy. In the history of a multi-ethnic state, domination may alternate so that in one phase a particular community holds pre-eminent political power but may lose it to another community over time. Further, a dominant community may not necessarily acquire power all by itself in competition with another community but in coalition with other smaller communities. Many cases exist of a minority communal group, by one means or the other acquiring power, dominating the state for extended periods of time. Fiji is an example of ethnic minority domination that existed until very recently. This chapter focuses on the dynamics of this type of rule in Fiji. In the narrative that follows, we shall present the ethnic composition of Fiji, its history, communal self-conceptions, the origins of the conflict among the communities, and in particular we shall examine how power was acquired, exercised, and lost by these minority regimes.

Fiji: the making of a multi-ethnic state

The ethnically segmented structure of Fiji (Table 12.2) is constituted of two main groups, the indigenous Fijians and the Indians, accounting for over 95 per cent of the total population. When Fiji was colonised on 10 October 1874, the Deed of Cession bound Britain to preserve the Fijian way of life. Three policies were initiated that laid the cornerstone of communalism. First, all land which was not yet alienated to Europeans, consisting of over 80 per cent of the country, remained under Fijian ownership. The second policy saw the recruitment of indentured labour from India so that from 1879 to 1916 some 60,537 Indians were introduced into Fiji, about half remaining under a scheme that allowed them to become legal residents (Gillion 1977: 70–1). The final policy was the establishment of a separate Native Fijian Administration and a Fijian Council of Chiefs through which the British governed the Fijians indirectly (France 1969). While this policy shielded Fijian culture by virtually establishing a state within a state, it so protected Fijians that they were unprepared to compete with the Europeans, Chinese and Indians once their circle of interaction had enlarged beyond the village. The upshot was the institutionalisation of Fijian economic inferiority. Fijian penetration of the business sector has been generally unsuccessful even with the aid of special programmes mainly because of the communal nature of Fijian culture (Watters 1969; Healy 1986: 2–10). Asian Indians from India came mainly as contract indentured labourers, most of whom opted to stay as permanent residents (Naidu 1980). In contemporary Fiji, while Fijians predominate in agriculture, most small and intermediate size commercial operations are Indian. As in the rural areas where Indians and Fijians live apart (Fijians live in small concentrated villages while Indian farms are dispersed on sprawling leased Fijian land), in the towns, such as Suva, similar ethnic residential self-selectivity occurs, thereby rendering city wards predom-

Table 12.2 Population of Fiji (ethnic origins), 1986 and 1996

	1986 (%)	1996 (%)
Fijian	322,920 (46.1)	393,575 (50.8)
Indian	348,704 (48.7)	338,818 (43.7)
Rotumans	8,652 (1.2)	9,727 (1.3)
European	4,196 (0.6)	3,103 (0.4)
Part-European	10,297 (1.4)	11,685 (1.5)
Chinese/ Part-Chinese	4,784 (0.7)	4,939 (0.6)
Other Pacific Islanders	8,627 (1.2)	10,463 (1.4)
Others	810 (0.1)	2,767 (0.3)
Total	715,375 (100.0)	775,077 (100)

Source: Bureau of Statistics, Government of Fiji (1996)

inantly Fijian or Indian (Walsh 1978: 1–2). Cultural features also separate the two major communities. While English is the cross-communal language, Indians speak Hindi among themselves and Fijians speak their indigenous languages. Finally, most voluntary social and economic organisations such as sports clubs and trade unions are predominantly uni-ethnic (Mamak 1978). Inter-marriage between Fijians and Indians is practically non-existent. Hence, racial, linguistic, religious and cultural cleavages fall one on top of the other in a pattern of coinciding reinforcements separating Indians from Fijians. Europeans, although numerically insignificant, had dominated the direction of the colony imprinting a capitalist economy, Christianity among Fijians, English as the *lingua franca*, and a variant of the Westminster parliamentary model. The remaining population categories were the Chinese, Mixed Races and other Pacific Islanders. While major cleavages divide the ethnic groups into cultural compartments, each segment in turn is not monolithically unified. Internal divisions within the Fijian and Indian communities have assumed salience in the last decade and a half. Within the Indian group, there are Muslims (15 per cent) with a further division between North and South Indians as well as separate sub-identities such as Punjabis, Gujaratis, etc. Similarly, significant regional differences separate Fijians into historic tribal communities.

The politics of ethnic pre-eminence and paramountcy

We shall focus mainly on the issue of representation since it emerged as the site in the contest over power, and, implicitly, the problem of domination. To understand the issue of the right to rule among the ethnic communities of Fiji, it is necessary to return to 1874, when Fiji was annexed by Britain. Fijians read into the Deed of Cession of 1874 a claim of 'paramountcy'. While the word itself is not mentioned in the Deed, repeatedly invoked, 'paramountcy' evolved into a mystical doctrine of Fijian supremacy (Lawson 1991) and lacking precision, it engendered imagined claims. When popular representation was first introduced in Fiji in 1904, the colonial council included two nominated Fijians representing an indigenous population of 92,000, six elected Europeans representing 2,440 persons, while 22,000 Indians were completely without representation. Indians demanded equal representation couched in terms of 'common' roll (one man, one vote) as distinct from the 'communal' roll (sectional representation). Because the Fijians were governed under a separate Native Administration, the Indian demand for a common roll initially only challenged European control, but in time Fijians came to share the European view that common roll would cause a fundamental alteration in favour of Indians in the distribution of political power and privileges in Fiji. When the Indian population surpassed that of the Fijian in 1946 and became a clear majority in the entire population by 1966, the concept of the Indian quest for hegemony became ominous to Fijians.

When in 1963 universal adult suffrage was introduced, a full-blown party system came into existence consisting of two major parties, the National Federation Party (NFP), supported predominantly by Indians, and the Alliance Party, supported mainly by Fijians, but also including Europeans, Chinese and others. As self-government approached, the struggle to correct these inequities and the debate over the relative merits of the common versus the communal system of representation, especially the Fijian claim of paramountcy, were carried on mainly by the two political parties representing Fijians and Indians. Independence meant that the country required a new constitution, and in turn this implied that the outstanding issues which separated Fijians and Indians had to be reconciled. Between August 1969 and March 1970, the representatives of the NFP and Alliance met to work out a constitutional solution for Fiji. The negotiations yielded agreement on the inter-related issues of representation, citizenship and land.

On the system of representation, the Alliance accepted the common roll as a long-term objective and acceded to the NFP demands that (1) a Royal Commission be established some time between the first and second elections after independence to re-examine the entire issue of common versus communal roll; and (2) common roll elections be held for the municipalities of Suva and Lautoka. In the meantime, a system of communal and cross-communal voting would continue. Parity of representation was accorded to the Fijians and Indian communities, while the European, part-European and Chinese sectors, referred to as 'General Electors', although constituting only 3.5 per cent of the population, continued to be over-represented with 15.4 per cent of the seats. On paramount rights for Fijians, the NFP conceded that additional 'weightage' should be allocated to Fijian interests through a Senate, where the amending procedure entrenched Fijian interests by requiring consent of the Fijian Great Council of Chiefs on matters related to Fijian land and custom. On the issue of citizenship, in a quid pro quo, the Indian negotiators successfully won acceptance of full Indian citizenship in a package that included a Bill of Rights which prohibited discrimination on the 'grounds of race, place of origin, political opinions, colour or creed'.

Along with the explicit written compromises, the 1970 Constitution contained two far-reaching extra-constitutional features: (1) a societal-wide power distribution formulation ('balance'); and (2) Comity Agreements. Under 'balance' (Premdas 1993: 271–4), sectoral pre-eminence was distributed as follows: (1) the Fijians controlled the government, the Prime Minister's office in particular, and predominated in the public bureaucracy. They also owned 83 per cent of all the land. (2) The Indians dominated the sugar industry and small and intermediate size business. They also enjoyed access to Fijian land via leases. And (3) the Europeans controlled the very large businesses, such as banks, hotels, factories, etc. 'Comity' referred to the varieties of informal devices by which communal leaders work out a *modus vivendi* to accommodate each section's interests.

The 1970 Constitution practically conceded Fijian minority domination of the government, at least temporarily. Following the compromises, there was a period of amicable relations between the Fijian and Indian party leadership. The honeymoon that followed the making of the 1970 Constitution and the elections in 1972 that confirmed the Alliance and Fijian political paramountcy did not last long however. Soon a basic challenge to the entire constitutional settlement emerged from the Fijian section of the population in the form of a newly organised Fijian Nationalist Party led by Sakiasi Butadroka. On 9 October 1975, Butadroka introduced a motion in Parliament calling for the expulsion of Fiji's Indians, sending massive waves of fear throughout the Indian community (Premdas 1979: 30–45). Their very existence was threatened for they knew that indigenous Fijian sympathy with the motion was widespread.

The Butadroka challenge would be followed by three critical events in the remaining part of the decade which saw the growth of new strains between the Alliance and Federation parties, throwing the entire set of understandings of the 1970 Constitution in turmoil. The first event in part came as part of the outbidding process with which Butadroka's Nationalists had confronted the Alliance Party, regarding the alleged inequitable benefits that Fijians derived from the constitutional agreements. In similar manner, a faction within the Indian community decided to challenge Koya's leadership of the Federation Party, claiming that he had sold out Indian interests at the 1970 constitutional talks. Hence, both Mara and Koya, moderate leaders within their own respective ethnic communities, were confronted by extremist outbidders whose actions pushed them to adopt extreme positions themselves to counter the challenge, triggering a resurgence of inter-communal malaise which deteriorated into outright Fijian–Indian animosity. The second event occurred as a consequence of the March–April 1977 general elections when the Alliance lost to the Federation Party but the Fijian Governor-General frustrated Indian accession to power. Had the Indian-based Federation Party assumed power, it would have broken the expectations of continued Fijian political paramountcy. The final event pertained to the Royal Commission Report of 1975 that reviewed the electoral system on the merits of the common versus communal roll. Containing the potential to redesign the electoral system in their favour, the Report was unceremoniously and unilaterally rejected by the Alliance government, thereby foreclosing Indian demands for an electoral system based on 'one man, one vote' and with it equality.

Towards the end of the 1970s, outbidder sniping had the desired results when Mara and Koya resorted to attacking each other bitterly. Like a set of falling dominoes, thereafter nearly all cross-communal acts of cooperation were strained, if not destroyed. Every major settled constitutional idea and compromise was in shambles by 1980. An unstable fluid state of affairs existed throughout the first half of the 1980s, which was exacerbated by growing inter-communal distrust. To be sure, at the beginning of the 1980s, one final attempt was launched at forming a government of national unity to rescue the ship of state from certain political disaster but this foundered when both leaders publicly traded charges of deception. Subsequent elections were bitterly fought and exacerbated ethnic tensions between Fijians and Indians. In the 1983 elections, the Great Council of Chiefs threatened that 'blood will flow' if Indians persisted in their quest for political power. The 1987 elections would actually bring things to a head when the NFP savoured victory.

The main actors in the elections of 1987 were the two old-established parties, the Indian-based National Federation Party and the Fijian-based Alliance Party. However, there was one major addition, the Fiji Labour Party (FLP), which grew out of a struggle between the Alliance-run government and the Fiji Trades Union Congress in 1985 (Howard 1991). The Federation Party was persuaded to join the Labour Party in a coalition arrangement under the leadership of Fijian labour leader, Dr Timoci Bavadra. Also, to the FLP fold was added the Western United Front (WUF), which represented the interests of disgruntled Fijians in the Western region of Viti Levu. With such a formidable combination of forces cutting across race and class, the Labour–Federation coalition won the elections. For the Alliance Party and a section of the Fijian population, the loss signalled a fundamental violation of Fijian paramountcy. The fact that a Fijian remained Prime Minister temporarily assuaged Fijian anxieties about the future of Fiji under a *de facto* Indian-dominated government. However, at meetings and demonstrations organised by an extremist Fijian group calling itself the 'Taukei Movement', indigenous Fijians were told that the Bavadra government was a front for Indian interests and that their immediate objective was to deprive them of ownership and control of their land. It culminated in a military intervention led by Lt. Col. Sitiveni Rabuka, proclaiming 'Fiji was for Fijians', and announcing that the old constitution was abrogated and a new one would be prepared to guarantee Fijian political paramountcy in perpetuity (Premdas 1991a; Howard 1991). With the ousting of the Labour–Federation government which had won the general elections barely thirty-three days earlier, representative parliamentary democracy was crippled. The military's coup motto, 'Fiji for Fijians', guided their action in separating the Fijian ministers from the Indian as they were dragged out of Parliament. In what must have been a shock to the soldiers, the Fijian and Indian ministers held on steadfastly to each other, refusing to be separated. The new military regime and its successor deliberately embarked on a course of action to fashion a polity and society around ethnic symbols of one community. Ethnic repression became systematic, imparting the defining feature of the new order. It was clear that the new governing powers were intent on preventing any breaches in the ranks of Fijians, this in their view being the main cause of the defeat of the Alliance Party in the 1987 elections. Dissident Fijians came in for special pressure but Indians as a whole, regardless of the network of friendships and shared activities between Fijians and Indians cultivated over a century of sharing the same space, were deemed the collective enemy. During the riots following the coup, indiscriminate violence was directed against Indians and their property, especially in the capital city, Suva.

Trade union leaders came in for special intimidation and harassment (Leckie 1997). To neutralise the power of the unions, several of which resisted the new regime, the new government embarked on a tactic of divide and rule along ethnic lines despite the fact that many unions, including the Fiji Trades Union Congress, were ethnically mixed. To combat union militancy, the new regime attempted to form new ethnically oriented unions which were parallel to the old. One such union was the Fijian-based Viti Civil Servants Association, which was formed to offset the multi-ethnic Public Service Association which opposed the regime. To neutralise Indian control of the sugar industry, which provided more than half of the country's foreign exchange, the government promulgated the Sugar Industry Protection Decree and the National Economic Protection Decree of June 1991 which criminalised legitimate trade union activities (ibid.). In all of these actions and counter-actions, the underlying tension in the main was between Fijians in a Fijian-dominated government and Indians in the National Farmers' Union. Indians feared for the loss of their leases, most of which were obtained from Fijians. Most Indian leases were due either for renewal or termination in the latter half of the 1990s and, given the state of Indian–Fijian relations, this did not augur well for the sugar industry and Fiji's future.

One aspect of the Rabuka military regime assumed remarkable insensitivity to the multi-cultural structure of Fiji society. As an avowed born-again Christian, Rabuka decided to translate the demands of his brand of Christianity into the official policy of the government. For Rabuka, a self-professed fundamentalist lay preacher in the Methodist Church, 'Indians are not Christians. They do not worship God and His Son Jesus Christ' (Dean and Ritova 1988: 37). He declared all of them 'heathens' and threatened to ban public celebration of their ceremonies. Rabuka proceeded to promulgate by decree the Sunday Observance law under which no commercial trading and work could be carried out on the day of Sabbath (Premdas 1997: 79–95).

Some opposition against the new government also came from the Western province, which was the home base of the deposed Prime Minister Bavadra. Western indigenous Fijians, possessing a distinctive sense of separateness from Fijians in the East, had long held grievances against the Alliance government which allegedly favoured the Eastern chiefly establishment. The seventeen years of Alliance rule had brought few benefits and patronage to the Western Fijians, who at various times had organised dissident movements against Alliance domination. It was in part because of this Western alienation that many Westerners chose to support their own home-grown son, Timoci Bavadra, in the 1987 elections. Hence, many Westerners were upset with Bavadra's overthrow, and joined demonstrations against the new rulers. Hence, the frontline of the counter-attack consisted of a visible cross-communal and multi-ethnic group derived from activists in the church, university, unions, and the media. In 1990, a new constitution was promulgated and with it the practices of minority ethnic domination were institutionalised. In December 1987 a semi-civilian government under Ratu Mara was installed, and the true groundwork for a more permanent system of repression and human rights violations was laid.

Ethnic inequality became the defining cornerstone of the new order (Ravuvu 1991). The Constitution was not based on majority rule; it was a document forged in the service of ethnic supremacy. In every area of political and economic life, explicit priority was assigned to Fijian interests above others. The 1990 Constitution reserved the top positions of President, Prime Minister, Chief Justice, Public Service Head, etc. for Fijians. Fijians and Indians and Others were placed into separate ethnic constituencies allowed to vote only for their own community's representatives. A veritable apartheid state was created, denounced internationally everywhere as racist and repressive.

Much evidence, however, suggested that the new dispensation harmed not only non-Fijians, but also most lower-class Fijians. The main Fijian beneficiaries of the coup were drawn from the chiefly establishment, notably from the Eastern Confederacy in the Fijian tribal system. A class and status dimension seemed to be built into the new constitutional order so that those lower income and lower-status Fijians who had so enthusiastically supported the military intervention of Lt. Col. Rabuka in the expectation of obtaining a better deal were about to be systematically excluded and frustrated. Overall, then, two types of exclusion were incorporated in the Constitution, the first being ethnic, which dealt with the alleged Indian menace, and the second which marginalised lower-income indigenous Fijians for equality. The claim to paramount rights of Fijians not only licensed a new system of oppression, but it was also clearly designed to preserve the privileges of a Fijian elite acting in conjunction with other privileged non-Fijian sections in the population. One of the major areas that demonstrated this practice was employment in the public service and state enterprises. While in May 1987 Fijians held 47.6 per cent of public service positions, two months later after the coup, the figure had increased to 53 per cent. About 99 per cent of Fiji's Armed Military Forces are Fijian, 75 per cent of the Police Force, 90 per cent of the Permanent Secretaries and most of the senior positions in the justice system (Premdas 1991a). Many appointments had become implicated in family and clientelistic networks, undermining the professionalism and neutrality of the public service.

The rationale for this system of inequality was the doctrine of 'affirmative action' which was implemented in a way that favoured the Fijian well-to-do. These so-called affirmative action provisions of the Constitution set off a storm of protest, especially from the excluded communities. Not only were a minimum of 50 per cent of public service jobs to Fijians involved but also similar discrimination was permitted in the award of schemes established by parliament for the allocation of government scholarships, the award of trade and commercial licences, loans and the distribution of other state services. It was the Coalition parties, made up mainly of the Fiji Labour Party and the NFP, that most vehemently condemned the programme, arguing that such discrimination should not be practised in relation to one ethnic community but in favour of those in need, regardless of ethnic affiliation. The argument was intended to destroy the myth that Indians as a whole were well off and Fijians were poor. The World Bank estimates showed that the income gap between Indians and Fijians was 'relatively moderate' with the average income of the Indian family at (F)$4,003 and the Fijian (F)$3,398. Analysis carried out by United Nations Development Program (UNDP) and published in *Fiji Poverty Report* revealed that while Fijian households had the lowest average income, Indians made up over 50 per cent of the households living below the poverty line (UNDP 1997: 25). The report pointed out that 'on average, lower incomes in Indo-Fijian households fared worse than Fijian Households' (UNDP 1997: 26) but that the average income of the upper 10 per cent of Indian households was so large that it tended to distort the average income of most Indians (ibid.: 26). This had largely accounted for the misperception of relative Indian wealth *vis-à-vis* Fijians, supplying the seed for the emergence of a breed of populist Fijian extremists who exaggerated the inequalities, demanding that government be placed under Fijian control and policies be designed to rectify Fijian disadvantage.

To offset non-Fijian pre-eminence in business, the Fijian-led government embarked upon a series of affirmative action measures also to encourage Fijians to enter into the private sector (Healey 1985: 2–10). The regime embarked on programmes involving the Fijian Development Bank to facilitate Fijian entry into the business world. Another scheme that the government embarked upon to put Fijians into the business sphere was through financial participation in the purchase of shares in companies. Through Fijian Holdings Ltd., a holding company formed originally in 1984 by 14 Fijian provinces, the Fijian Affairs Board, and the NLTB, an interest-free loan of (F) $20 million was secured from the government to purchase shares in ten private companies. Since independence, especially in the 1980s and after the military coup in 1987, Fijian-dominated governments had offered training programmes and various incentives to Fijians to get them into business but with limited success (Sutherland 2000). Indigenous Fijian academic Dr Sitiveni Ratuva concluded after examining these programmes that they have only 'served to produce the exploitative hegemony of a minority of Fijians. Meanwhile poverty among Fijians deepens' (2000: 247). Many other analysts had come to the same conclusion, arguing that while 'a small Fijian elite did well ... but there was hardly anything like a successful Fijian business class. Fijian political power had not translated to economic power' (ibid.). The Minority Rights Group

International based in London in a recent report also described the record of this policy failure, saying that the various programmes:

> did little to increase the Fijian participation in commerce and came at a considerable cost. For example, the Fiji Development Bank provided concessionary loans worth slightly more than $192m(F) to indigenous Fijians between 1975 and 1999. By 1999, its annual loan portfolio for this purpose was reduced to $3.3m(F), mainly due to bad debts associated business failures. Further, the scheme has tended to benefit only a small number of well-connected individuals and families.
>
> (Persad *et al.* 2001: 3)

While it can be persuasively argued that cultural differences between Fijians and Indians account for a measure of the disparities between them, this cannot set aside the equally compelling view that the emergence of a significant Fijian economic elite has been substantially thwarted by the traditional Fijian leadership itself.

For dominance to be complete, it was necessary that not only the legislature and the executive be preponderantly Fijian-staffed, but also the judiciary. Immediately after the coup, it was the Supreme Court judges led by Fijian Chief Justice and his Indian associates who declared that the coup was illegal and advised the Governor General accordingly. The courts had proven to be an embarrassment to the military so that when Rabuka seized the government in the second coup of 25 September 1987, he proceeded to reorganise the judiciary to suit his own needs. Several of the judges, mainly of non-Fijian descent, as well as magistrates, were intimidated and, like many lawyers in the country, decided to leave Fiji.

The views on Fijian pre-eminence fostered an atmosphere of discrimination and intimidation that compelled citizens mainly from one ethnic group to relinquish their homeland and seek refuge in another country by legal and illegal means. By 1990, over 30,000 Indian citizens of Fiji had left Fiji, selling their properties cheaply and abandoning generations of labour and industry invested in building their homes and homesteads. Non-Fijians as a whole became nervous about their continued residence in Fiji. A small trickle of Fijians also left Fiji. The exodus persisted as thousands of Indians sought refugee status in host countries, especially in Australia and in Canada. The interim government placed no hindrance against mass Indian emigration and actually extended low cost government loans to Fijians who wanted to purchase low-priced Indian homes and properties so that Indians could leave immediately. The intimidatory and repressive acts of the coercive forces seemed to bear the character of a premeditated tactic designed to drive Indians out of Fiji. Because most loans granted to indigenous Fijians in the past tended to lapse into default and were forgotten or forgiven, these new loans which were granted in particular to a select set of well-placed Fijian middle-class civil servants appeared to be gifts and payoffs for political loyalty to a strategic stratum of Fijians.

Rabuka actively promoted the exodus of Indians, arguing that they were only 'guests' in the country of their birth even though they were third and fourth generation citizens. Insisting that he was not a racist, and 'not an Idi Amin', and that in fact he wanted Indians and other non-Fijians to stay in Fiji, he nonetheless viewed them as 'guests in this country' (Dean and Ritova 1988: 119). The systematic harassment of Indians, the discrimination against their entry into the public service after the coup, and an array of policies and practices aimed against the Indian community had the ultimate impact of levelling the ratio of Indians to Fijians in the population by 1990. The Fijian population level, which had been surpassed by the Indian level since 1946, was now getting close to the latter. To reduce or eliminate an entire population group marked by distinctive racial and ethnic identity, even though this was not done through physical extermination but by intimidation and discrimination, it could be argued, borders on a variant of genocide. It is paradoxical that an indigenous group, accustomed in other places in Australia and North America of making similar changes, of being victims of indirect forms of genocide, was committing the very acts that it had itself condemned. At various conferences the policies of the Fiji government under Rabuka and Mara had been endorsed by indigenous Pacific island groups as well as those in North America and Oceania. It seemed to be a case of displaced aggression against a vulnerable group as compensation for the inability to attack the powerful settler communities that have usurped indigenous lands elsewhere.

Overall, looking at the Constitution as a whole, the reception that it received from the international community was one of universal condemnation. This condemnation was focused mainly on the ethnically unequal and discriminatory provisions of the Constitution, but also aimed at the authoritarian features generally which also discriminate against lower-income and low-status Fijians. The power-holders were not only ethnic supremacists but had also cordoned themselves off from lower-income Fijian commoners, whose name they invoked to execute the coup and on whose backs they expected to maintain power.

International actors and pressures in a new globalised order

Many pressures had accumulated in the years following the promulgation of the 1990 Constitution, compelling the return to a more democratic and inclusive political order. To dislodge an authoritarian regime and force it to undertake reform required the critical assistance of international actors. Economic measures were deployed which led to the withdrawal of domestic and foreign investment, as well as diplomatic sanctions which isolated the regime as a pariah state. The most telling diplomatic and symbolic act was the expulsion of Fiji from the Commonwealth of Nations and the withdrawal of the Queen as the Head of State. Subsequently shunned by many states, Fiji was embarrassed at international forums and placed in the same category as the racist apartheid government of South Africa. For the next decade, Fiji was continuously lectured about returning to democratic practices in particular by its main regional trading partners, Australia and New Zealand. Added to the pressures from these external forces were Australian and New Zealand trade unions, which, responding to a request from the Fiji Trades Union Congress, implemented a firm embargo and passenger ban on ships and aircraft bound for Fiji. This had an immense effect since Australia and New Zealand were the main sources of Fiji imports and exports. Tourism was also struck a devastating blow since it had emerged as Fiji's second most significant source of foreign exchange after sugar. The disruption of trade and shipping by overseas union boycotts led to a steep decrease in government revenues, which in turn led to a major currency devaluation of 17.5 per cent, the first since independence. Military expenditures had escalated and a lot of foreign aid had dried up. In effect, while a set of domestic NGOs, labour unions and political parties pummelled the regime at every turn, their action was backed up by international organisations.

The greatest damage, however, was done by international financial institutions such as the World Bank and the International Monetary Fund. After the 1987 coup and the 1990 Constitution, there was a dramatic fall in investment. A World Bank Report said: 'With an adequate supply of financing in Fiji, private investment is not constrained by lack of finance' (World Bank 1995: 11). Rather, 'the roots of the investment shortfall can instead be found in the domestic environment: political uncertainty' (ibid.). The source of most internal private investment was Indian entrepreneurs who joined the boycott of the governing regime by withholding their capital. To add to the investment and unemployment crisis was the loss of vital skills caused by the mass exodus of some 50,000 to 70,000 people by the late 1990s (Chetty and Persad 1993). The World Bank as well as Fiji's trading partners continued a barrage of unrelenting pressure for democratisation. According to the World Bank:

> In the aftermath of 1987, two political issues need to be resolved. First is the issue of political rights: the constitutional review will be closely watched by the private sector. The second is the impending sugarcane land lease renewals which if mishandled could further aggravate relations between ethnic groups.
>
> (1995: i)

In the new globalised economy, Fiji's sugar, which enjoyed special preferential prices in the European Union under the ACP–EC agreement, was in danger.

Towards a new order

Two other internal political changes crystallised, pushing the process of constitutional review towards democracy. First, the Fijian population had grown, coming progressively closer to becoming the absolute majority. Second, the Prime Minister, Sitiveni Rabuka, and the Opposition Leader, Jai Ram Reddy, developed a new rapport, pushing the effort towards redemocratisation successfully. Under the new Constitution of 1997, Fiji was officially proclaimed a multicultural society even though it simultaneously accorded symbolic recognition to the 'paramountcy' of indigenous Fijian interests. Any person and not exclusively a Fijian could now become Prime Minister. The Constitution provided for a bicameral legislature with an elected House of Representatives, derived from a combination of communal and cross-communal seats and a nominated Senate. To protect Fijian interests, the Senate was endowed not only with overwhelming numerical preponderance to Fijian representatives but also veto powers on issues that affected Fijian interests.

Despite its consensus orientation, the new Constitution was sitting on a set of festering problems stemming from Fiji's non-integrated multi-ethnic structure and history of inter-sectional conflict. Equally troubling was the state of the army, police and public service during the seven-year rule of Rabuka, which saw these institutions overwhelmingly overstaffed by Fijians through family and clientelistic connections. In particular, practically all of the top senior echelon positions fell by patronage under Fijian control, rendering these bodies deeply politicised. The problem for the new government under the Constitution was to restore professionalism and honesty.

On 19 May 1999, Fiji went to the polls, resulting in an unexpected dramatic victory for the Labour-led People's Coalition. Mahendra Chaudhry was named Prime Minister, the first Indian to hold this position. The cabinet consisted of a majority of Fijians, who also held both of the Deputy Prime Ministerial positions and the most critical ministries related to Fijian Affairs. Despite these concessions, on 19 May, a civilian-instigated coup occurred, resulting in the removal from power and the kidnapping of Prime Minister Chaudhry for fifty-six days. The leader of the intervention, George Speight, a mixed race Fijian, proclaimed 'Fiji for Fijians', condemning the ascension to power of an Indian. After the crisis, the trek back to restoring democracy commenced with the appointment of a new all-Fijian Interim Government. New elections were held in 2002 under the old 1997 Constitution, throwing up startling results. The most important was the defeat of the Fiji Labour Party and the acquisition of power by Laisenia Qarase, the former head of the Interim Government, who formed his own Fijian-based party, the Soqosoqo Duavata Ni Lewenivanua (SDL) Party. Entering the elections, Chaudhry's FLP was divided and, moreover, it lost several of its Fijian allies. With this event, Fiji was re-accepted in the Commonwealth and the various trade boycotts and sanctions mounted against it by Australia, New Zealand, the European Union and the United States were eventually withdrawn.

This rosy picture was, however, marred by a development that did not augur well for ethnic equality and democracy in Fiji. Prime Minister Qarase, even in victory, proclaimed that his government was intent on institutionalising Fijian political dominance, promising to jettison the 1997 Constitution. To underscore his intention, in appointing his cabinet, contrary to the constitution which stipulated that any party with 10 per cent or more of the votes was entitled to participation in the executive cabinet, he decided to exclude the FLP and Mahendra Chaudhry from the new government. Chaudhry's FLP had won 27 seats and proportionately was entitled to 8 of the 20 cabinet positions. Qarase's SDL had gained only 31 seats, less than half of the 71 seats in the House of Representatives, but was able to attract support from two very conservative anti-Indian smaller parties. With the exclusion of the Indian-based FLP, the act represented a return to Fijian paramountcy, except on this occasion it was enacted when Fijians had become an absolute majority of the population.

Conclusion

The problem of managing ethnic diversity in order to satisfy all major interests through institutions, policies and practices is the most outstanding and unresolved issue in governance today (Stavenhagen *et al.* 1996). The Fiji case illustrates some of the difficulties in finding solutions for these states (Premdas 2002: 16–26). The chapter does not argue that it is inevitable that cultural diversity leads to inter-ethnic conflict and to ethnic dominance. In part, while the Fiji case suggests the need for consensus political systems of power-sharing, requiring special kinds of institutional arrangements which deviate from standard western zero-sum adversarial parliamentary models, it points to their limitations in an inflamed communal society (Young 1999). While the 1997 Constitution incorporated several consensus mechanisms that attempted to contain the centripetal forces of division and restore stability, it was erected on a society that was still deeply at odds with itself, triggering an ethnically driven coup.

Ethnic domination, and particularly by a minority, was the cornerstone on which the Fiji state was founded. From the inception of the colonial state in Fiji, its operations were converted into an instrument in the service of alien planter and imperial interests. The state that was created was neither neutral nor representative. It became imbued with the priority accorded European and imperial interests and the stratification system that was implanted was plainly ethno-centric as well as racist. It presided over an order that was unequal and unjust, but, more significantly, it institutionalised practices which laid the foundations for communal conflict and the struggle for ethnic ascendancy. Initially, the state utilised its monopoly of violence to enforce an economic, social, cultural and political order to promote the needs of the minority European interests. All of this was, however, achieved through a system of ethnic manipulation that pitched Fijians against Indians. The claims of Europeans to superordinate power could not be sustained over time and they were replaced by Fijian claims to political paramountcy, in 'balance', an arrangement that sought to reconcile Fijian, Indian and European interests. To be sure, a 'balance' in the distribution of spheres of influence and rewards was informally put in place but it was unable to withstand the challenge from outbidders. With the breakdown of the independence understandings, a struggle for ethnic pre-eminence proceeded apace. The state was then thrown into perpetual crisis, expressed in perennial ongoing tensions which periodically exploded into ethnic confrontation and violence.

Ethnic minority dominance in Fiji has displayed some interesting peculiarities. To begin with, while the slogan 'Fiji for Fijians' was effectively deployed to mobilise Fijians, the benefits of acquiring power accrued mainly to a select set of Fijians. This was a case of double minority domination, one against an ethnic adversary and the other against its own community. Hence, ethnic domination combined a communal feature with a class dimension. Not all Fijians accepted the chauvinism of the minority ruling regime with many joining ranks with others against it. In addition, minority ethnic domination in Fiji showed an obsessive preoccupation not only with 'minoritising' the ethnic adversary even by intimidation and forced migration, but also by attempting to destroy their economic welfare. Domination had to be complete and all the disparate pillars of economy, polity, culture, and demography had to be totally conquered. Domination clearly was not limited but sought total control of the ethnic 'Other'. Hence, even when the Fijian leaders regained power with a demographic majority, they persisted in promulgating policies that continued to harass the Indians. Finally, in the context of a globalised world where a trajectory privileges individual human rights and liberal democracy, the claims of Fijians as a group for paramountcy found little support. A thicket of NGOs committed to the spread of democratic rights, already robustly present in Fiji, renders the outcome of the conflict in Fiji an international affair to the present.

References

Chetty, N.K. and Persad, S. (1993) *Fiji's Emigration: An Examination of Contemporary Trends and Issues*, Suva: University of South Pacific Population Studies Program.

Dean, E. and Ritova, S. (1988) *Rabuka: No Other Way*, Sydney: Doubleday.

Durutalo, S. (1986) *The Paramountcy of Fijian Interests and the Politicization of Ethnicity*, Suva: South Pacific Forum.

France, P. (1969) *The Charter of the Land: Custom and Colonization in Fiji*, London: Oxford University Press.

Furnivall, J.S. (1948) *Colonial Policy and Practice*, London: Cambridge University Press.

Gillion, K.C. (1977) *The Fiji Indians' Challenge to European Dominance 1920–1946*, Canberra: Australian National University Press.

Gurr, T. (1994) *Minorities at Risk: A Global View of Ethno-Political Conflicts*, Washington, DC: United States Institute of Peace.

Healey, J. (1985) 'The politics of entrepreneurship: affirmative action policies for ethnic entrepreneurs', *Small Enterprise Development*, 2(2): 2–10.

Horowitz, D. (1985) *Ethnic Groups in Conflict*, Berkeley, CA: University of California Press.

Howard, M. (1991) *Race and Politics in an Island State*, Vancouver: University of British Columbia Press.

Lawson, S. (1991) *The Failure of Democratic Politics in Fiji*, Oxford: Clarendon Press.

Leckie, J. (1997) *To Labor with the State: The Fiji Public Service Association*, Dunedin: Otago University Press.

Lewis, W.A. (1965) *Politics in West Africa*, London: Allen and Unwin.

Lijphart, A. (1977) *Democracy in Plural Societies*, New Haven, CT: Yale University Press.

Lustick, I. (1979) 'Stability in deeply divided states: consociationalism and control', *World Politics*, 31(3): 325–44.

Mamak, A. (1978) *Color, Culture and Conflict: Pluralism in Fiji*, New York: Pergamon Press.

Milne, R.S. (1982) *Politics in Ethnically Bi-Polar States*, Vancouver: University of British Columbia Press.

Naidu, V. (1980) *The Violence of Indenture* (World University Series, Fiji Monograph No.3), Suva: University of the South Pacific.

Persad, S., Dakuvalu, J. and Snell, D. (2001) *Economic Development, Democracy and Ethnic Conflict in Fiji*, London: Minority Rights Group International and Citizens Constitutional Forum.

Premdas, R. (1979) 'Constitutional challenge: nationalist politics in Fiji', *Pacific Perspective*, 9(2): 30–45.

—— (1991a) 'Fiji: ethnic conflict and indigenous rights under a new political order', *Asian Survey*, 31(6): 540–58.

—— (1991b) 'The politics of inter-ethnic accommodation', in R. Premdas and E. St Cyr (eds) *Sir Arthur Lewis: An Economic and Political Portrait*, Jamaica: Institute of Social and Economic Research, University of the West Indies, pp. 71–93.

—— (1993) 'Balance and ethnic conflict', in J. McGarry and B. O'Leary (eds) *The Politics of Ethnic Conflict Regulation*, London: Routledge, pp. 251–74.

—— (1995) *Ethnic Conflict and Development: The Case of Fiji*, Aldershot: Avebury.

—— (1997) 'The Church and reconciliation in ethnic conflicts: the case of Fiji', in G. Baum and H. Wells (eds) *The Reconciliation of Peoples: Challenge to the Churches*, New York: Orbis Press, pp. 79–95.

—— (2002) 'Seizure of power, indigenous rights and crafting democratic governance in Fiji', *Nationalism and Ethnic Politics*, 8(4): 16–26.

Premdas, R. and Hintzen, P. (1982) 'Guyana: coercion and control in political change', *Journal of Inter-American Studies and World Affairs*, 24(3): 337–54.

Rabushka, A. and Shepsle, K. (1972) *Politics in Plural Societies*, Columbus, OH: Merrill Lynch.

Ratuva, S. (2000) 'Addressing inequality? Economic affirmative action and communal capitalism in post-coup Fiji', in A.H. Akram-Lodhi (ed.) *Confronting Fiji Futures*, Canberra: Asia Pacific Press, pp. 226–48.

Ravuvu, A. (1991) *The Façade of Democracy*, Suva: Oceania Printers.

Smith, M.G. (1969) 'Institutional political conditions of pluralism', in L. Kuper and M.G. Smith (eds) *Pluralism in Africa*, Los Angeles: University of California Press.

Stavenhagen, R. *et al.* (1996) *Ethnic Conflicts and the Nation-State*, New York: St Martin's Press.

Sutherland, W. (2000) 'The problematics of reform and the "Fijian question"', in A.H. Akram-Lodhi (ed.) *Confronting Fiji Futures*, Canberra: Asia Pacific Press, pp. 203–25.

United Nations Development Program (1997) *Fiji Poverty Report*, Suva: UNDP.

Walsh, A.C. (1978) 'Fiji's changing population: implications for race relations', *Unispac*, 8(1): 1–10.

Watters, R.F. (1969) *Koro: Economic Development and Social Change in Fiji*, Oxford: Clarendon Press.

World Bank (1995) *Fiji: Restoring Growth in a Changing Global Environment*, Washington, DC: World Bank.

Young, C. (1999) *The Accommodation of Cultural Diversity*, New York: St Martin's Press.

Index